Politicians —
Owned and Operated
by Corporate
America

Politicians — Owned and Operated by Corporate America

Why Campaign Reform is Crucial to the US Economy and National Security

Jack E. Lohman

Politicians - Owned and Operated by Corporate America

Why Campaign Reform is Crucial to the US Economy and National Security.

By Jack E. Lohman

Published by:
Colgate Press
P.O. Box 597
Sussex, WI 53089
Phone: 414-477-8686
Fax: 262-432-0271
Email: CorporateAmerica@execpc.com
Website: www.MoniedPoliticians.com

Copyright © 2006, Jack E. Lohman, First Printing, 2006

ISBN, print edition: 0-9768906-3-1

Library of Congress Control Number: 2005903925

Printed in the United States
0 9 8 7 6 5 4 3 2 1

Cover design by One-On-One Book Production

Table of Contents

"Never doubt that a small group of thoughtful, committed people
can change the world. Indeed, it is the only thing that has."
Margaret Mead

Acknowledgments

Special thanks go to **Michael Hodges**, another grandfather who cares about where the politicians are taking the country and whether it will be here for our grandkids. Michael publishes "The Grandfather Economic Report" at http://mwhodges.home.att.net — a must-visit web site. It includes many graphic presentations (many of which are included in this book) reviewing economic issues facing today's generation. If what Michael has shown doesn't trigger your anger, nothing will.

Chapter 6: The nation's health care system is one of the leading victims of our moneyed political system, and I want to thank the following experts for their help in achieving a focus for this chapter: My friends, **Drs. Gene and Linda Farley**, two retired physicians with nothing to gain but a system they can pass to their grandchildren, are members of *Physicians for a National Health Program* and the *Coalition for Wisconsin Health*. Gene and Linda travel the state of Wisconsin educating citizens, politicians and business leaders on the benefits of a single-payer health care system, and we couldn't have better people advocating for the public. And another longtime friend, **Ron Milhorn**, who spent 34 years with Medicare and is now a health care consultant in Finksburg, MD. Ron specializes in Medicare coverage policies and understands all too well why the train is off the track.

Chapter 8: Much thanks to **Mike McCabe** of *Wisconsin Democracy Campaign*, Wisconsin's leading campaign and electoral reform group, for his valuable input and fight to right the system. The grass roots efforts of WDC and **Ed Garvey**'s *Fighting Bob* group drew over 1000 activists to the first rally of the People's Legislature in Madison, WI. They learned one major thing: that people are mad as hell and want change. Today! (If you want to help, see **www.wisdc.org, www.PeoplesLegislature.org**, and Garvey's site at **www.FightingBob.com**.

Chapter 10: John Bonifaz and **Jamin R. Raskin** describe the *Wealth Primary* so well that this chapter is almost a verbatim but shortened version of their book of the same name (with permission). This phenomenon is extremely critical to understanding the impact of money in politics. If you've got money, you can run for office; if you don't, there may be wealthy interests who will fund you (for a price). But without money or substantial financial backing, don't even try. The Wealth Primary can be downloaded for free at the Center for Responsive Politics:
www.opensecrets.org/pubs/law_wp/wealthindex.htm.

Chapter 11: Thanks, too, to **Barb Lubin** at the *Arizona Clean Elections Institute* **www.AZclean.org** and the *Maine Citizens for Clean Elections* **www.mainecleanelections.org**, both of whom set the gold standard in 1998 for the rest of the nation to follow. And more recently the *Clean Up Connecticut Campaign* **www.cleanup connecticut.org** and the grassroots *Citizens for Election Reform* **www.cfer.us** won Clean Money reform in Connecticut.

These activists have proven that Clean Money Elections both work and pass constitutional muster. Freedom of speech is now available to all citizens in Maine, Arizona and Connecticut, not just to the rich. Arizona and Maine were implemented by voter ballot, thus the excuse that "voters don't want to be taxed for political elections" is just that, an excuse for politicians to avoid doing the right thing.

Chapter 12: And finally, thanks to political comedian **Will Durst** for his take on the subject, which turns out not to be very funny at all. It is really hard to laugh when your government has its hand in your pocket and a finger in your eye.

Note: Since the web pages referenced here cannot be guaranteed to be operational at the time you read the book, you can see the backup page on this book's site. Just add the final page name (following the last "/") to **www.MoneyedPoliticians.com/**. For example, the above would be **www.MoneyedPoliticians.com/wealthindex.htm**.

*To my wife, our four children
and seven grandchildren.
I can only hope that Congress quits giving
away their country before they get to enjoy it.*

*And to my mother,
who at 89 understands all too well
that neither political party fends for
the elderly. You don't want to hear
what she has to say about politicians.*

About the Author

Jack E. Lohman

Before retiring in early 2004, Jack spent 25 years operating his own medical services laboratory with 70 employees in four states. The company provided cardiac monitoring services on a sub-contract basis to hospitals and clinics, thus his concern about the direction of the health care system and the role political money has played in it.

His body resides in Milwaukee but his heart remains in beautiful western New Jersey. He has voted Republican 80% of the time, is center-right on most issues, but favors certain liberal proposals. He voted for Ross Perot and John Anderson – mainly because he objected to the stranglehold our duopoly has on the country – and he supported Ralph Nader. He favored John McCain over George Bush, but having lost that battle he nonetheless held his nose and voted for Bush, the lessor of the evils, in two presidential elections. Unfortunately, they don't allow do-overs in voting.

He's not at all happy with the current moneyed political system and the fact that it costs taxpayers thousands of dollars every year to repay the special interests that fund the political campaigns. His business sense says that the costs of full public funding for campaigns — at $15 per taxpayer per year — would be a major bargain as it saved each taxpayer $3000 to $4000 in government asset giveaways every year. That's an investment most taxpayers would gladly make, if the politicians would give them the chance to vote on it.

Lohman volunteers time to help the campaign finance and health care reform efforts and is on the national advisory board of Public Campaign, a Washington, DC-based public advocacy group. He currently serves as Executive Director of the *Wisconsin Clean Elections Coalition* (**www.WiCleanElections.org**), volunteers for Wisconsin Democracy Campaign (**www.wisdc.org**), and authored the websites **www.wi-cfr.org** and **www.SmokeFreeDining.net**, the latter of which gets a little plug later on. (You are invited to add your favorite smoke-free restaurant to the database for others to enjoy, though recognize that only a handful of states have been listed so far.)

Foreword

First, the disclosures: I've been called a progressive conservative, whatever that is, but I am a lifelong Republican and vote for the GOP 80% of the time. These pages could give you a different impression of my political allegiances, however. I'm liberal on some issues, conservative on others. My left wing friends call me right wing and my right wing friends call me left wing, so I guess I'm somewhere in the middle. I like it that way.

Secondly, I am not happy about using words like corruption, bribery, payola, conspiracy and greed — it makes me sound like a wild 50's radical, which I was not then and am not now. But that's exactly what describes today's politics, and to ignore the words would be to roll over and accept the system. I'm not ready to do that.

And lastly, I receive no payments from any company, institute or entity outside of my social security checks and income from my investments (though those investments are diverse and may even include industries I chastise here, like the pharmaceutical industry). No organization has paid me to write this. Such is life.

The results of a recent poll by the *Wisconsin Policy Research Institute* shows that only 6% of the public think state politicians are working on their behalf, while 47% believe they represent their own interests and 41% believe they represent special interests. That's very sad, but how can that surprise anyone when the thing that most frequently gets legislators elected is money and the people most willing to give them money are the special interests? Money buys power, thus those with money will continue to win the allegiance of the politicians. Our electoral system is trash and it must be fixed.

I consider myself center-right and a fiscal conservative, but it is precisely because I'm fiscally conservative that I want to stop the money that flows between private and public leaders, and I'm willing to invest $15 per year in a state/federal Clean Money campaign finance system to get us there. Moreover, I am betting that the vast majority of Americans are also willing to invest in this worthy cause.

That investment will save every taxpayer $3,000 to $4,000 per year in government giveaways, which is a dramatic return on investment.

I am not happy that my political party is the biggest offender when it comes to accepting money from special interests, and Republican leaders come under intense fire in this book. Simply put, I will not hide my head in the sand because those causing today's problems are the Republicans that I (usually) support.

That said, the Democrats don't get off easily within these pages either. Though being out of power at the time of this writing limits the harm they can do, when in power and money was flowing their way they were as guilty as the Republicans! Even when they had the chance, they refused to pass campaign finance reform, and they will not attack the Republicans now because they do the same corrupt things when they have the chance, even now lapping from the same corporate money troughs as their political adversaries.

It's the system that is bad. Politicians need campaign money to get elected and there are just two sources for it, public and private. The current system virtually demands the private money corruption that drives it because public money for elections is not available. Politicians have no choice but to take money from special interests and give favors in return so that more money will be made available in the future. Though they can make the choice to change it, both parties have refused to do anything constructive on this front.

It's not the amount of private money that is of concern. It's who's giving it, who's getting it, and what taxpayer assets are swapped in the process. In some cases we are lucky. It's just government services that get traded away, frequently with higher taxes included in the bargain. In other cases we are not so lucky and more important assets like national security and troop safety are being exchanged.

It is also not what is "illegal" that's bad, because most of that is well hidden. It is the unapologetic flow of legal campaign cash that is corruptive. If illegal money passes hands, people go to jail, and a few have and more will. But when legal money flows politicians get elected and taxpayer-funded favors get passed to the private funders. So it is the flow of this mislabeled legal money that we must stop. We cannot continue with a public electoral system that is funded by private investors, as that perpetuates the most corruptive conspiracy ever lobbed against the American public.

When a government that is supposed to protect the masses — the poor from the rich and vice versa — but when only one side can afford to fund the political elections, it is pretty clear as to who will come out on the top and who will be on the short end of the stick when laws finally get signed by governors or the president.

Forget about the "trillions of dollars" of U.S. debt and start thinking about it in "people" terms: $25,000 is the amount of debt every American owes today because of government mismanagement and special interest giveaways; and that number is growing rapidly. Every year we pay the interest on that debt, about $1600 per person annually at a 2% interest rate, plus an added $3000 to $4,000 per taxpayer to cover the costs of corporate welfare. That's the amount of taxpayer assets the politicians give to special interests each year to protect and ensure their future political contributions and election advantages. That's the amount the current electoral system is costing every citizen, and this money comes out of your paychecks and yearly budgets in the form of taxes and fees and lost services.

Our country is in a slow financial decline. We cannot survive as a consuming nation only and without any manufacturing of our own. If all manufacturing is outsourced, we will be in no better shape than other third world countries that depend on others to produce. Even now, we depend greatly on foreign investors to fund our $500 billion annual deficit. Our economy will collapse under the current weight.

Too many people and organizations, like the *Cato Institute* and *Heritage Foundation,* focus on government overspending — the symptom — and virtually ignore the disease, which is our moneyed political system. Politicians taking money, bribes and payola. Only by stopping the flow of cash from those who want money spent to those who spend it will we eliminate the burden it creates on our nation's economy and our personal finances. And not to be forgotten, the finances and security of our children and grandchildren.

The U.S. Congress consists of two houses — 100 senators and 435 members of the House of Representatives — all of whom want to stay in power with the vast majority of them believing that the best way to do that is to accumulate large stashes of campaign cash to fend off challengers. Looking after the good of the country in order to stay in office has dropped to a distant second behind protecting the interests of those who fund their elections. Money buys those elections. Money buys political power. Get used to it.

You must understand the full dynamics here. It is not just that politicians receive money from corporations and lobbyists that keep them in power. Beyond their present government job looms their future occupation: lobbying. They certainly don't want to pass any campaign reform laws while in Congress that would curtail their next source of income, the lucrative lobbying profession. In many cases their stint in Congress is just the training ground, the place to learn the legislative and lobbying ropes and to develop friendships that will fuel their future profession. Today there are 26 former congressmen and 342 ex-staff members working as lobbyists, virtually all of whom had a hand in perpetuating the campaign abuses that would have ultimately affected their future jobs.

Take Rep. **Billy Tauzin** (R-LA), for example, though he's just one of the dozens. After years of carrying the water for the pharmaceutical industry he landed a $2 million per year job with the nation's pharmaceutical lobbying association. He leads the organization now, and that position will surely entail being lead lobbyist with full access to the House floor during congressional debates. Get that? While an important bill regarding pharmaceutical legislation is in progress, Tauzin can still walk the House floor and pat his ex-colleagues on the back, sometimes even slipping them a campaign contribution just to make sure he has their attention (and vote). Only our current crop of politicians would accept this as legitimate.

Tauzin's lobbying job would likely never have been offered had adequate campaign reform been in place, and he consistently voted against it during his tenure as a U.S. representative. Others to make the leap from government to cushy lobbying jobs are Democrat **George Mitchell** and Republican **James Baker,** but most of our government "servants" (and I use the term lightly if not derogatorily) have their eye on multi-million dollar jobs in the industries they were once charged with regulating, and that makes their desire to change the system virtually zero. The phenomenon is also present in state legislatures, whose members often also move on to lucrative lobbying jobs. In our state, former Democratic governor **Tony Earl** is a registered and active lobbyist, and now that Republican **Tommy Thompson** is on the loose don't be surprised to see him land a lucrative lobbying position. He knows all the ropes, having once serving as Wisconsin's governor with very close ties to industry.

This book has but one focus: to connect the dots and demonstrate the disastrous effects our moneyed political system has on America and how we can fix the problem. Indeed, there will be some who will become incensed that I blame their own contributions or political party for corrupting the system and causing havoc in America. Perhaps you don't care because you support the special interests that are currently giving the most money and getting what they want more often than not. But that will change when your party is out of power and the other guys are buying your congressman.

As **Robert W. McChesney** and **John Nichols** describe in *Our Media, Not Theirs*, "The traditional distinctions of Left and Right are not decisive categories. The more accurate split is between up and down, those who benefit materially from the corrupt status quo, and those who do not."

It is totally mind-boggling that the right wing has drawn voters from the low- and middle-income categories when these people should know that the Neocons' agenda is to maximize their own wealth at the expense of the lower classes, or at the very least, to eliminate major portions of our societal needs. It's also terribly puzzling that the same right wing politicians that promised to bring values and morality to the White House, and their right wing constituents who so vehemently tout the morality of the Republican party, have all been so forgiving of the political corruption that has been prevalent in the Bush administration.

It should surprise no one that this book will discuss our health care system, which is terribly broken because politicians have allowed campaign contributions to affect its regulation. Billions of dollars are being squandered annually through overuse, misuse, excessive CEO salaries and corporate profits, and even outright fraud. A universal health care system must be established, yet getting around all of the special interests will prove difficult, and hence the inclusion of this topic in a book about campaign finance reform.

One thing remains constant in American political life: those with the deepest pockets seem most comfortable with the way things are going, and no matter how corrupt the system they'd prefer no changes at all to ensure the flow of money into their own coffers. Those with empty pockets are a bit more concerned. That's probably understandable given their place in the economic hierarchy, but the members of both groups should look at those in the other category and study how they really got where they are. Regardless of which category you represent, the haves or the have nots, think about where our country will be when the dominoes finally fall and you finally wake up and do something about our corrupt system. Your kids and grandkids deserve better.

And think about how little of your personal money it would take. For $5 per taxpayer per year, we can fully fund elections at the state level with public money and save each taxpayer over $1300 per year in special interest giveaways. That's a bargain investment that any good businessman would jump at. Another $10 per taxpayer per year would publicly fund the federal elections and return over $3000 per year in aborted government giveaways. That's a $4300 return on a $15 investment, money that would be better spent on family needs.

When are we going to wake up? How many jobs must leave the country before we stop this nonsense? When are we going to stop letting the politicians and their wealthy buddies pick our pockets and those of our kids? When are we going to dump the corrupt congressmen amongst them? Why must we wait for the prosecutors to do it? Or let them move to lobbying the system, as **Tom DeLay** will do? We must get serious and throw the bad apples out of office. Sure, I know. That's most of them, but they gotta go. They are so adept at giving meaningless lip service, telling us what we want to hear but without any intentions of acting accordingly that we can't tell who's good and who's bad. We really need a complete turnover. Now! Whether they are Republican or Democrat, they should be ousted from office, and the best time to do that is in the primaries where you can replace them with a candidate from the party of your choice.

As I write this the Bush administration is concocting yet another ploy to take from the poor and give to the rich. The IRS has an *Alternative Minimum Tax* (AMT) that was originally aimed at wealthy wage earners. Despite the hoops their crafty tax experts had to jump through to minimize or totally eliminate their tax liability, the wealthiest among us had to pay an alternative minimum tax. Trouble is, over the years the AMT started affecting even those wage earners in the $50-75,000 category. The easy solution would have been to simply decree that the AMT affected only those with gross incomes of, say, over $150,000. Whatever. Easy. Over and done with!

But instead, Bush's tax committee wants to eliminate the AMT altogether — to "make the system simpler" — even for the multi-millionaires and **Grover Norquist**s of the world. And to make it revenue neutral the committee wants to eliminate the tax write-offs home mortgage holders take for the interest they pay over the year. So, you guessed it, housing costs will go up, house values will go down and fewer people will be able to move into their first house. That's Bush's "ownership society." Disposable income will decrease and some people may even be forced to downsize as a result. Fewer new houses will be built and the housing market will collapse. What will that do to the total economy? I don't even want to think about it.

This, all to give the wealthy another tax break. If he wanted to offset the AMT losses he could have simply rescinded his two earlier tax cuts for the rich. Or do the opposite! If trickle-down economics works so well, let's reduce the taxes for the wealthy to ZERO! Can you then imagine how all of the wealthy multi-millionaires would then reinvest their booty to help the U.S. economy? (Don't even think about it; their investments would go overseas.)

If Bush's proposal passes congress perhaps it will then wake up our sleepy and complacent taxpayers. I don't believe that it will, but that's because I understand the politics behind it. At the very least Bush has started the cash coming in from both sides of the battle. Lots of cash; from the wealthy taxpayers on one side to the Realtors and builders on the other side. It's funny how all of this works.

But SuperPresident will come to the rescue. Sometime shortly before the 2006 elections, after both sides have been bled dry, Bush will threaten to veto the bill and come out of it as a hero. This is his "rabbit out of the bag" before the mid-term elections, most certainly planned to keep the Republicans in power. Problem solved.

If President Bush really believes in an "ownership society," he should start by letting the citizens own Congress and the electoral system.

When President Bush took over in 2001, the US had a budget surplus projected to be $5.6 trillion over 10 years. In his first four years, Bush transformed that into a budget deficit of $5.2 trillion, a $10.8 trillion reversal. The so-called corporate "turn-around artists" certainly have nothing on him, but Bushnomics was clearly not the type of turn-around the country was looking for.

Note that some citations will conflict with others because of different sources reporting their data within different periods.

1
Where are our heads?

If you have ever been drawn to the idea of "privatizing" Social Security, or the privatization of any other government program for that matter, just think about what allowing private interests to fund our state and federal political campaigns has already done to society. It is a remarkable example of how things can go terribly wrong when private money is allowed to influence the political system. The results are not a pretty sight.

When the issue of privatization comes up, always remember one thing: private contractors and their executives can give campaign contributions to politicians and their parties to influence government spending and regulations — government entities cannot give money. It should surprise no one that most politicians therefore favor privatization of most government services.

As you read further, you'll either get very mad at the political system or walk away thinking I'm a nut case and that your favorite politician simply wouldn't do this for personal gain. If the latter is the case, I urge you not to throw the book away, but to set it aside and read it 10 years from now to see where America is then.

Clearly, not all congressional or state representatives are self-serving, but even if yours is one of the precious few who are principled, he is terribly outnumbered by those who are not.

Not only will he be unable to make meaningful progress in fixing the system, but he'll have a tough time even representing you, which he has sworn to do and is paid a handsome wage from our tax dollars to do. Nor do all CEOs lust for wealth and power to the extent that they are willing to give away their homeland to foreign interests in return for cash. But enough are.

I think about the 80-20 rule, and if only 20% of politicians are bad players, that's enough to create total havoc with our economy, increase our taxes, cause job losses and wage depression, perpetuate political corruption and threaten national security. Unfortunately there is strong evidence that the numbers are reversed; that 20% are good guys and 80% are in it for themselves and the special interests that fund their elections. And 90% of the public believes so, as the poll described earlier attests. Maybe the 80% of Pols once went through the "clean" stage and the shades of gray to get where they are, and a small percentage remained pure. But there is every indication that the rest are self-serving. Do I believe that it really could be as high as 80%? Indeed I do, or I wouldn't have written this book.

> *"You're either on the outside or the inside, and the only*
> *thing that can get you on the inside is money."*
> **Former Rep. Joe Scarborough (R-FL)**

It's easier than you think

To get what they want, special interests need only corrupt the few politicians in leadership or the swingers in the middle who cast the deciding votes, and their campaign cash has easily managed that and more. There is a fix to this sad state of affairs, but it will not occur without the full understanding and pressure from the public. People will have to pressure their government representatives, even those they feel are properly representing them, and they may even have to throw some of them out of office. In many cases, political jobs will have to be threatened before action is seen. But how close to rock bottom must the nation get before the public demands serious change, before the politicians are willing to allow their secure political positions to be open to fair and competitive elections? Sadly, things may have to get worse before they stand a chance of getting better.

The issues

Whether your concern pertains to

- ➤ our nation's economy,
- ➤ the war on terror,
- ➤ border protection,
- ➤ the outsourcing of jobs overseas,
- ➤ the exploitation of illegal immigrants,
- ➤ exorbitant health care and pharmaceutical costs,
- ➤ high income and property taxes, or
- ➤ corporate environmental abuses,

....if you follow the money, you'll virtually always find a direct link from one or more special interest groups or executives to the politicians who need their dollars to get re-elected. These politicians write the laws that directly affect the issues, and they respond best to campaign dollars. Big dollars; not your $10 or $20 contribution.

> *You'll hear this over and over, so get used to it: We live in a cash society, and those who have the cash will control our politicians and political system, even without ever being voted into a government position themselves. If they can't pass laws, they can buy those who do.*

Special interests are, very simply, people. They are people like you and me, but with two important differences: they are very rich and very powerful. How they got money and power is sometimes questionable — some achieved it honestly but some rode in on the backs of the poor or through outright corporate or health care fraud. For this latter group, campaign contributions have brought wealth to people who otherwise would not have earned it on their own, but they gave political cash where the returns on investment were good.

How the rich and powerful use their wealth is of great concern. Some outright bribe politicians to further build their assets, while others advocate for fair trade and honest government, even fighting against unfair tax breaks that would benefit themselves. My hat is off to **Bill Gates Sr., Warren Buffet** and **Ben Cohen** (of Ben & Jerry's fame), who are three successful business leaders who openly object to the massive tax breaks that benefit even themselves.

Interestingly, at about the same time the tax break bill was being passed, a budget with $15.8 billion in local pork barrel projects greased its way through Congress and was signed by President Bush. It just doesn't stop. And in January 2006 a bill to cut $30 billion out of Medicaid and other lifeline services moved through Congress, a political contingent obviously more willing to take from the poor before rescinding the gigantic tax breaks they gave to the rich.

According to *BusinessWeek Online* (May 9, 2005) one tasty slice of pork went to FastShip, Inc. a year after its company executives gave $8,500 to **Senator Arlen Specter** (R-PA). Specter tucked a tiny sentence into a 312 page emergency spending bill that would award a $40 million contract to a "Philadelphia-based company" for cargo ships. That company turned out to be FastShip. **Senator John McCain** (R-AZ) called it pork because the Secretary of the Navy even said his department did not want the money or the ships. But Specter and FastShip did.

Do the math: that's a 4700-to-1 return on investment, well worth $8,500 in campaign contributions. If the taxpayers had given Specter the $8500 instead, we wouldn't have had to pay the $45 million for the useless ships! That's the Clean Money way I discuss later.

The Left or Right

You'll hear a lot of people call environmental and labor organizations "special interests," and indeed they are in the strictest sense. But they are not the problem of which we speak. They do not have the hoards of cash necessary to buy and own their own Congress members, or to outbid the business and other wealthy campaign contributors for political favors.

These groups never have had the cash to compete with them, and they never will have it. But it is entirely likely that, **if** they were wealthy, they'd be just as free with their campaign cash as everybody else — because that's the only strategy that works with our trusted political leaders and the good guys know it all too well.

Some special interests are trying to fix the system while others are corrupting it. You can decide which side you're on.

Pick your side.

The most effective contributors are the executives of profitable corporations and other wealthy Americans. The top 20% of American households control over 80% of the nation's wealth, while the bottom 80% controls only about 17%, according to the U.S. Census Bureau.

According to the *Americans for Democratic Action*, the richest one percent of Americans has an average net worth of $5.5 million, and the bottom 5 percent own a whopping $2,000 in assets (See **www.inequality.org/incineqada.pdf**). Not surprisingly, the richest 1 percent contributes 80 percent of the campaign contributions.

These select few executives are not elected by the people, yet they nonetheless drive the political system and the peoples' business. They have a financial motive in seeing that laws are passed in a way that wealth transfers from the pockets of others to their own, and they are willing to share that wealth with those who make it all possible — the politicians who write the laws.

There is simply no major issue that affects the American economy in which money does not change hands at the political level. Without true campaign finance reform, few of these issues will ever be resolved to the benefit of the public.

You'll hear people claim that campaign finance reform is not possible without violating the Supreme Court ruling in the **Buckley v. Valeo** case, where the spending of political cash was determined to be "speech" and therefore could not be restricted without violating the First Amendment of the U.S. constitution.

But these people are wrong. Campaign finance reform measures are in effect in several states and they pass constitutional muster because the reforms are voluntary. And they work! So beautifully, in fact, that the special interests in Arizona sued the state to get the reform measures reversed. Fortunately, they lost, and I'll talk more about that particular situation later.

"When the Supreme Court ruled in Buckley vs. Valeo that money equals speech, it in effect ruled that those with no money have no speech. Gone are the days when one man truly equaled one vote."
Former Sen. Max Cleland (D-GA)

Simply put, the fat cats don't like the little guys to have equal speech, or equal anything. It interferes with their plans.

How it happens (and how it doesn't)

Former Senator **William Proxmire** (D-WI) once said that "campaign contributions not only influence Congress in terms of how members vote, what issues they raise, what programs they push, and in what fine-print they include in their bills; but contributions also influence Congress in terms of what congressmen do not do, in the issues they do not raise, the speeches they do not make, and the influence they do not exert."

As an example, cigarette giant Philip Morris has opposed all laws that restrict smoking in workplaces and restaurants, that limit their efforts to get kids to smoke, or that in any way increase tobacco taxes to discourage smoking. The company has had great success snuffing out its opposition and making sure that anti-smoking legislation does not get discussed. It has just cost the company a bit of money, and they were more than willing to pay it because the return-on-investment warranted it.

Smoking bans, incidentally, have had very positive effects on restaurant and bar revenues. Not only have they reduced the deadly effects secondhand smoke has on restaurant workers, they have prompted nonsmokers to start eating out more, and nonsmokers represent 75% of the potential restaurant customer base.

In the state of New York, a year after they banned smoking in public places, the state's *Department of Labor* reported 10,000 new restaurant jobs. That is not the sign of a failed policy, but Philip Morris tends to be more interested in its own profits than the restaurant operators' financial or physical health. Thus the tobacco giant has consistently fought these bans with campaign cash — and quite successfully I might add. They have also given millions of dollars to restaurant and tavern associations, which has encouraged them to fight against the best interests of even their own members. Is it any wonder that restaurants have an 80% chance of failing in the first two years operation? Why these owners can't see through the smoke and discover the obvious is unfortunate.

Philip Morris was one of the nation's largest campaign contributors to the Republican Party in 2004[1], and when **Tommy Thompson** was governor of Wisconsin, the company contributed over $160,000 to his re-election campaigns and funded numerous personal trips for the governor — to ball games and to Australia, England and South Africa[2].

The governor and Wisconsin legislature were (and unfortunately still are) for sale to the highest bidder, and it should surprise no one that it took over three years for advocates to get smoking out of daycare centers. How ironic that Thompson went on to head the *Department of Health and Human Services* in Washington, the government organization charged with keeping the populace healthy, yet his history of protecting the deadliest product in the world, a product that kills over 2 million humans a year, and with two immediate family members (wife and daughter) threatened by cancer, would leave you wondering where his allegiances really are. What does it take to get a politician to ignore the financial interests of his funders and make the right decision for mankind?

As is usually the case, those on the side of public health didn't have the financial resources to outbid the world's largest cigarette manufacturer. Money in the political system stops regulation and wins deregulation, and the only thing that can protect an industry with such a deadly product is cash. Over $53 million in campaign dollars since 1990 seems to have helped the tobacco giant puff up its profits, and the company's cash flows to politicians even today. Large amounts flow out as campaign contributions but far larger amounts flow into its coffers as profit.

If tobacco killed its victims faster, smokers would quit overnight. But it takes its toll over many years. The same can be said of political corruption, where the public pays for it in dribbles. Send taxpayers one bill for the $4000 per year the moneyed system costs them, and they'd descend on the politicians like a tsunami. But like the tobacco industry, the politicians take it out of taxpayers a little at a time.

It is interesting to see the new Philip Morris strategy of "helping" parents talk to their children about the health risks of smoking. Every parent knows what happens when they "talk" to their kids about not doing something that is bad for them: they immediately go out and do it!!! Thus the tobacco giant has enlisted unsuspecting parents to do their job for them; to get the kids to experiment with smoking! Only Philip Morris could develop a strategy so clever, or better, sleazy, and a lot of people have fallen for the apparent trick.

Let me say a bit about smoking in restaurants that has nothing to do about campaign finance reform and everything to do with common sense. If this is boring, move on to the next chapter. I recognize that us former smokers are the worst of the bunch when it comes to this subject, but the following is for both nonsmokers and restaurant operators who want to eliminate the problem but are afraid they'll lose business if they go smoke free. First, they won't, if they convert the right way: with a splash. Over 75% of the population are nonsmokers and the vast majority of the remaining are smokers who want to quit. They know it bothers nonsmokers because they get nagged about it at home. Only 3% of the public are hard core smokers who don't care about the affects on others and might stay away from a restaurant that does not let them light up. Let them leave. For every smoker that stays away, two nonsmokers will take their seats. That's a good swap.

Smoking in restaurants chases away business. Every smoking customer will, over time, chase away five or more nonsmokers. But restaurant operators only see the smokers who return; they never see the nonsmokers who leave and never come back. So they are misled as to where their real customer base is; a costly misinterpretation.

Smoking is voluntary and breathing is not. As the *American Lung Association* says, "Nothing else matters when you can't breathe," and that's a problem for those with asthma. The interesting thing about a smoke free restaurant is that they have chosen clean air, which 100% of the population can enjoy. Smoky restaurants have chosen dirty air which at best only 25% will enjoy (however, even 20-30% of smokers prefer smoke free dining).

Smokers light up in restaurants not because they have to, but because they are allowed to. If they weren't, most would be okay with it. They'd just light up after they leave, and the smoker's friends and family would love the restaurant because of its clean air policy (and they'll be back soon). Most smokers do not stay away from their favorite restaurant because it is smoke free, they just quit smoking in it. Virtually all restaurant operators that I have spoken with not only have reported from zero to 5% revenue increases; almost none have reported losses. If they lost money, they converted the wrong way (that is, too quietly), though even those losses will be temporary. To be more effective they must convert with a splash; let the world know that they are now smoke free.

In Appleton Wisconsin we had a family-run pizza restaurant. They were the first in the city to go smoke free, and when they did they received gobs of free press. TV, newspapers and talk radio wouldn't let loose of the story. The place was mobbed, and in the first 6 months they increased their sales by 60%. But the husband and wife — still with their 60% gain — closed up shop and moved to Dallas. Good reliable workers became hard to get and the 18 hour days the couple were working nearly destroyed their marriage. Now if that kind of success scares you, allowing smoking is your answer. It will surely limit your growth and expansion costs.

Another success story is Applebees in Kentucky, a tobacco state. The owner of that franchise took all 77 of his stores smoke free and increased business in the process. I refuse to go into Applebees in Wisconsin, but when I go to other restaurants that are smoke free, and there is a waiting list, I spend the time having a drink at the smoke free bar. That's business they otherwise would not get, and I'm surely not alone. Nonsmokers are not necessarily non drinkers, they just seem that way because they stay away from smoky bars.

Good resources are:

➤ If you are a nonsmoker looking for smoke free dining in your city, visit **www.SmokeFreeDining.net.** If your favorite restaurant is not listed you may add it. Note that all states are not well represented here, but with your help the list will grow.

➤ If you are a restaurant operator looking for ideas on how to go smoke free profitably, download the file from the Wisconsin Initiative on Smoking and Health at **www.wish-wi.org/operators.pdf.** You'll never regret making the change, but follow the suggestions rigidly.

➤ **www.tobaccoscams.org**

The saga of Randy "Duke" Cunningham (R-CA) promises to blow a hole in the House and Senate infrastructure. Look for a number of face-saving lobbying reforms to be introduced before the 2006 elections. But don't be surprised if some of those which pass are spiked with unconstitutional provisions designed to be shot down by the courts after the election.

"Politics is the gentle art of getting votes from the poor and campaign funds from the rich, by promising to protect each from the other."
Oscar Ameringer

Taxes – He who pays the piper

The story behind President Bush's tax breaks is not very pretty, mainly because of what motivated them, who got them, and most importantly, where they will lead the country. Like many taxpayers, I would have preferred that the money had been spent on something the country needed, like national security or universal health care.

These tax cuts certainly weren't needed by the wealthiest Americans. These people already spend all they want to spend and still have millions, even billions, left over to invest. Moreover, much of their newfound wealth (or should that be called "booty?") goes to offshore tax havens or industries that build products (and hence transfer jobs) off shore. After all, they are the most profitable companies and, of course, a portion of those profits gets kicked back to the political campaigns of those who made it all possible.

It doesn't take an economist to recognize that it would have been better to cut payroll taxes for the middle and low income wage earners who would have invested in securing their families' future by buying new homes, cars and products that would have grown our economy and helped create U.S. jobs. Tax cuts to the lowest income group would also help them get off the government dole and back to work or school, or to improve their kids' education. But the greedy and shortsighted portion of our citizenry won the hearts of the politicians who write the laws.

Laments Canadian physician **Dr. Michael Rachlis** in his book *Prescription for Excellence,* "Of course, the vast majority of the tax cuts go to people who pay a lot of taxes. In Canada, the rich are getting richer and the poor are getting poorer. As of 1999, the poorest 10 per cent of Canadian families collectively held –0.4 per cent of the country's wealth—they owed more than they possessed. In the meantime, the top 10 per cent held 53 per cent. The poorest 50 per cent of Canadians collectively held only 6 per cent of Canada's assets. Why is it that we fervently believe that the best way to make poor people productive is to pay them less but the best way to make rich people productive is to pay them more, in advance?"

> *Let's not lose sight of that question: "Why is it that we fervently believe that the best way to make poor people productive is to pay them less but the best way to make rich people productive is to pay them more, in advance?"*

Economy.com reported that, for every dollar spent extending unemployment benefits, our *Gross Domestic Product* (GDP) would grow by $1.73 — and that same dollar tax cut for low income earners would increase the GDP by $1.34. When giving money to high-income folks, however, a dollar increases the GDP by only 59 cents, and by phasing out the taxes on stock dividends, it rises just 9 cents.

What should that tell us, besides that this trickle down sleight-of-hand nonsense is just that, a trick? These numbers clearly demonstrate that "trickle-up" is far better for the economy than is trickle-down! With tax relief, our poorer people will buy more products and will be a better stimulus to the economy. An increase in the minimum wage would also have a strong trickle-up effect as more products are purchased and the economy grows.

But look at who's giving the campaign money.

To rub salt into the wound, on September 23, 2004 Congress blocked tax cuts to the poor as we now head toward a record $10 trillion deficit over the next ten years, all so we can pay for the tax cuts already given to the rich — and all of which will bury us in increased interest costs and the loss of the dollar's value. The only upside to this is that, as the dollar crashes, so will the value of our work and we'll become more like the third-world countries that make cheap products. If we can't bring Chinese wages up so our workers can have jobs, maybe we can just lower American wages to the Chinese level. Problem solved! We'll all be very poor, but we'll have jobs. If that's our goal we are on our way to achieving it. Some interesting headlines recently ran in the media. Note the dates.

Bush Policies Drive Surge in Corporate Tax Freeloading
82 Big U.S. Corporations Paid No Tax in One or More Bush Years
www.ctj.org/corpfed04pr.pdf, Sept. 22, 2004

Bid to Save Tax Refunds for the Poor is Blocked

"Congressional negotiators beat back efforts yesterday to expand and preserve tax refunds for poor families, even as they added $13 billion in corporate tax breaks to a package of middle-class tax cuts that could come to a vote in the Senate today."
Washington Post, Sept. 23, 2004

Over $13 billion in corporate tax cuts paid for by the elimination of the child tax credit for the poor! Eliminating a tax break for families making less than $10,750 per year, so we can give more to the rich? That's, apparently, family values Republican style. These are poor people who chose children over abortion, that are getting screwed by the GOP. Certainly, if we refuse them bread, some will have an incentive to get off the bread lines. Others will simply steal. But mixing a little compassion with such a basic conservative ethos might be in order here. We are spending billions of dollars per year venturing into outer space, but we cannot protect our borders because political cash comes more from spaceship builders than from family builders. We can no longer afford the government educational (Pell) grants that went to low-income families, and Congress has blocked the tax cuts for the poor, all because the resources are needed to fund tax breaks for the rich. This all makes sense as economic policy to someone, I imagine, but they must be on the receiving end.

As *United for Fair Economy* points out, "tax cuts" for the rich is really a misnomer; tax shifts to the poor is more accurate. "The choice to send nearly $200 billion to the top 1% rather than to state governments highlights just one way in which the federal tax cuts of 2001 and 2003 are actually tax *shifts*, not tax cuts, for the vast majority of Americans. While many of the tax shifts are not yet well known, a majority of Americans sense the bait and switch nature of the tax cuts. In a recent poll, only 19% of Americans said that their tax burden had actually been eased by the Bush administration's economic policies." Source: **www.FairEconomy.com**

Katrina; will it be the last?

Though tax-cut apologists will not want to hear it, the cuts in earlier tax revenues — and ultimately the reductions in state revenue sharing to communities — played at least some role in the toll Hurricane Katrina took on Louisiana and Mississippi. This in no way excuses the inept response of the New Orleans mayor or Louisiana governor, or even FEMA, but in 2002 — after several independently written papers predicted a Katrina-type disaster — the U.S. Army Corps of Engineering sought money for a study to determine how the region could be updated to withstand a Category 5 hurricane, most critically by strengthening the levees that protect the below-sea-level New Orleans from overflow and flooding. The money was denied to the engineers, thanks in part to the massive tax cuts and corporate tax breaks and subsidies doled out in recent years.

But they did get some money. As *The Washington Post* reported, over the past five years Louisiana received $1.9 billion for civil works, more than any other state including California, but spent hundreds of millions of dollars on unrelated pork barrel projects — one, a city fountain. The Louisiana congressional delegation must be very proud of that fountain, as well as the other $200 billion that will be spent this year on our nation's corporate welfare and special interest pork, rather than rebuilding and fortifying the south.

We can only guess as to how things would have been different if the national surplus in 2000 had been used wisely instead of being gifted mostly to the wealthy.

Thus the lucky individuals and corporations that got their big tax cuts and subsidies should do some serious soul-searching about their inadvertent but predictable role in this country's worst national disaster, however remote or minor it might have been. This is what happens when tax money is diverted from critical to unneeded and sometimes stupid projects, all because someone in the upper bracket wanted more than their share and the politicians were willing to give it to them. For a price, that is.

Not to be forgotten is the local corruption and graft that shrouded city and state politicians — taking money that should have gone to protecting their constituents. Also not to be forgotten is the mantra of the poor and downtrodden to remain poor and downtrodden. As one writer lamented, people in other parishes were in boats saving their neighbors while those in New Orleans were hollering for the federal government. But that's all they knew in the past. Let's hope that these people can now start new lives in the cities they've relocated to, and learn to do more for themselves.

It will be interesting to see if the Katrina, Rita and Wilma disasters are enough to prompt the president and congress to rescind Bush's 2001 and 2003 tax cuts to help pay the horrific costs that the nation now faces. The Iraq war certainly wasn't enough to do it; let's see if hurricanes are, even despite the bigger burden on the wealthy.

Perhaps this means that some of the $15 billion of pork that he approved in the 2005 budget will be given back to the people, like the $223 million "bridge to nowhere" in Alaska that serves 50 local residents who chose to live on an island. With that kind of money we could have replaced their ferry with individual hovercrafts and still had millions left over! But a look at **Rep. Don Young**'s (R-AK) contributions from transportation contractors will give you a clue to how the game is played. His campaign take of $1.5 million was second only to George Bush's $7.2 million.[1] Young, incidentally, vows not to give up a penny of his pork for the Katrina victims, and you can be sure that he had a hand in the no-bid contracts already received by Alaskan contractors to help rebuild New Orleans. Wouldn't those contracts have been better directed toward Louisiana companies and Louisiana workers? Not if you follow the money!

Let's also not forget that the pork number is really $200 billion per year when you include all corporate welfare, enough to totally rebuild the south, though like Young the fat cats will fight any demands to give it back. Moreover, this is an excellent opportunity for President Bush to "match willing workers with willing employers," as he always likes to gush. Congress has authorized 10,000 new border patrol agents, and displaced Katrina victims are his answer. Those qualified can be trained for border patrol in the southwestern states, and those who are not qualified can replace the illegal immigrants in the jobs that apparently are so hard to fill. These employers can now become true humanitarians (wink, wink!). We can also temporarily house the homeless in the military bases that are soon to be closed, and some bases can be set aside for future disasters, like a potential avian flu outbreak. Not all need be lost on Katrina.

As an aside, Congress should also reconsider its recent weakening of bankruptcy protections, at least as they apply to the poor people affected by Katrina. Hopefully the compassionate right will force this issue. These people need help.

Long term effects

Katrina should send another important message. What will we do when the whole world runs out of oil, not just New Orleans? Isn't it time to mandate alternative fuel technologies to be created by the transportation industry, or are their campaign contributions too important to the electoral system to alienate the industry? If they are not willing to do this voluntarily, let's have the taxpayers fund the research and ourselves own it! We can then lease it to the manu- facturers! And what about finally tackling global warming, which is believed to have had a significant effect on the increased strength of Katrina, Rita and other recent hurricanes? Isn't now the time to go against the energy interests and make the Kyoto accord happen?

We must now consider three important things: With the continuing rise of water caused by global warming, we should not rebuild the low-lying parts of New Orleans. This is going to be an expensive moving target for decades to come, as the icebergs melt and the water rises and warms. Does it really make sense to rebuild against the wishes of Mother Nature, who took millions of years to lay out the south? Let's turn the land into golf courses and other entertainment options. Secondly, we must refocus on a safe and well-protected form of nuclear power (as France has done) and drastically reduce our use of fossil fuels. Lastly, we must get the money out of our political system and go to public funding of campaigns, as they have in Maine and Arizona. These problems are all about money and they will always be about money, at least until that money comes from the public rather than private interests.

Even after Katrina the Republican Party wants to totally repeal the estate tax that doesn't even benefit today's wealthy; it benefits their kids when they die. One trillion dollars over the next decade! Trust me; the estate tax doesn't hurt the Paris Hiltons of the world who still have all the money they could ever hope for.

It's also hard not to criticize the fact that Halliburton received a $500 million no-bid contract to help in the cleanup process, and that Bush suspended the Davis-Bacon Act so they could maximize their profits with low wage workers. That Act required government contractors to pay prevailing wages to their workers, and with a lucrative cost-plus contract you'd think that cutting the worker's wages would not be necessary. These workers need more help, not less. In fact, good worker wages would help to rebuild the region's economy. You can be sure that Halliburton's CEO will not see a decrease in his wages. But let's also say something about the opportunities ahead for the victims who have been jobless for so many years. There will now be thousands of jobs available during the cleanup process and there is virtually no excuse for not working. These people will be given new opportunities and now is the time to accept the challenges.

It's hard to argue

Instead of spending money on better Kevlar bullet-proof vests and Humvee protection for our troops, instead of providing better care for their families when troops are killed, we are giving tax breaks to the wealthy. Instead of developing GPS, laser or RF technology to eliminate friendly fire incidents in war, we are exporting our treasury to Jupiter and Mars. Go figure.

Instead of hiring more border patrol guards, we are spending billions on building a missile defense system that will not protect us when the next WMD enters the country in a suitcase or backpack — as London and Jordan have recently experienced. All this thanks to the defense and space contractors who found a fast track to congressional approval of their own projects. American citizens would be better off if they were protected from rocket-propelled grenades and car bombs coming into this country rather than from missiles falling from the sky, but that means border control, which won't make corporations who benefit from low wages very happy.

The trick in Trickle Down

I've always maintained that, if "trickle down" economics really worked as right wing politicians and their cash constituents claim, we could all just write a $3000 check to our favorite CEO and eliminate the middleman. Let's give the CEOs the money directly and let them trickle it back down to us as they see fit. I've not gotten many takers on the idea.

As an aside, the 2001 tax cut saved Bush $31,000 in federal taxes and Vice President Cheney $11,000. For those with incomes over $1 million per year, their tax savings averaged $88,870. Source: http://hope.journ.wwu.edu/tpilgrim/j190/richgetricher.html

> *According to Citizens for Tax Justice (ctj.org), Bush's 2001 tax cuts gave the richest 1.3 million taxpayers an average of $53,120 each, while the lower 78 million got a humongous $347 each. Actually, if trickle-down really works so fantastically, why don't we quadruple the pork and create even more corporate growth? That's what the nation really needs!*

So what's wrong with this picture? Why did most of the tax cuts go to the rich? I don't think I need answer this, but the unemployed and low-to-middle income citizens do not give campaign contributions, so they don't deserve any tax breaks, at least by the strange logic by which the American system currently operates. But the top 1% of wage earners provide over 80% of campaign funding. Get used to it. That's the way the moneyed political system works.

I think most Americans feel as I do. I don't care what the issue, I don't want my congressmen or state representatives bought or sold by anyone, not even the special interests I agree with. I would rather have politicians beholden to the people and the well-being of the American economy and adequate national security than to the fat cats who fund their elections. I want my political representatives more concerned about my grandchildren than their political pocketbooks.

As a business owner, if I had an employee giving company assets to outsiders in exchange for money on the side, I'd fire him — perhaps even have him jailed. We call this bribery, payola and theft in the business world. But in the American political system it is called freedom of speech. We don't jail them, we re-elect these jokers. Where are our heads? Most business owners are honest and would respond the same way, yet they tolerate these same dishonest actions by their political representatives; and even contribute to them.

Our current electoral system virtually demands this conflict of interest when it should demand honesty instead. If CEOs and wealthy contributors did not receive more assets from the taxpayers than they gave in campaign contributions, the political money would dry up virtually overnight. But politicians like the benefits and don't want to deter them, and the corporate interests like the benefits too. They get a huge return on the money they give to politicians.

In the end, tax breaks are bought and paid for, and if you believe in that kind of government, you should be overjoyed because you've got it. If you don't like it, do something to stop it. If we starved the campaign system, public financing of campaigns would happen overnight. If you are a contributor, withhold your money and demand that your friends do too. (You can find the names of Wisconsin contributors at **www.wisdc.org/wdc.php** and national contributors at **www.opensecrets.org**.)

In a strange twist of fate, the very campaign contributions that companies use to undermine the public interest are, like all expenses, added to the price of their product and the buying public then reimburses the company at the cash register for the very expenses it incurred to stick it to us.

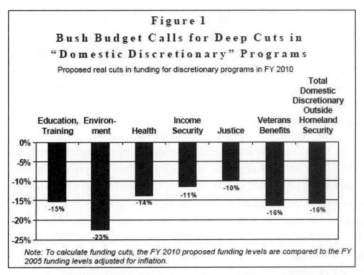

Figure 1: Who's getting cut? Apparently these are not projects that affect campaign contributors. Source: www.cbpp.org

The Bush definition of "compassionate"

The *Center on Budget and Policy Priorities* (**www.cbpp.org**) has dissected the president's budget, and the cuts seem more conservative than compassionate.

Their findings include (reprinted with permission):

➢ Education: The overall level of funding for education and training programs would be reduced in 2006, with the reductions growing larger in subsequent years. In 2010, funding for education programs would be cut 14% below the 2005 level when adjusted for inflation.

➢ Low-Income Programs: Programs targeted at low-income families that provide food assistance to pregnant women, infants, and young children; early childhood education and child care; and home energy and rental assistance would all be subject to substantial cuts by 2010. These cuts could significantly reduce the number of low-income people who are served by these programs.

➤ HIV/AIDS Treatment Funding: The federal government provides funding to states and communities for HIV/AIDS treatment services, including funding to help those with HIV/AIDS purchase drugs. Under the budget, this funding would be cut by $550 million over the 2006-2010 periods, and by $191 million, or 10%, in 2010 alone.

➤ Environmental Protection: The reductions to environmental protection and natural resource programs (including national parks) would be severe. Overall, environmental and natural resource programs would be cut by $27 billion over the 2006-2010 period, and by $8 billion, or 23%, in 2010 alone. This would require widespread, deep cuts in these programs. For instance, the set of EPA programs that support state and local environmental efforts related to ensuring clean drinking water, upgrading sewage treatment facilities, and reducing air pollution (known as the State and Tribal Assistance Grants) would be reduced by $1.1 billion — a cut of 28% — in 2010.

➤ Community Development Funding: The Administration is proposing to consolidate 18 community development and community service programs — including the Community Development Block Grant and the Community Services Block Grant — into a single block grant with reduced funding. Under this proposal, funding for community and economic development to states and localities would fall by more than one-third in 2010.

➤ Impact on States and Localities: The impact on state and local budgets would be substantial. In 2010, federal grants to states and localities provided through discretionary programs would decline by nearly $22 billion. The cumulative reduction over the five-year period from 2006 to 2010 would amount to $71 billion. In effect, the federal government would be shifting a sizable amount of program costs to other levels of government. *To cope with the drop in federal funding, states and localities would have to choose between reducing services and raising taxes.* (emphasis mine)

Bush is not all wrong

But I wish he were doing it for the right reasons. Clearly, some entitlement cuts are justified. We all hear stories of unmotivated and lazy people working the state or federal system to their benefit, either feigning injury in order to spend months at home at public expense, staying on unemployment to milk the system, moving to welfare when work is not attractive, and milking the hundreds of other freeloading mechanisms that must be paid for by the working public. If clever, they can receive $30,000 per year in taxpayer-funded welfare benefits, and as long as the government (read, the public) is willing to fork over the cash, they are just as willing to take it.

Few would argue that these leakers must get off their duffs and contribute to society, at least to pay their own way. There is absolutely no reason why they can't do something to contribute, and if they don't want to work it should be mandated if they are to continue receiving public support. President Bush indeed may be helping the rest of us by starving the welfare system and not collecting the taxpayer dollars that enable unfair entitlements. I look at all of the community services that are terribly underserved, such as non-profit nursing homes and homes for the disabled and mentally retarded, and wonder why these unemployed people can't spend 20 hours a week — the 20 hours they are not looking for employment — working in exchange for their unemployment check or food stamps. They will do this if they are sincere, and it must be mandated if they are not. If nothing else they'll gain experience and motivation to get a better paying job.

But hopefully, Bush's forced cutbacks will not impact those truly unable to work, though this seems unlikely; and even if these drastic cuts were the correct decision, I'd much prefer that his actions were not because he is answering the calls of his financial supporters. Most of us can accept even bad legislation if we know that money is not passing hands in the process. Importantly, this is the first time in U.S. history that the government has given substantial tax cuts in a time of war, when money to defend the country is most needed. Only George Bush could pull that one off. But we should not be so gullible as to believe Bush did this all to motivate the unemployed. His campaign contributors seem quite happy with his tax cuts.

Starving the system doesn't seem to be working. The government grew by only 3% in Clinton's 8 years, and already by 10% in Bush's first 5 years. Something has gone awry.

What price glory?

All the blame should not be placed on CEO and executive greed, though these offenders are on top of the list. Labor leaders must take their share of the blame for pricing their members' services out of the market, driving the hardest bargain possible, and otherwise making manufacturing in the U.S. very unattractive.

Labor leaders do not suffer here, but the union members do. Their true competition is not management but the foreign laborers who are forced to accept low wages and benefits. Corporate managers are really only the facilitators and the benefactors. It is clear that Labor did not take seriously the threats from management that high labor and benefit costs would ultimately drive the work out of the country, but those threats have come to fruition.

It would seem prudent that labor should now be finding ways to keep companies in America, rather than bleeding them for whatever they can get. Having lower paying jobs is better than none at all; and the overly aggressive labor leader may not be doing his members a favor by driving the toughest bargain possible. In this era of globalization he may instead be hastening the day when those jobs will be exported, if they are the type that can be. In the meantime, Labor should help management pressure Congress to pass a meaningful universal health care plan that, admittedly, goes against the wishes of the for-profit side of the medical industry and the right-wingers who want to limit the size and scope of government. But universal health care is vitally needed, as I will discuss later.

Despite my criticism of labor leaders, it is not easy to ignore the overly aggressive and even greedier CEOs who rake in tens of millions per year all while chastising those at the bottom for wanting a better wage. Most certainly, for all of the corporate welfare the low-wage workers now must support they deserve far more than they are getting. As Figure 2 demonstrates so well, even *with* a 32% increase in worker wages, corporate profits still increased by 116%, so the corporate claims of poverty are a bit hollow. CEO pay increased by 535%, so corporate leaders didn't do too badly either.

You'd immediately think this is not fair, and it isn't. But life isn't fair. It is controlled by those who have pushed their way to the top.

To digress a little on the labor issue, of concern should be the teaching profession and the negative impact its unions (and campaign contributions) have had on the quality of services delivered to students (and the resulting quality of students, of course). Compared to other industrialized countries, we spend more dollars but lag seriously in education. There is no financial incentive for teachers to excel, but instead, every incentive to reduce class sizes and teacher workloads. I'm not a teacher but I think their average salary of $45,000 per year is not horrendously bad, especially when they have 2 to 3 months in the summer to make additional money.

Smaller classrooms do not seem to be the answer, and the tenure that protects even the wildcards like **Ward Churchill** and his distasteful leanings at the *University of Colorado* must be eliminated. People like him have every right to free speech, but not on the taxpayer's dime. Most of us do not want to pay for our children to be taught a teacher's arrogant prejudices. We want them to learn history and skills that can lead to a profession. Not hate, belligerence and disloyalty to America. We must minimize the administrative bureaucracy and put good teachers more in charge. We must pay teachers well but make them more accountable, or the drive to turn the system over to the private sector will continue (though I'd be terribly concerned that it would follow the same road that our private health care and campaign funding systems have taken).

Back to taxes, according to **Robert B. Reich**, former Secretary of Labor under Bill Clinton, "The Bush administration's fiscal policy is deeply flawed. At a time in our nation's history when the gap between rich and poor is wider than the Gilded Age of the 1890s, and every rung on the income ladder is wider apart than its been in more than a century, giving a giant tax cut to people at the top is socially and morally shameful. It's also economically senseless." Reich also charges that Bush's tax cut was not to stimulate the economy but to reward his wealthy contributors and to starve the government of resources so free services to the lower income brackets would have to be eliminated. "Privatization of such services becomes a more palatable alternative when there's no money for public provision." Reich is generally right, but Bush may be the pendulum on its way to the other side.

And of course, privatization means the opportunity to reward the same private campaign contributors who seek to control these services. It's a win-win situation for the rich: First they win lower taxes for themselves and then they win the opportunity to partake in the spoils. It's funny how that works.

Look at the effort to bring all airline security guards under the federal Air Transport Association after 9/11 to ensure strong security and safe skies. The only thing that saved this private industry was the $65 million in campaign contributions from the airport security contractors and union members in years previous (though federal screeners were initially employed, a loophole remained that allowed private screeners to take over these duties later). But importantly, private funding trumped national security and also went miles to fuel the $15 billion airline bailout provided by Congress in 2002 and the United Airlines pension bailout of 2005. Frankly, it probably would have been better to see United sell off its assets and routes and employees to other carriers, because now we've sent a regretful message to other companies with poor management: get into trouble and the taxpayers will bail you out. I don't particularly like the long term prognosis of a bailout policy. Precedent is hard to reverse.

It is comical that, despite their bankruptcies, the airlines are nonetheless able to make their PAC contributions to the politicians on time. *PoliticalMoneyLine* reported contributions in the 2003-4 cycle from Northwest (186,833 with 59% to Republican candidates), Delta ($91,500 with 77% to Republican candidates), and United ($111,500 with 42% to Republican candidates). They obviously know on which side their bread is buttered. (**www.FECinfo.com**)

Worse, look at all of the pension plans that have dried up and forced retired employees onto Social Security or Welfare (*The Broken Promise*, Time Magazine, Oct 31, 2005). The federal *Pension Benefit Guaranty Corp.* (PBGC) is supposed to guarantee these plans, but so many companies have declared bankruptcy (which allows the company to keep all of the money in their pension plan), that the PBGC now has a deficit of $450 billion, which means that we taxpayers will ultimately be on the hook for these corporate losses. Thus, CEOs who have ripped off their companies can now rest assured that their ex-employees and taxpayers will pick up the tab.

The bottom line...

This is about money! It's always been about money, and it will always be about money. Political money! Again, federalized entities cannot give campaign donations, but private contractors can. That's why politicians are trying to shove privatization down our throats even when public funding is the more sensible method.

While Americans have their right hand on their heart, they had best keep their left hand on their wallets, because their congressional leaders are making hay while our attention is diverted to national terrorism. Following 9/11, Congress should have immediately mandated federalized airport security to get people flying again, and then passed campaign finance reform to get the money out of our political decisions so reasonable security and immigration laws could be passed later. But these are just a couple of the hundreds of issues that are bought and sold at the congressional level. We may not even agree with each other on this or the others, but it is not the "issues" that really count. What matters is that virtually every issue we could even dream of debating is driven by the political system and the moneyed interests. Our personal debate simply doesn't matter.

What really prompted the tax cuts?

Labor organizations are not as big an influence on the political system as many claim. According to **Micah L. Sifry** and **Nancy Watzman** of *Public Campaign,* a Washington DC based public advocacy group, Labor is outspent by business interests by more than 14-to-1 and rarely wins on the issues. In 2000 and 2002, for example, labor unions contributed just over $187 million while business interests gave $2.2 billion (that's Billion, with a "B"). It should be very clear that Bush's tax breaks would not have occurred had money not changed hands in the electoral process, and that should bother all citizens and businessmen who value honest government.

The GOP cleverly attached the misnomer **"death tax"** to what is officially the **estate tax**, which affects only 2% of the wealthiest American children upon their parents' deaths. It should instead be called a **"windfall tax"** because it goes to children who in the first place didn't work for the money that is being passed on by their parents. Even the *National Farmers Union* argues that the estate tax does not affect small family farms, as the Republicans so forcefully claim, and that not one family farm has been lost due to the estate tax! (**www.nfu.org**) Where are the Republicans getting their information?

Yes, the wealthy won again, but this is not the only area where cash buys votes for the moneyed interests. Hide your wallet when the politicians begin debating the privatization of the Social Security system, which is being pushed by the Wall Street Barons who contribute millions of dollars to politicians each year. And don't even think about fixing the high-cost and high profit health care system when physicians, for-profit hospitals and HMOs, insurance companies and the mega-profitable pharmaceutical industry spend over $100 million annually on lobbying and campaign contributions, a pot of gold that is growing wildly at the time of this writing.

It simply doesn't matter what your core issue is — follow the money and it will virtually always lead you to a politician. The common denominator in all issues that impact our lives is virtually always the dollar bill, and if you've got money and are willing to share it, you can join in the political process. Throughout your daily life, ask yourself if that one societal issue you are most concerned about would even be a problem if money wasn't changing hands at the political level. Follow the decision-making process up the ladder of power, and you will almost always identify moneyed influence along the way.

As we'll discuss in more detail later, public financing of campaigns (again, at $15 per taxpayer per year for both state and federal elections) will fix the problem, and in the process, it will eliminate the over-$3000 per year we all pay to offset corporate welfare programs. (This is an average and the number varies depending on whether you include both state and federal elections and your tax bracket. In any case, it is costing you hundreds of times more than if you simply paid for the elections up front.)

Again, let's eliminate the middleman, and the trickle down method is not what I am talking about here! Let's get back to the point where the politicians we elect are serving their constituents, you and me, and not the corporate interests. We cannot export democracy unless we first have it in our own system.

If politicians are to be responsible to the public, then the public must fund their elections. Only then will lower taxes and balanced budgets return to our daily vocabulary. If we can eliminate the effect of the fat cats who benefit from the government giveaways, we can pay for publicly funded elections hundreds of times over.

The current system pays off, for some!

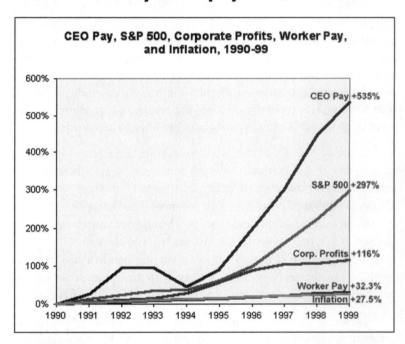

Figure 2: This chart dispels one argument made by corporations. In spite of worker pay increasing by 32% between 1990 and 1999, corporate profits nevertheless increased by 116% and CEO salaries went up by 535%. It would appear that American workers are not gouging their companies as much as the CEOs are. Source: www.faireconomy.org

According to United for a Fair Economy, if the minimum wage had risen as fast as CEO pay has since 1990, today's minimum wage would be $15.71 rather than the paltry $5.15 it is today. (www.FairEconomy.org)

It is well known that the rich pay more taxes than the poor, and the rich don't like that one bit. They often advocate a flat tax where everybody pays, say, 15% of their salary. But this is a highly regressive tax that results in a decrease in taxes for the rich and an increase for the poor. Serious thought must be given to the long-term effects such a shift of the tax burden would have on the country. The progressiveness of the current tax system helped build our strong nation. To reverse a system that has worked this well is not wise.

James K. Galbraith[3] had it right when he said "There is irony here for America's wealthy. While Bush may leave them untaxed, he will not leave them rich as they were... An economy that fails for working Americans cannot work, in the long run, for the wealthy... **To our friends among the wealthy in this country, let us say plainly: You are better off being wealthy and taxed, than going down in the first class cabins of a sinking ship."**

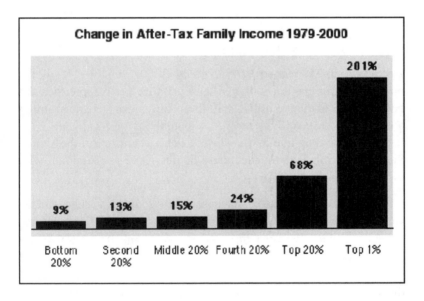

Figure 3: It's not hard to understand how this happens. When the bosses are calling the shots, their wages continue to go up while the lower echelon remains stagnate. Source: www.faireconomy.org

He is dead right. We have seen what happens in countries where the vast majority of people are poor and unemployed, compared to the few that are filthy rich, and I don't think we want that for our country. But if you follow the direction of the dominoes that are now falling, we have a good start in that direction. The rich would be wise not to demand too many riches and be happy with only a marginal spread.

More sources on income gap can be found at:

http://hope.journ.wwu.edu/tpilgrim/j190/richgetricher.html
www.ncpa.org/pd/economy/ecob1.html
www.inequality.org/incineqada.pdf
www.cooperativeindividualism.org/dodson-wealth_of_our_nation2003.html

"If Stupidity got us into this mess,
then why can't it get us out?"
Will Rogers

Who's getting the raises?

According to **www.inequality.org,** by 2000, the top 1% of the population was getting a bigger share of after-tax income than the bottom 40%. In other words, 2.8 million Americans were out-earning a combined 110 million people. "Generations of Americans have been told that they live in the world's richest nation. But the United States today might more accurately be described as the nation with the world's richest rich people."

A good argument can be made that "the strong get stronger and the weak get weaker," but the bottom line is a nation with a great and unhealthy divide between the classes, and some day we will see massive social unrest as a result, perhaps even anarchy. We must find ways to raise the standard of living for those at the bottom, and those at the top might want to spend time thinking about how to do that.

It is hard to argue against the realities of the political scene. As **www.MediaMatters.org** points out in *Misstating the State of the Union:* "While many in the media continue to mislead the public about the causes of the Bush deficit, falsely claiming [it was] brought about by the terrorist attacks rather than by reckless tax breaks for the wealthy, the facts are clear: We're experiencing massive deficits because George W. Bush cut taxes for the wealthy while increasing [government] spending nearly 30 percent in just four years. To sum up: Reagan doubled the deficit, Bush the elder nearly doubled it again, and Clinton slashed the red ink and produced a surplus of more than a quarter of a trillion dollars."

However, we cannot ignore that **Bill Clinton** had a Republican Congress and wielded the veto pen frequently, but as of this writing, Bush hasn't vetoed the GOP spending spree even once since his 2000 inauguration. It would have done some good to send Congress to the woodshed a few times, just to let them know that they are not spending their own money. It is also worth noting that a total shutdown of Congress occurred during the Clinton years, and Clinton's Congress spent much of its time impeaching him rather than spending money, so maybe political diversions aren't so bad after all.

We should also remember the promises of the GOP to close down the Department of Education and return that funding and function to the states. Instead of closing down the DOE, Bush doubled its budget so they could waste it away on his *No Child Left Behind* plan. (You can do that when you are spending other people's money.)

Bush and company missed an excellent opportunity to close the DOE after 9/11, when its employees could have been transferred to the Department of Homeland Security rather than hiring and training new employees and growing the size of government by 10.5% in just four years. Conversely, government grew by only 3% in Clinton's eight years in office. Instead of eliminating 101 domestic programs, as the Republicans promised, they did just the opposite and increased spending by 30%, again, without veto.

And speaking of media matters, another consequential issue is the relatively few mainstream media stories about our corrupt political system. Sure we hear about **Tom DeLay**, but *not* saying anything about the $500,000 given to DeLay by contributors and passed to his wife and daughter would have been such a glaring omission that even Big Media could not have weathered the resulting storm. It is hard not to call this exorbitant amount of cash a lesson in "money laundering." Ties to the contributors and the special favors given by the embattled ex-Speaker, along with the blossoming scandal of lobbyist Jack Abramhoff, appear to be the straw that broke the camel's back, though there are as many examples of Democrats crossing the same ethical line.

At the very least, Tom DeLay should have been thrown out of office by his constituents, if not sent to jail by the prosecutors, rather than letting him simply resign. He has been indicted and has resigned his leadership position in order to spend time defending the charges; but even if he does that successfully, the voters should execute the only power they have left; vote him out!

When looking at the massive amounts of congressional indiscretions reported on the unregulated Internet Blogs and web sites — reports missing from daily TV broadcasts by Big Media — it becomes all too clear why the mega-broadcasting companies might want to keep a low profile on the campaign reform issue: they are part of the corruption as they filter hundreds of millions of dollars to the same congressional members for favors just like other business sectors do (you'll read elsewhere about the $70 billion digital spectrum that was given to the industry absolutely free). In short, don't expect a major expose' by Big Media. They'd soon have to expose their own part in this national disgrace.

According to The American Prospect, April 2005:

➤ Between 2002 and 2004, state budget gaps forcing tax increases and service cuts totaled approximately $200 billion. During those same years, Bush's tax cuts for the wealthiest 1% of Americans totaled $197.3 billion.

➤ In 2003, 252 Fortune 500 companies shielded 2/3 of all profits from state corporate income taxes, and 35 paid no state taxes at all during that year.

➤ Between 1988 and 1999, audit rates for the poor increased by 33% and declined by 90% for those making over $100,000. In 2002, for every audit of a taxpayer making $100,000 or more, 5 taxpayers earning below $16,500 were audited. The tax returns of one in every 47 of the working poor were audited in 2002, compared with one in every 145 of those making $100,000 or more.

3
Who pays?
We all do – Some more,
some less.

The cost to business

Business leaders must wonder where their companies will market when the final domino falls and the consumer base can no longer afford their products and services, or worse, as the country faces the prospect of anarchy. Today's problems are mild in comparison to what could lie ahead if we don't fix these economic imbalances today. We would hope that the politicians would fix it but there is little chance of that as long as the campaign money keeps coming in.

The cost to the public

An increase in national debt means an increase in U.S. interest payments and a subsequent increase in taxes accompanied by a decrease in government services, all because of congressional mismanagement and the lust for reelection and CEO wealth.

I have yet to understand how political conservatives can hate our bloated, inefficient government, excessive laws and high taxes — the symptoms — but still favor our cash-and-carry political system, the disease. These ideals are mutually exclusive, and yet so many people on the right claim to hold both. They support a system that is terribly lacking in the integrity and morality they espouse.

As contributions increase, so goes the national debt

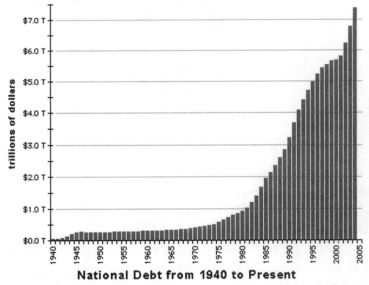

National Debt from 1940 to Present

Source: U.S. National Debt Clock
http://www.brillig.com/debt_clock/

Figure 4: Note the last three bars that represent the Bush administration's contribution to the problem, and also note the slowing during the Clinton years (when presidential vetoes were still in fashion).
Source: www.brillig.com/debt_clock

"Ninety eight percent of the adults in this country are decent, hardworking, honest Americans. It's the other lousy two percent that get all the publicity. But then, we elected them."
Lily Tomlin

The per-person debt costs

Figure 5: How our debt affects every American, each of whom currently owe over $25,000. It's sort of like owning and paying for a car that you cannot drive, but the payments (taxes) go on forever. Source: Grandfather Economic Report, http://mwhodges.home.att.net

Imagine that you have just purchased a $25,000 car that you have to park in the garage. That's right, you can never drive it, but you must make monthly payments totaling over $1800 every year. Moreover, you will <u>never pay it off!</u> You'll never own it. That's what your political leaders have done for you. Send them a thank you note.

"I don't make jokes. I just watch the government and report the facts."
Will Rogers

Total American Debt

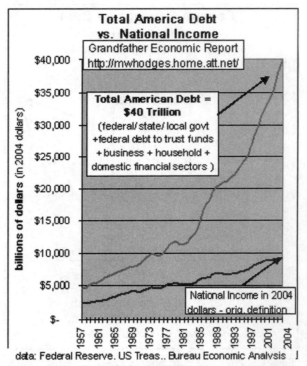

data: Federal Reserve. US Treas.. Bureau Economic Analysis

Figure 6: A comparison of the total national debt versus national income is just as revealing. Source: Grandfather Economic Report,
http://mwhodges.home.att.net

Who do we owe the money to?

We must also be concerned with where the money is coming from, and in America's case, the cash is increasingly coming from foreign investors, much of it from Asia and Europe. If we must rely on foreigners, and they start getting nervous about their U.S. holdings and backing away from investing here, interest rates will be driven higher to attract them, which will also increase the interest we pay on homes and automobiles — and the end result will be a decrease in ownership, just the opposite of what George Bush teases us with. His ownership society will be kaput!

Who's growing and who's not

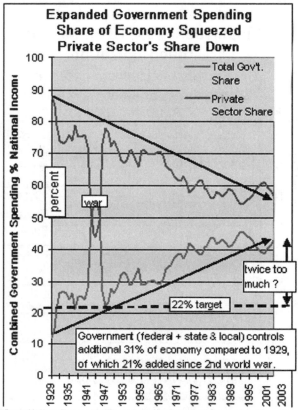

Figure 7: As a percent of total U.S. spending, government spending (bottom line) is rising while private spending (top line) is decreasing. Soon our government will be bigger than the private sector.
Source: http://mwhodges.home.att.net

*"I am not worried about the deficit. It
is big enough to take care of itself."*
Ronald Reagan

Who's gaining the jobs? Government workers.

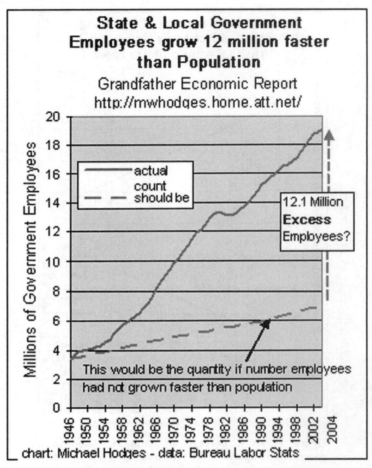

**Figure 8: As government spending increases, so must
the number of employees the taxpayer must pay for.
Source: http://mwhodges.home.att.net**

*Good legislation does not need cash
to flow; only bad legislation does.*

Another look at spending.

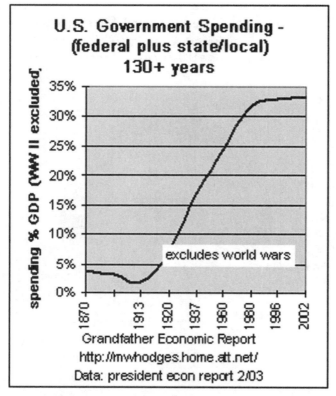

Figure 9: Government spending as a percent of U.S. Gross Domestic Product.
Source: http://mwhodges.home.att.net

Under the Clinton team, government grew by 3%. Under Bush's "conservative" administration, the president has not vetoed even one spending bill since his first inauguration in 2000 and the size of government has grown by over 10% and spending has increased by 33%. While in 2000 the federal government spent a little under $19,000 per household per year, today they spend $22,000.

Where the Feds spend your dollars

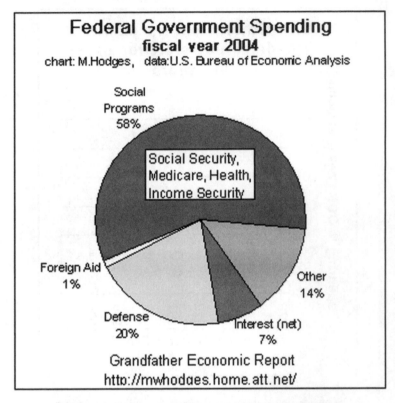

Figure 10: Where the Feds are spending your dollars.
Source: http://mwhodges.home.att.net

The failure of politicians to address the concerns of society is the symptom of a runaway disease; political corruption. Eliminating our moneyed political system is its only cure. If government is going to be owned by anybody, it should be the taxpayers. Ownership requires investment, and that investment would total less than $15 per taxpayer per year for a Clean Money campaign finance system.

Where you are spending your dollar

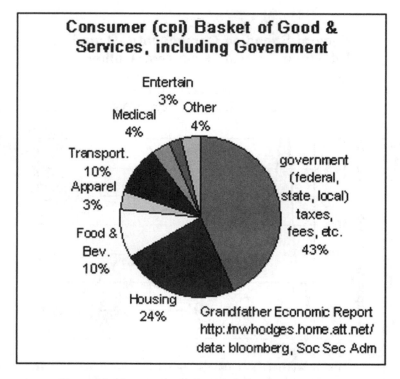

Figure 11: How you spend your dollars.
Source: http://mwhodges.home.att.net

Our moneyed political system is the only thing standing in the way of good government. That politicians can face their friends and family with the shadow of corruption hanging over their head on a daily basis is puzzling. It's like, "all of the other guys take private money and may be corrupted by it, but I am not. Trust me!"

Yeah, right.

Federal spending trend

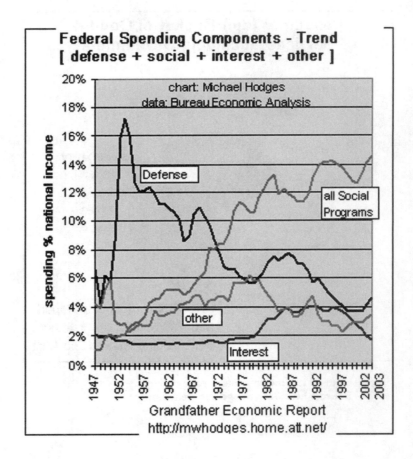

Figure 12: Social spending is on the way up, which lends strong credibility to the Right Wing's argument that it is totally out of control.
Source: http://mwhodges.home.att.net

"If you tell the truth you don't have to remember anything."
Mark Twain

4
Corporations — Necessary evils?

T he short answer is: Yes.

Corporations are legal entities that were originally established to allow average citizens to pool their resources in order to develop products and services they could not otherwise fund by themselves. The first corporation funded a national railroad system.

There is no question that job growth, the overall economy, and the strength and security of America would be a pitiful fraction of what they are today without the advent of corporate opportunities. When the government extended "limited liability" status to shareholders, which limits their personal liability to the amount of their investment, the nation's economy soared, though also at the sacrifice of corporate responsibility.

But too much of a good thing has become a major, national problem. The axiom "be careful what you ask for because you just might get it" comes immediately to mind. Corporations have become unwieldy. They have grown more than ever expected and have taken on a life of their own. If allowed to continue unchecked, corporations will destroy America and its democracy.

Our moneyed political system allows corporate executives and CEOs to influence politicians and obtain the laws needed to weaken the rights of shareholders and employees, to jeopardize retirement accounts, to weaken trade laws between the countries, and to even limit states' rights. Worse, they have succeeded in buying their way out of corporate fraud prosecutions by controlling the Securities Exchange Commission laws that govern their actions. Shareholders, employees and community stakeholders have been put at the total mercy of corporate leaders whose only interest is in maximizing their own personal wealth.

We are not very far from complete corporate ownership of America. Even today, politicians often quietly check with their major corporate benefactors before moving forward with new legislation. The issue is not how any pending legislation will affect the citizens of the United States, but how it will affect their funding sources. Tobacco and energy legislation are two prime examples. In my state, major energy suppliers were allowed to merge, thus eliminating energy competition altogether. The electric and gas companies are now one company and those seeking to compare gas versus electric heating before building a home should give it up. Those choices are no longer meaningful.

Though establishment and growth of corporations led to our strong industrialized nation, they unfortunately have also allowed a select few executives to pick the pockets of the public and to hoard personal wealth, which has in turn fueled the outsourcing of jobs to poorer nations and lower-wage workers. Outsourcing reduces costs and increases profits, of course, which many company directors use as a carrot for higher CEO salaries and stock options. It also provides an incentive to illegally pad the books to make profits artificially high, which is a major fraud against the public.

CEOs of companies that outsource the manufacturing of their products to other countries enjoy salary and benefit packages that, on average, are twice that of CEOs who have kept jobs in America. Killing jobs in America by sending work to cheap-labor countries provides the extra cash to double their salaries, so it is not difficult to understand why CEOs think hard about transferring the manufacture of their products abroad (though these companies often lose control of their intellectual property and product designs, a pretty dumb thing for an executive to do if he plans on staying with the company).

These wealthy recipients of tax breaks do not create American jobs, as some would like us to believe. In truth, high CEO salaries help drive the transfer of jobs offshore, but since executives have seized control of the corporations from their owners, the share-holders, and they now essentially own the politicians that control corporate laws, there is not mush hope for positive change soon.

I equate these few abusive executives who rape the system with the computer hacker and virus distributor. It's a small percentage of business leaders who do this, but enough of them behave badly to throw a giant monkey wrench into the nation's economic system. Hackers, spammers and the exporters of American jobs for personal gain should do hard time in jail.

Export to whom?

As **Kenneth A. Buchdahl** describes in *Dismantling the American Dream*, our standard of living will eventually become depressed and equalized with third world nations like China and India, the countries presently benefitting the most from the bulk of our job losses. Buchdahl argues that, with China's $0.40 hourly wage rate and the US's $15.50 hourly wage in the manufacturing sector, if nothing dramatic is done to change the current dynamics, we'll see American wages lowering and China's increasing, meeting somewhere around $2.00 per hour in 30-40 years. This is not the bright future that I have always envisioned for my children and grandchildren, and probably not the future you have envisioned either.

The more outsourcing that occurs, the more the recipient third world country strengthens its technology and military resources at the expense of our own. What used to be a dominant U.S. economy will disappear, and America's ability to attract the world's better scientists will go with it, a process that will jeopardize a vital aspect of our national growth and security. Buchdahl is absolutely correct.

But it doesn't stop there. Other U.S. trading partners — like Australia, Canada and Europe — are now beginning to buy Chinese rather than American products, and this will substantially reduce our future exports and add even more to our unemployment crisis. Even if our jobs were to increase, they will suffer with reduced earnings.

When are America's politicians going to wake up and smell the coffee? If the CEOs aren't going to change their stripes — and given the enormous profits they are currently reaping for themselves, that seems unlikely — then our elected officials must! And if our politicians don't take the initiative, and given their lucrative relationship with the corporations, this seems unlikely as well, then the voters must! A complete turnover in Congress may indeed be necessary before we elect a group of politicians who are smarter than those in the countries that are walking away with our economy.

What also is it going to take before corporations and their shareholders realize that outsourcing their products to unstable countries could someday cost them their products and investments when that country has social, military or political unrest and can (or will) no longer deliver product?

On corporate ownership, or the transfer thereof

Imagine yourself as one of a hundred neighbors that pooled their money to develop a man-made lake and a community recreational center. You collectively hired a CEO and board of directors, and as the years passed, the facility and organization grew to ever greater proportions. It was a great achievement.

Soon the CEO and directors changed the corporate rules and the shareholders lost control of their own facility. Then the association dues went up and the CEO began padding the salaries of the board members, and they in turn increased the CEO's salary and stock options. A sweetheart relationship ensued, and the CEO was now getting a percentage of the profits. So, he started to cook the books to make the profits look bigger than they really were.

Even as the CEO's salary escalated out of sight, he and the board decided that the lake would be more profitable as a commercial fishing attraction, thus improving their own salaries substantially. These greedy people have taken a good idea and perverted it to hijack your community.

Silly? Not totally. That's a not-too-far-out example of how CEOs can wrest power from the shareholders, the owners of the company, though in this case one would hope that the city would come to your aid. But I wouldn't count on even that simple and logical act of intervention. When you look at the power of imminent domain and follow the history of the *Wal-Mart*s and *CostCo*s of the world as they have convinced community after community that their commercial businesses create more jobs and pay more taxes than the private property owner that wants to keep his farm, the odds are not on your side. These companies have also been known to make contributions to the local mayor in his re-election bid, and more often than not, they win any disputes involving property rights.

This is also not unlike what is going on in some U.S. corporations today. The **Kenneth Lay**s and **Bernie Ebber**s and Enrons and WorldComs of the world have shown that the mechanism is there to do exactly that, to steal from shareholder owners, employees and their retirement funds, and even the community itself. All of this is made possible because the moneyed political system has prompted Congress to lift key SEC requirements for corporate responsibility. At the turn of the Y2K century, cooking the books became the norm, as company after company "restated their earnings" (read: corrected their earlier lies) — all while the SEC watched from the side. Even executives of failing companies enjoyed the benefit of massive bonuses and severance packages, all carried to them on the share-holder's back. This is often "hush money" to make sure the departing CEO does not blow the whistle on the company's shenanigans.

Call this the "kinder, gentler SEC" that then-Speaker of the House **Newt Gingrich** and his Neocons of 1994 promised us. Unfortunately, the government's kid-glove approach with corporations hit home in a big way, as millions of workers lost major portions, and sometimes all, of their retirement funds. But what else would you expect? The budget of the SEC is controlled by Congress and Congress is controlled by the corporations through campaign money. Money is driving the system, but it isn't taxpayer money.

Also from **Robert McChesney** and **John Nichols**: "Although it is clear that the Enron affair is a stunning example of supreme political corruption, the [media] coverage increasingly came to concentrate upon the business collapse of Enron and the chicanery of *Arthur Anderson*, rather than the sleazy methods, legal as well as illegal, in which the company used the political system to make billions of dollars ripping off consumers, taxpayers and workers."

McChesney and Nichols have demonstrated all too well that there is absolutely no business entity that our trusted congressmen cannot penetrate and control, and the most important to them has been our national media.

While other corporations just give campaign cash in return for taxpayer assets — sometimes even policies affecting national security — politicians have sealed this deal by receiving both media cash AND the ability to control their lifeline to the voting public. Not only do they get Big Media cash with this swap, they also get a media that is not very likely to report on their daily corruption or that of their soul mates. Sure, the **Tom DeLay** campaign's $500,000 payments to his wife and daughter will be reported (how could they not report that?), but the meat of our corrupt moneyed political system will continue to rot on the shelf unreported.

Why? Because the media is now a major player in the moneyed political system — it is not just part of the problem, it has become a major part of it because it was at one time our trusted link to the discovery of sleazy government actions. It is no more.

With the blessing of Congress (in return for cash), big media conglomerates have been able to acquire most of the local broadcasters and press outlets without monopoly interference from the *Federal Trade Commission* (FTC), thus there are no longer any checks and balances. While the FTC goes after Microsoft for antitrust violations, it has a total hands-off policy when it comes to the media. Now that NBC is owned by GE, don't expect any investigations of GE's defense contracts or environmental abuses and superfund cleanup violations. And don't expect any investigation into violations by the parent companies of CBS and ABC either, because they are also owned by giant corporations.

Our free press is now free only to those who control it, and that's the government protection citizens must now expect. Until congress begins to control the Internet in the same way it controls other media, Blogs and newsletters from public interest groups will be our only accurate access to political news. If you get Brittan's BBC on cable, they tend to have a free tongue as it relates to American politics.

Where is the public outrage? Not only do we see fewer CEOs in charge of increasing amounts of public information, a monopoly of gigantic proportions, they are less forthright. Even when the Republicans and Democrats took over the presidential debates from the *League of Women Voters*, the media essentially sat out the discussion regarding the third-party candidate loss to the public. There was no outrage. The media moguls like the two-party system just as it is because it gives them greater access to both the public and politicians. They've joined the team.

Tariffs

The early tariff system protected American industries from aggressive foreign competitors whose labor costs and lack of environmental, health care and employee safety obligations provided them unfair cost advantages. That is, it protected them until the CEOs of multinational corporations discovered that, by offshoring their own manufacturing, they could decrease their costs and increase their profits (and their own salaries and wealth in the process).

The rest is history. As the campaign contributions from multinational corporations and their executives began to flow, so-called "fair trade" laws became the norm. GATT, NAFTA and the *World Trade Organization* (WTO) began to rule American trade. Finally added to America's demise is the *Central American Free Trade Agreement* (CAFTA), which will cost us even more jobs.

Despite the rhetoric from politicians, NAFTA has failed and has cost millions of American jobs — CAFTA will also fail. But when corporations are funding the political elections, it is the corporations who will win this battle. Only public funding of political campaigns would have reversed these political priorities, but that's the last thing corporations or politicians want to see. The voters must speak out!

The spin at the time

Politicians justified these trade laws on the basis of the increased exports that would result, but none seemed to realize that people making $4 per day in other countries couldn't afford to buy products made by people who earn $120 per day here; or they simply didn't care that the trade would be in only one direction, as long as the CEOs and politicians got their money and they got a piece of it.

Thanks to those at the top of the corporate world and the congressional representatives who served as their puppets and approved this trade process in the first place, the U.S. now cannot pass trade laws to protect the American public unless the proposed laws do not violate WTO, NAFTA, GATT or CAFTA regulations. Our national sovereignty has been sacrificed to appease U.S. corporate heads. Even state governments are now being restricted by WTO regulations, which means that a One-World government is right around the corner.

Worse, this world is ultimately going to be driven by corporations and their CEOs because they drive the WTO. All of this is on our economic horizon because we've allowed private cash to fund our political system, yet it is somewhat puzzling that our congressmen have not seen the writing on the wall. Why they would accept WTO governance over our democracy is hard to understand. And to those who believe that greedy and seedy CEOs could better run our country than do our cash-compromised politicians, that takeover will be a sad day in our history.

Relocating offshore

According to **www.citizenworks.org**, corporate accountants from over two dozen major companies have found tax loopholes that allow them to move their corporate headquarters offshore to Bermuda and other Caribbean countries, which in turn allows for the transfer of U.S. profits off shore where the taxes are virtually zero. The practice of avoiding taxes via offshore havens is estimated to cost U.S. taxpayers $70 billion per year. Citizen Works also cites the U.S. General Accounting Office report of four of the top 100 federal contractors — Accenture, Foster Wheeler, McDermott International and Tyco — are incorporated in a tax haven and were awarded U.S. contracts worth $2.75 billion in 2001. While Dick Cheney was CEO at Halliburton, that company's tax havens grew from 9 to 44 and its taxes shrank from $302 million to $85 million. Also moving off shore were Global Crossing, Tyco International and Ingersoll Rand, moves that cost taxpayers $30 million, $60 million and $400 million, respectively.

Interestingly, even though they are now essentially operating as foreign companies, they can still give campaign contributions to U.S. political parties and the companies themselves can still bid on U.S. government contracts. It's funny how that works.

Enron pulled a cool, but legal, move. They reported losses of $3 billion to the IRS and paid no federal taxes, but they reported profits of $2 billion to the shareholders, which of course made its directors very happy. You'd think that only **Kenneth Lay** could work a deal like that, but it is legal for any company to carry two sets of books, one for the IRS and another for shareholders. That loophole must be closed, but political money is on its side.

Of course, while paying no taxes increases profits and executive salaries even further, Bermuda is also a potential Wild West for executive crimes against shareholder owners. Our laws do not protect American investors there, a fact that should greatly concern both shareholders and pensioners.

While most CEOs have high ethical expectations of their own employees, those who give the big bucks to political campaigns are very willing to turn a blind eye to the corrupt politicians that help them maximize their booty, which of course they gladly share with those politicians. Somehow this double standard does not shock me, given how embedded in the culture this system has become.

One congressman's battle

There aren't many of them out there, but U.S. Rep **Bernie Sanders**, the Independent congressman from Vermont, is a politician who wants to fix the system. Following is an excerpt of an editorial he wrote for the *Rutland Herald*, called "Ending Corporate Welfare":

"While corporate America is selling out the working people of this country and moving millions of jobs abroad, the taxpayers of this country continue to provide tens of billions of dollars a year in corporate welfare — loans, loan guarantees, grants, low-cost insurance and tax breaks — to the very same corporations that are throwing American workers out on the street. Here are just a few examples:

➢ Since 2001, Motorola has laid off 42,900 workers and invested $3.4 billion in China while receiving over $190 million from the U.S. Export-Import Bank and $16 million from the Advanced Technology Program.

➢ Since 1975, General Electric eliminated more than 260,000 U.S. jobs and invested over $1.5 billion in China, while receiving more than $2.5 billion from the U.S. Export-Import Bank, more than $100 million from the Fossil Energy Research and Development Program, and $8.2 million in corporate welfare from the Advanced Technology Program.

➢ Since 1990, Boeing laid off 135,000 workers increasingly outsourcing design work to China, Russia and Japan, while receiving over $18 billion in corporate welfare from the Export-Import Bank.

➢ Since 2001, General Motors has laid off 37,500 workers and invested $3.5 billion building manufacturing plants in China, while receiving over $500 million from the U.S. Export-Import Bank, $9.1 million from the Advanced Technology Program, and more than $8.5 million from the Partnership for a New Generation of Vehicles. GM has recently announced that it will be buying $6 billion in auto parts from China every year, up from $2.8 billion last year.

➢ Since 2001, IBM laid off over 15,000 U.S. workers and signed deals to train 100,000 software specialists in China over the next three years, while receiving more than $20 million from the U.S. Export-Import Bank.

➢ While Halliburton laid off 10,000 workers when they merged with Dresser, and has used foreign subsidiaries to evade U.S. taxes, they and their subsidiary Kellogg, Brown and Root received $551 million in corporate welfare from the Export-Import Bank since 2000.

And the list goes on. Dozens of America's largest corporations are on the dole while they move our jobs abroad."

Yes, and the list will continue growing as long as political money drives the political system. Politicians will never be answerable to the public unless we change their campaign funding mechanism.

Corporate responsibility

This is simply too big a subject to cover in a chapter of a book. It really requires several complete books, but a good one on the subject is *The People's Business* by Lee Drutman and Charlie Cray.

I am constantly amazed at the number of businessmen and politicians who tout "morality" and "values" and "principles" as if they trump everything else, as well they should. But then these same executives turn a blind eye to the daily corruption of their business and political colleagues, and they oppose things like unpaid family leave (but take paid time off themselves anytime they want to), an increase in the minimum wage (though their own wages escalate routinely), and worker safety laws (which they are not affected by). Where are their hearts? Their "values?" Their own morality?

They must have taken a page out of Congress' book. Congress members recently received an automatic pay raise that was adjusted for cost of living increases, and all while the minimum wage must undergo a congressional fight to be changed.

Papers on corporate lack of responsibility abound, and one of the most revealing web sites by **Russell Mokhiber** and **Robert Weissman** is called "The Ten Worst Corporations of 2004." **www.MultiNationalMonitor.org**. (As with this and other web pages, search on the title of the document.)

From their list (reprinted with permission):

➢ Abbott Laboratories raised its prices on the AIDS drug Norvir by 400% (unless the drug is used in conjunction with other Abbott products, in which case the price increase is zero).

➢ Merck, maker of Vioxx, was charged by Dr. David Graham, an FDA safety official, of being responsible for between 88,000 and 139,000 patients experiencing heart attacks or stroke as a result of using the drug. Of those, 35,000 to 55,000 are said to have died [That's worse than 9/11 by a factor of more than 10!]. The potential risks of this drug were exposed in 2000, four years prior to the company's withdrawal of the product from the market. The editors of Lancet wrote that the FDA too often sees the pharmaceutical industry as customers rather than a sector of society in need of strong regulation. Graham, following his testimony, said his bosses threatened to throw him out of the drug safety unit.

➢ **Wal-Mart** — A February 2004 report issued by Rep. **George Miller,** D-California, encapsulated the ways that Wal-Mart squeezes and cheats its employees, among them: blocking union organizing efforts, paying employees an average $8.23 an hour (as compared to more than $10 for an average supermarket worker), allegedly extracting off-the- clock work, and providing inadequate and unaffordable healthcare packages for employees.

Miller's innovation was in documenting how Wal-Mart's low wages and inadequate benefits not only hurt workers directly but impose costs on taxpayers. The report estimated that one 200-person Wal-Mart store may result in a cost to federal taxpayers of $420,750 per year — about $2,103 per employee. These public costs include:

➢ $36,000 a year for free and reduced lunches for just 50 qualifying Wal-Mart families.

➢ $42,000 a year for Section 8 housing assistance, assuming 3% of the store employees qualify for such assistance, at $6,700 per family.

➢ $125,000 a year for federal tax credits and deductions for low-income families, assuming 50 employees are heads of household with a child and 50 are married with two children.

➢ $100,000 a year for the additional Title I [educational] expenses, assuming 50 Wal-Mart families qualify with an average of two children.

➢ $108,000 a year for the additional federal healthcare costs of moving into state children's health insurance programs (S-CHIP), assuming 30 employees with an average of two children qualify.

"There's no question that Wal-Mart imposes a huge, often hidden, cost on its workers, our communities and U.S. taxpayers," Miller said. "And Wal-Mart is in the driver's seat in the global race to the bottom, suppressing wage levels, workplace protections and labor laws." (Remember, that's the old "Buy American" company.)

The extent to which Wal-Mart will go to block a union shop is unprecedented. When workers voted to unionize one store in Canada, Wal-Mart had the last laugh: they shut down the store! Completely! Costly, perhaps, but it sent a strong message to employees all over the world: unionize and you will be without a job! Wal-Mart will recoup those lost dollars without fail.

Perhaps Wal-Mart's bigger offense is that its great pressure on manufacturers to low-ball prices sends them overseas for more competitive manufacturing, and thus outsourcing becomes virtually required if they expect to do business with the world's largest retailer. This from the company that once prided itself for its Buy American mandate, and combined is the reason I avoid them altogether. And while I applaud their contribution to the victims of Katrina, it is difficult not to wonder about the motives of an otherwise non-altruistic company.

See also: **www.citizenworks.org/corp/tax/taxbreif.php**

Let's not forget *IBM*, our nation's loyal leader in technology. According to **www.faireconomy.org** IBM reported profits of $14 billion between 2001 and 2003, paid a minuscule 1.3% in taxes, yet paid its CEO **Sam Palmisano** $19.5 million, and then chose to sell its personal computer division to a Chinese manufacturer. And *Time Warner* reported $6 billion in profits from 2001-2003 and claimed federal tax refunds of $457 million, for an effective tax rate of -7.3%. *Saks Fifth Avenue* paid a whopping -2.2%. It just doesn't get any better than that.

An interesting experiment would be to tie the corporate tax rate to CEO salaries: as the CEO-to-worker wage gap widens, the higher the corporate tax rate. Of course, such a strategy would have to include other forms of compensation in the calculation, like stock options and other benefits, like CEO departure bonuses. (Sorry, I'd just like to see our unworthy but overpaid CEOs squirm.)

Global warming

When it comes to the issue of global warming, I am simply not qualified to judge whether the contending claims have merit. I do know that most credible scientists believe that it is a clear and present danger and the only issue is *when* the results of increased global temperatures will come crashing down on us. Speaking personally, however, I can envision that, if there is a building envelope of gases around the earth, it will indeed eventually raise the world's temperature — it simply stands to reason.

Whether our food sources, and ultimately our civilization, are jeopardized as a result, I do not know, but the scientists with stature are absolutely certain that these terrible things will happen. It's just a matter of when.

On the other side of the argument are the corporations who are polluting our air and poisoning our water resources and want to continue doing so. Their CEOs reject all forms of regulation on the grounds that it would increase their costs and decrease their profits (and salaries, I forgot to say).

I simply don't know the answer, and too few do; but I do know that if political money were not changing hands our government representatives would find the right answer to this issue, and damned fast. As it is, we can only be assured that the special interests will win no matter what the damage, just as they do on every other issue. And most certainly the withdrawal from the Kyoto treaty by President Bush made a lot of these guys very happy campers. You can imagine the parties they threw. It is unfortunate that the scientists who are raising the red flags, the men and women who are in a position to make this critical judgment, are not on the list of big contributors.

Free speech, the Trojan Horse

As mentioned earlier, in any other country we'd call our current political system bribery and payola; but in American politics, we call the transfer of money from powerful constituents to state and congressional policy makers freedom of speech. But speech is not free when only the wealthy can afford it.

Should the wealthy have greater freedom of speech than any other citizen? Should I be able to spend my wealth to drown out your speech? Boston Attorney **John Bonifaz** of the *National Voting Rights Institute* (**www.nvri.org**) calls this moneyed speech a violation of the Fourteenth Amendment right to equal protection under the law, and it is difficult to imagine how this perversion of democracy is anything other than precisely that.

Even if you believe the politicians when they say that campaign contributions do not buy favors, only access to the politicians, that is an explicit admission that the poor do not have the same access as the rich, and therefore do not have equal representation under the law. Thus our politicians are blatantly violating the 14th Amendment of the U.S. Constitution while they simultaneously tout the First Amendment.

Contrary to what many CEOs and politicians believe, or at least want citizens to believe, corporations are not people. Not even my corporation. They cannot go to jail for their wrongdoing or even vote for the politicians they own. They are artificial, paper entities given privileges by the state (read, the people) to perform lawfully to benefit the citizenry of that state. They are things, possessions. But somehow the Supreme Court, in its infinite wisdom, has bestowed upon these "things and possessions" the right to finance our political system under the premise that money is speech.

Importantly, nobody denies the CEOs and shareholders, individually, their freedom of speech. But "things and possessions" should not have the same rights as people and should not be allowed to drown out the speech of citizens. Nor should I have the right to double influence, once as a voter and again as a shareholder. Nor as a shareholder should I be forced to accept the political influence the corporation in which I am invested has on politicians. Citizens should take precedent over corporations, not the other way around, and this is an issue the courts should reverse.

Nonetheless, the rich guys prefer the current moneyed system to regular voting. The money that they or their companies provide buys television time, which for the politician builds name recognition, the number one reason people vote for candidates. To be frank, if the fat cats can influence the votes of many, they need not vote themselves because they in essence vote over and over again by proxy. What those with money are really doing is using the corporate structure, which was in effect given to them by the people, against the people themselves. And then they add their political costs to the price of their product and they get reimbursed at the cash register by the very people they stuck it to! This is a great system we have.

Political responsibility

Can our current state legislatures and Congress change this unfair and undemocratic drain on the public?

Of course they can, but don't hold your breath waiting for action. The ability to outspend their challengers gives incumbents a 94% re-election advantage, and they like things just as they are, thank you.

Clearly, corporations should be controlled by government and not the other way around. And while the CEOs have the right to hire and fire their own employees, they should not have the right to hire and fire our elected officials and control the wealth and spending of the taxpaying public, which they have obtained surreptitiously through the direct ownership of state and federal politicians.

Congressmen will deny this relationship, even get offended at the suggestion, but a detailed look at the campaign contributions they receive compared to the resulting votes they make on behalf of their cash constituents will readily justify this charge. Political loyalties are not directed toward the public they have sworn to serve.

Corporations are responsible for delivering profits to share-holders, and neither the corporations nor their CEOs represent the will of the public. Nevertheless, they control the public, our very lives, by virtue of the legislation they purchase. Weakening government control to the benefit of corporations, which many right wing apologists advocate, jeopardizes the very system that sustains our government structure and democracy. That's what got our great nation to where it is today; going backward is not my choice.

The answer is not to eliminate corporations, but instead, to eliminate the financial power they have over the politicians.

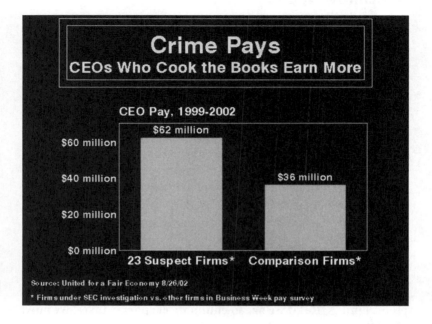

**Figure 13: Corporate cooking of the books pays off big.
Courtesy: www.pnhp.org**

Corporations have an absolute need to lobby Congress and have their side of the issue heard, as Congress needs to hear all sides of all arguments. That kind of interaction in itself is good, and we should all support debate. What is bad is that corporations are, in effect, allowed to lobby with cash in hand. (Oh, yeah, that's illegal. They have to send the check a week in advance of, or following, their meeting.)

Public funding of campaigns, as will be detailed later, a system wherein the politicians are beholden to the public rather than the special interests, a system wherein laws are passed on the basis of what really is in the best interest of the public rather than multi-national corporate interests, will only come to be when the public demands it. This type of honest representation will also, automatically, take into account the interests of the corporations that bring jobs to the people. But the representation will not be unbalanced, as it is today.

Alternative tax methods

It is easy to vacillate on the corporate tax issue, but the bottom line is that our tax system is broken because it can be manipulated by campaign contributions. And since corporate taxes are providing an even smaller percentage of federal revenues anyway, from 21% in 1962 to 8% of overall government revenues today, and with some of our most profitable companies paying no taxes at all, why do we tax corporations at all?

I've come to believe that we should just eliminate corporate taxes altogether, and the loopholes they foster, and put the entire tax burden on the public. We pay the corporate taxes anyway, when they add their expenses to the price of their product, so why not just pay them more directly and make US products more competitive and US jobs more plentiful? That would reduce the lobbying for loopholes and the complexity of the tax system and the company moves to Bermuda. The expense of avoiding taxes via a costly accounting department and consulting firm would also be eliminated, all of which would reduce product prices. **But if we are to eliminate corporate taxes, we must also eliminate state and federal subsidies to corporations!**

Or better yet, totally eliminate taxes for corporations that have reduced the total compensation gap, including all stock options and bonuses, between their highest paid and lowest paid workers, to below 100-to-one! *Now the overpaid CEOs can really squirm.*

Other proposals:

Low-income: Those making below $25,000 per year should not pay taxes at all, but those without a job and collecting unemployment, welfare or food stamps should have to preform community services for the 20 hours per week they are not seeking a job.

Middle income: I favor a flat tax on incomes between $25,000 and $150,000 per year, though the tax preparation and accounting firms might not like having to then find other sources of income.

Upper income: They should pay on a progressive basis, any even more so than they are today. Let me restate that: This could be righted by simply repealing Bush's unfair tax cuts he's given since 2000. By and large, a fair tax system will ensure longevity for our democracy.

These tax rates are starting points and should be indexed to inflation. They should apply equally to all income: profits on savings and investments, stock dividends, capital gains, estate taxes, and even to lucrative stock options. It would also eliminate the games that are played, like the **Google Boys** taking only $1 in wages and all of their income in stock so they can pay taxes at the lower capital gains rate.

To argue that these ideas would stifle investments is baloney. The rich will put their money where it draws the best return, and investments have always outperformed bank interest rates. If the wealthy CEOs don't like this approach, their boards can vote them another $10 million or so to cover their taxes. Let it come out of company profits, as their salaries do today. (Hello.... shareholders!)

This simplified tax system would free a lot of IRS employees to apply for jobs at the Homeland Security Department or border patrol and leave a few to handle the few tax returns from the wealthy. It would also cut the tax preparation costs for those 90% who are flat-taxed, though it would have a negative employment effect on the accounting profession (which in recent cases is being off-shored anyway). But these savings by the lower classes will be spent on product that will help the economy grow, in sort of a "trickle up" basis. (Sorry Mr. Norquist; you might have to look for other employment too.)

But the rich will continue to complain about getting taxed at a higher rate. When I hear of rich people — especially those few who have elevated their incomes on the backs of the poor — complain that they have to pay too much in taxes, my heart really bleeds for them. If their intelligence was more substantial than their greed they would want to do everything possible to narrow the wealth gap between themselves and the very poor.

Unlike Japan's current wage gap of 10-to-1 (between CEO and lowest-paid worker), America's wage gap has grown from 40-to-1 in 1982 to over 400-to-1 today. Over 13,000 households now have an average annual income of $10.8 million. How much money do these people really need? When is enough enough? For many of these people it is pure greed; not a rising tide that is lifting all boats. Many of those at the top are depressing the wages of those at the bottom, all to build their own wealth. I stress again that I am not against wealth, only that which has been acquired inappropriately.

If the wealth gap keeps widening at the current rate, there will be a major backlash as the lower classes revolt against the upper classes long before mid-century. There is just no way to stop that eventuality under the current set of political-corporate circumstances.

The logical conclusion is that government will collapse and anarchy will ensue. It may not happen in my lifetime or perhaps yours, but it is unavoidable if the U.S. stays on its current path. Remember the WTO demonstrations? Multiply that by hundreds of thousands of angry citizens and you have a likely scenario for America's future if wage inequity is allowed to continue to grow.

Cream of the crop

It is hard to believe that the corporate scandals involving **Kenneth Lay** at *Enron*, **Bernard Ebbers** at *WorldCom*, **John Rigas** and his sons at *Adelphia*, **Richard Scrushy** at *HealthSouth*, and **Dennis Kozlowsky** at *Tyco* could ever have happened in the United States.

But thanks to the groundwork laid by Congress, they did. **Micah L. Sifry** and **Nancy Watzman** of *Public Campaign* discuss the effects of corporate irresponsibility in their highly-recommended book *Is That a Politician in your Pocket? Washington on $2 million a day.*

They write that, "The first reckless change made by Congress was the treatment of stock options. Back in 1994, the *Financial Accounting Standards Board* (FASB) was preparing to rule that the granting of such options be treated as a company expense. That step would have reduced corporate earnings and thus deflated stock values. But it would have also tempered the rise in CEO pay and it would have reduced the incentive for CEOs to artificially inflate their company's stock price through all sorts of deceptive accounting schemes. However, most CEOs simply saw the proposed change as an attack on their compensation and convinced lawmakers that it would stifle incentives. In response, the Senate passed a nonbinding resolution sponsored by Senator **Joe Lieberman** (D-CT) calling on the FASB to back down, which it did."

Arthur Levitt, then-chairman of the FEC, told PBS's *Frontline* "There was no question in my mind that campaign contributions played the determinative role in the Senate activity." Senator Lieberman was very high on their list of campaign recipients.

Thank you, Senator Lieberman. I had always thought that corporate giveaways was only a Republican problem. Now we know that the Democrats are just as bad.

The authors report that, when the SEC attempted to force the accounting industry to stop selling consulting services to the same firms they did accounting for, which was a clear conflict of interest, letters from 47 Congress members forced the SEC to back down, and the corporate looters breathed a sigh of relief. Ultimately, 700 corporations restated their earnings after the roof fell in. (This is what Senator Proxmire would call "what members of Congress do not do" as a result of receiving money from the right people. They did not regulate the industry as they were obligated to do because they did not want to turn off the money spigot.)

Another look at corporate responsibility by the Cato Institute can be found at: **www.cato.org/pubs/handbook/hb108/hb108-22.pdf**

The *Cato Institute*, a Libertarian think tank in DC, has done excellent work exposing unnecessary government spending (the symptom), but I have yet to see it identify and condemn the reasons politicians give away taxpayer assets in the first place. The disease, i.e., the private corruption of our public electoral system, seems not to resonate with Cato's concerns, which has long opposed fixing the system with public funding of campaigns.

I am mindful that at least a portion of its financial support comes from the very entities that benefit from writing the campaign checks, so Cato may not want to harness its own supporters, one of which has been Philip Morris. But in my mind it is ridiculous to complain about government spending and ignore the catalyst — campaign cash. What is it about our cash-and-carry political system that these people do not understand? I would advise Cato (and the Concord Coalition) to attack the corruptive political process; not protect it or ignore it. As to Cato's book "Welfare for Politicians," I would argue that there is no better system of "welfare for politicians" than the one we already have, where re-election rates are over 90% and incumbents have a 4-to-1 fundraising advantage over challengers. Its editor, **John Samples**, implies that the Clean Money system does not increase competition when it clearly has done so in Arizona and Maine, where 78% of its current legislature are Clean Money candidates. He argues, in essence, that only unpopular candidates take public money for campaigns, when in both 2002 and 2004 the Republicans won more races under Arizona's Clean Money system than did the Democrats. Samples posits that taxpayers should not have to support candidates with beliefs different than their own, when in fact that is exactly what happens in the current system when taxpayers are forced to pay, through the hidden tax system, that which results when opposition politicians give state or federal assets to the special-interests they do not support. Samples and I are clearly on different wavelengths.

When I hear that our political system *is not really so corrupt after all*, I am reminded of the arguments by the tobacco companies when they wanted us to believe that cigarettes were not really hazardous. But people are smarter today, on both counts.

Think about it

Why have politicians become numb to the fact that every time their name is mentioned along with a company, it only has to do with how much money that has changed hands between them? Why don't they want to become known as a politician that helped clean up the political system?

Public elections should not be financed with private money. Period! If public office holders are to be beholden to anybody, it should be to the taxpayers. But then, as mentioned repeatedly here, the taxpayers will have to fund the elections (at a cost of about $15 per year for both state and federal elections).

Note that the taxpayers are already funding the elections through the back door as politicians trade public assets for campaign cash. But if we were to pay for the elections more forthrightly we could reduce those costs to tens of dollars per year as opposed to the current thousands it is now costing us.

5
Social Security:
Bent or Broken?

Y ou have surely heard the arguments on both sides of the Social Security issue. What stands out most is the massive political commitment President Bush has made to push his privatization agenda through Congress. (Sorry, the word "privatization" didn't poll well so he now prefers "personal savings accounts.")

Bush's logic escapes me. Social Security needs tweaking, but it is not in a crisis. The lack of affordable health care for the public is a crisis situation, however. So is guarding our borders and increasing military intelligence and providing Kevlar vests to our troops and armoring their Humvees. There must be heavy political money behind the SSI privatization effort, or he wouldn't be staying up nights figuring out how to make it happen.

When this discussion began, I really liked the idea of "personal accounts" for Social Security. After all, if anyone's going to control my money, I'd rather it be me than a government department. But then I started putting all of the pieces together and wondered: why would a president who is so concerned about leaving massive debt for future generations give massive tax cuts to the wealthy that would cause that massive debt he so despises? That's what his Social Security plan would do.

Then I looked at our privatized campaign finance system, which has turned our country upside down — in fact, virtually trashed any ethical values we might hope for in the political arena — and decided that I didn't want anything like the Bush plan for my retirement. I don't trust the motives of private banking contributors and I don't like the motives of the investment bankers supporting this system.

Next on the right-wing cut list will likely be Medicare, Medicaid, Welfare and the many other societal parachutes that keep the needy from crashing headlong into the ground (though many of these programs are abused and probably deserve cutting or reorganizing). These programs are paid for by working Americans yet they support mostly non-working Americans. Sometimes even illegal immigrants. The *Cato Institute* has calculated that the whole package of welfare benefits is equivalent to a $30,000 per year job, thus encouraging people not to look for work.

Recent government reports claim widespread welfare over-payments totaling $45 billion per year, or over $400 per working household. That must be fixed. Able-bodied people must be made to work, somehow, somewhere, even if in a low level public position to help transition them back into the mainstream workforce.

Improper and fraudulent Medicare payments cost taxpayers over $21 billion in 2004 alone. Medicaid fraud could reach into the billions for the state of New York alone, according to a July 18 2005 New York Times investigation. And though Medicare-for-all is a reasonable health care solution, the clamp on these abuses must still be tightened. And incidentally, Medicare and Medicaid fraud are not the only problems — private insurance fraud exists too, and likely to a much higher degree. In addition, more than 10% of food stamps are fraudulently issued to people in prison or to people who are deceased. This too must stop, and the states should open their systems to private investigators willing to work for a 24% or 50% discovery bonus.

But as far as Social Security is concerned, it is a program that was bought and paid for by the workers themselves, and the majority of people would accept a tax increase to save it. But the right wing has different ideas, and the special interests would like to control that money themselves. Social Security is not Welfare for the elderly. It is in most cases their own money, an involuntary savings account that people invested in so they could live their later years without going on the public dole. The workers and their employers paid into this system and they deserve at least to get their investment back (Bush promises that those over 50 will, a clear effort to quiet a major senior constituency).

The question now is: Does Social Security require massive change or a little tweaking, and how should that change or tweaking be accomplished?

The system clearly needs adjustment, but regardless of the outcome, many of us would feel a lot better if we knew that the they were being made without political money changing hands. Because people are living longer, the beneficiaries will have to contribute more. (Most of us do not like the alternative to "living longer.")

And we have yet to analyze the not-so-obvious: with Bush's propensity for allowing illegal immigrants into the country, does that also mean that those immigrants over 65 are going to qualify for Social Security? How about Medicare and Medicaid and federal housing and food stamps? All funded by taxpayers!

Follow the money (again!)

It seems that the people who want to destroy Social Security are mostly the more affluent right wing. They have already made it in life and don't need financial support, and perhaps as a result, see SSI as a drain on the economy and their investments. Then there are the corporations who must pay an equal amount of FICA taxes on behalf of the employee. This obligation cuts into profits and executive pay and perks, so diverting money away from FICA reduces their costs. Both of these groups are heavy campaign contributors.

The people who want to protect SSI are the poor and middle class who have paid into it for years and wish now that they didn't need it. They would prefer being rich, but about 65% of the elderly depend on that check for at least half of their income. Unfortunately, this group does not make campaign contributions, at least not in sufficient amounts to get anyone's attention, or clearly they would not have to worry about their future benefits.

An editorial in the February 7, 2005 edition of *U.S. News & World Report* stands out: "A Cure Worse Than the Cold," was written by its publisher. **Mortimer Zuckerman** cites 10 studies by the Securities and Exchange Commission that indicated "a disturbing level of financial illiteracy. For example, only 12 percent of the investors studied could distinguish between a load and a no-load mutual fund; only 14 percent understood the difference between a growth stock and an income stock; only 38 percent knew that when interest rates rise, bond prices fall; almost half somehow believed that diversification guarantees that their portfolio would not suffer if the market dropped; and 40 percent thought that the trust fund's operating costs would not be deducted from their investment return." He ends with: "Privatization thus gets things upside down. Social Security was not meant to re-create the free market; it was intended to insure against the vagaries and cruelties of the market and to permit Americans to count on the promise that the next generation will take care of them in their old age."

So that leaves a large number of workers dependent on the advice of the very foxes who want free run of the henhouse to get at their money and maximize their own wealth. Today 1% of the public owns more corporate stock than the bottom 90%. They know how to deal with their money, but much of the public does not. *The Nation* magazine charges that "the hope is that every private-account holder will see trial lawyers, government regulation, corporate taxation, and union drives as a threat to his or her retirement security." [And presumably they will join the fight against their own interests.]

It's the economy, Stupid!

This whole thing is just politics as usual, and very few of us trust politicians — especially those who are supposed to represent us but instead take money from the guys who want to get at our wallets.

For 70 years, our Social Security dollars have been protected from private interest manipulation, but the politicians have finally found a way to free these funds to benefit their cash constituents. Create a "crisis" and then offer a way out; let workers opt to put 4% of their FICA taxes into a safe part of the financial market.

Why can't we ever learn? Privatizing our campaign finance system led to massive corruption in Congress that plagues every aspect of our lives. Privatizing Social Security would drastically compound that problem.

Who's got the gold?

Remember the golden rule: he who has the gold, rules. In the case of private social security accounts, the rulers would be the Wall Street Barons and financial institutions that are funding the political campaigns. They gave President Bush over $20 million in 2004 to watch after their interests, not yours.

I can hear it now: "Too much government control; not enough options." The slippery slope begins. Once they have their foot in the door and the campaign cash starts flowing, hold on to your wallet. Today it is "4% and safe" investments, but when the campaign cash begins flowing to the congressmen who control the rules, the rules will change. But don't expect them to change in your favor. When Congress is further weakened by their money, the regulation of the financial industry will be slim.

Look at it now

Privatization of Social Security accounts means billions of new dollars coming into the stock market from millions of new investors, all going to Wall Streeters who give tens of millions of dollars in campaign contributions. The public must ask: if campaign cash were not flowing from the financial institutions to politicians, would the social security issue even be on President Bush's to-do list?

Probably not. As we've learned, good legislation does not require cash to flow from businesses, only bad legislation does. And this should worry every citizen that pays taxes. A hoard of cash is flowing to ensure that this bad legislation gets passed into law, which is all the more reason it shouldn't be. The politicians are drooling at the thought of this new source of income from the financial institutions, as it opens the door to millions more in contributions every time rule changes are proposed or debated in the years to come. This is a new political money machine the likes of which we've never seen.

We must also wonder: since President Bush says his proposal for citizens is "something like" what he and Congress and the federal employees have, why doesn't he simply propose changing the rules to allow us peons to opt into the federal retirement system? It's because the financial interests don't want the same strict government rules to apply to the rest of us. Right now their commissions for these federal investment programs are limited. Loosen the rules and such a program offers options to get rich, or rather, for the rich to get richer. Another "unmentionable" is the side effects of privatization of the Social Security system. What used to be cheap money for the government — SSI money went into low interest loans to the government for spending elsewhere — will now be diverted to the financial industry. Government financial resources would decrease and the U.S. must then get its money from outside sources — either from these same Wall Street financiers or from foreign investors — at much higher interest rates. So the public pays again and private interests win again, and the competition for money drives up interest rates for all taxpayers.

Privatization

I like the idea of privatizing a lot of things, but not while the private interests control the rules through campaign cash. That's a severe conflict of interest that ensures that the public stands no chance of winning. I wouldn't allow this conflict of interest in my own business, and few businessmen would. The political system is no different.

That said, Social Security should be an insurance to protect those who weren't as lucky in life. Admittedly, some work harder and are luckier than others, but if we do not create a solid safety net providing at least minimal living income, we'll end up supplementing it later with welfare payments. Besides, there are ethical considerations that have to do with our values. That's what Americans do — we take care of our elderly and we do not abandon them.

Though that age is behind me, I don't favor forcing people to wait until they are 68 or older to retire. That just keeps them in jobs that could be filled by younger workers when we could be reducing unemployment costs in the process of turning us old folks out to enjoy our final years.

One easily digested fix is to extend the amount of salary that is applicable to FICA withholding, say, from the current $90,000 to $500,000 annually, and indexing it to inflation. **Or better yet, eliminate the cap altogether!** That would give the system a big boost and would increase the contributions for less than 10% of the public, those at the top of the wage scale who can well afford it. We could even limit benefits to only those whose outside income is less than $100,000 per year, which is 90% of the people. Admittedly, the higher wage earners may squeak a little on this, but the compassionate among them will not. (Wait a minute! I forgot that Congress members and their funders fall into this category. Forget I said that.)

Privatizing government functions will make sense only when our political campaigns are funded by the public. If the politicians are going to protect their funders, let those funders be the taxpayers!

Those darned Baby Boomers

Yes, as the Baby Boomers age, the Social Security system will run a deficit at some point in time, just as the president claims. But the previous proposal will get us through that era, and soon after, we will see a baby bust and taxes can be appropriately reduced. In fact, some argue that if the economy remains on the upswing, we'll do just fine without any changes at all. But somehow it is hard to trust the economy, given the massive loss of American jobs due to outsourcing to other countries and the expanding influx of illegal immigrants. I'd rather pay more taxes if I knew they were being properly used.

It is interesting how these issues draw political money to the table, and continue drawing money into the political campaigns long after. President Bush has called the Social Security issue a crisis, and I'm sure the moneyed folks would like us to think that it is.

But is it really? At the very least, the discussion over what to do will keep the campaign money flowing, both from those who support the idea and from those who don't but want a seat at the table. Again, I don't know who is right, but I do know that Congress would find the answer to this issue pretty damned fast if they weren't receiving cash from financial interests.

That said, I can actually see these private retirement investments encouraging corporate growth, but given the direction that corporations are moving in today, growth tends to mean that mostly foreign jobs will be created and, most certainly, corporate CEOs will grow stronger than they are today — and neither development is in the best interest of the country.

We must fix the political system so these problems do not continue eroding the American economy.

How Social Security rolls are expected to grow

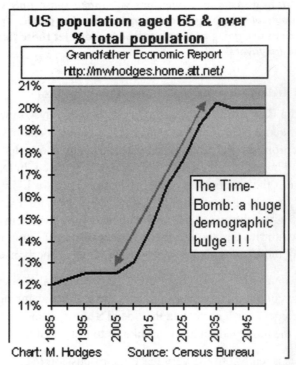

Figure 14: As a result of the Baby Boomer generation, the percent of eligible retirees is expected to increase by over 20% between 2005 and 2035. Indeed, the system must be tweaked, but it doesn't have to be destroyed.
Source: http://mwhodges.home.att.net

6
High health care costs are just the symptom of a terrible disease; eliminating our moneyed political system is the cure

Employers continue to pay double-digit increases in health care costs, and small businesses struggle to find ways to pool their resources to bargain for lower insurance premiums, but few understand the real dynamics of the problem. Consumers continue to push from the top, but the for-profit health care interests on the other end keep winning more and more political concessions — and costs continue to rise at astronomical rates.

People are focusing on the wrong question. They ask, "How can we pay for these high medical bills," when instead they should be asking: "Why are medical charges so high in the first place? What is driving the increases at five times the rate of inflation?"

First, understand the factions within the health care system. According to one industry survey (**www.pnhp.org**), the majority (64%) of physicians (though not necessarily their medical associations) favor a fair, single-payer system that would greatly reduce the bureaucracy and let them practice medicine instead of filling out paperwork and arguing with gatekeepers and paper pushers. Only 26% of physicians support the current system.

But the other faction — the for-profit hospitals, insurance and drug companies, and a few physicians raking it in at the top — are deathly afraid that we are going to implement an efficient health care system like that in Canada, where costs are 40% less than America's and their system covers all citizens rather than passing over 15% of its population as we do. The 40% savings that we'd experience in a similar system will mostly come out of these inefficient for-profit entity's pockets, so it should surprise no one that they are spending over $100 million annually trying to convince the public and politicians that the Canadian system is terrible and long wait times for care will result in gobs of body bags.

Even in Canada, their for-profit interests are lobbying to eliminate that country's universal health care system because they'd like to open their system to the profit taking enjoyed by their brethren south of the border. Canada has reduced the costly inefficiencies that these interests would pocket if they could have a US-type of open-ended for-profit system. Good for Canada. Also understand that American for-profit interests are waiting at the border for Canada to change to our system, then they'll pounce with a copy of NAFTA in their hand. Canadians are sitting ducks unless that country's politicians fix their system and lock it into place. As the U.S. health care interests take over the Canadian system, there is virtually no way for Canada to go but down. It doesn't have to be that way if their politicians ignore the lobbyists, increase their taxes to a level that will support their system and lock it into place.

Where are the body bags?

The Canadian horror stories are, simply, not true. The bodies of dead Canadians are not lined up on their streets. Wait times for medical services in Canada are usually short or nonexistent when truly urgent, just like in our system. They do have waiting times for non-urgent procedures, because they push their system more to the limits, but we many times do too (though our waits are still not as long). When their system's opponents really want to make things look bad, they count everybody with a future appointment as being on a waiting list, even if someone speculatively places themself on the list for knee surgery they aren't sure they are going to have.

Using that tactic we'd look bad too, but we also have problems. Physicians at USC Medical Center in California reportedly complained that emergency room patients can wait for up to four days for a hospital bed and others may die before receiving care. Perhaps we aren't always as lucky as we think we are. Americans are much more likely to be denied care altogether, if not because of excessive cost then for having poor or no insurance at all.

Over 90% of Canadians prefer their system over America's, as do most of their doctors (though some have departed for the bigger bucks south of the border). But if the U.S. switches to the Canadian system those doctors will only have South Africa without a universal system to migrate to. All other industrialized countries have universal health care coverage, putting us terribly behind the rest of the world.

Canadian employers pay a small health care tax ($800 per employee per year) and leave the health issues to the single-payer contractor to administer. In the US, we pay higher medical costs and often find our employers stuck between an unhappy employee and an insurance company trying to deny that employee his or her health care. And while Canada's unionized companies do not have to bargain for health care benefits, that's a frequent issue here.

What's wrong with this picture? Why are we so hung up on our out-of-control system? Because for many right wingers, they have an ideological bent against government involvement in health care, even when it makes the most sense and even when they are getting ripped off by the private health care sector.

The current U.S. health care interests will get the same amount of money for treating 45 million more patients, obviously cutting into their lucrative profits. No wonder they don't like the idea!

The fix for the U.S. is simple; we need a universal health care system like Canada's. Not socialized medicine, but a system of private non-profit hospitals and independent physicians that get reimbursed by one publicly-paid contractor instead of the mish-mash of 1500 insurance companies and health care plans that we currently have. Think about it as Medicare-for-all but without the wait times and still with better payments to physicians. As I cover our own system's problems you'll be able to tie them to this solution, which is supported by thousands of physicians and public interest groups.

Think about it.

The U.S. has less than 5% of the world's population, and yet spends 50% of the world's health care dollars. According to the *UN 2004 Human Development Report* and to **Dr. Stephen Bezruchka** of the *University of Washington*, Americans are less healthy than the residents of nearly every other wealthy nation. But as Bezruchka suggests, our higher investment in health care is not buying us better health. The United States ranks 26th in life expectancy, behind countries like Japan (81.5 years), Australia (79.1) Switzerland (79.1) and Canada (79.3, even with its notorious wait times for scheduling non-emergency operations). The U.S. is a dismal 26th at 77 years. By comparison Canada is in fifth place. Fifty years ago, the U.S. was in the top 5 in life expectancy. But today, even if we eradicated heart disease, our number one killer, as a cause of death, we still wouldn't be the healthiest country in the world.

Look also at the dialysis centers in the U.S., where 85% of them operate under the for-profit corporate structure. According to **Dr. David Himmelstein**, et al, in *Bleeding the Patient: The consequences of Corporate Healthcare,* the death rates for American dialysis patients is 47% higher than in Canada, and more than half of Americans are treated with reprocessed dialysis, a very unsafe practice. As well, twice as many patients get kidney transplants in Canada than in the U.S. What are they doing right?

In a study of 26,000 hospitals and 38 million patients between 1982 and 1995, **Dr. P.J. Devereux** showed a 2% higher risk of death in the growing for-profit hospital segment of health care. (Canadian Medical Association Journal CMAJ 166:1399-1406, 2002)

Before we get too far, let's make one thing very clear. When we say that the U.S. *spends* twice the amount of money on health care than what most other countries spend, it makes it sound like these are wise and elected expenditures. They are not. It is more accurate to say that the U.S. is being *charged* twice as much for its health care than any other country — charged by the medical providers that have been given too much freedom in what they can bill the system for the tests they order and drugs they prescribe. And they are getting away with it because the consumer (patient) is not qualified to oversee the medical decisions, nor would they even second-guess decisions that affect their health. They must trust their doctor. What we are really seeing is the stark difference between controlled and uncontrolled health care, and "more expensive" does not necessarily make it "better." We are also seeing a medical system that has been allowed to run amok by the politicians who are, effectively, on the health care payroll.

The 80-20 rule

As an aside, 15% of our sickest population consumes 70% of our health care costs, and that may be the case in Canada too. Though Canada spends 40% less per patient, that country still has far healthier people, *two years longer life expectancy*, and a *35% lower infant mortality rate* (primarily because mothers are not deterred from getting prenatal care), and their system *administration costs are 8% compared to up to 30% in the U.S.* And one more time just so you don't miss this fact, they cover 100% of their patients compared to 85% coverage here. There certainly does not seem to be anything wrong with their system, and in fact, it seems downright successful compared to ours.

One physician friend of mine complains that in spite of major complaints from the physicians at his clinic, the clinic administrators have overridden the physicians' advice with regard to which outside lab they should be using, that in spite of deep concerns in quality. Non-physicians should not be in charge of health care!

While we pay more for health care than countries with unified plans...

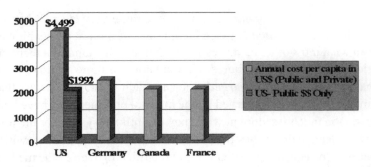

Figure 15: Courtesy: Wisconsin Citizen Action
www.CitizenActionWI.org

...we aren't as healthy.

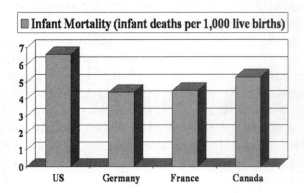

Figure 16: Courtesy: Wisconsin Citizen Action
www.CitizenActionWI.org

And we don't live as long...

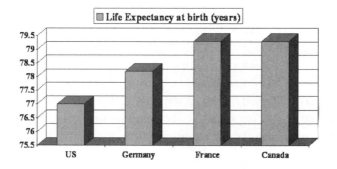

Figure 17: Courtesy: Wisconsin Citizen Action
www.CitizenActionWI.org

One source (that I've misplaced) charges that when you add up all of the citizens in the 14 states of Massachusetts, Alabama, Iowa, Oregon, Connecticut, Mississippi, Vermont, Arkansas, Montana, West Virginia, Louisiana, Indiana, Maine and Nebraska — all 45 million of them — they equal the number of Americans without health care insurance. Another 50 million Americans are poorly covered because of loopholes, caps, pre-existing diseases and exclusions. These U.S. citizens are a mishap away from financial disaster and the bankruptcy phenomenon that plagues America.

In fact, approximately 50% of all personal bankruptcies involve or result from exorbitant health care costs. Health care is not an elective purchase, like buying furniture or a boat. It is necessary and all too often requires a choice between saving the life of a loved one and remaining solid financially. That is a choice no human should have to make. Mothers are foregoing critical blood pressure and cholesterol medicines so they can keep food on the table for their children, and some die of stroke or heart attack as a result. Follow the political money and you'll see why we allow this to happen.

Fareed Zakaria reported in *Newsweek* (4/18/05) that Ontario now makes more cars than Detroit. GM and others of the Big Three have already moved some of their auto manufacturing to Canada because an American worker costs them $6,500 per year in health care compared to $800 in Canada. That's because their taxpayers pick up most of the costs. This adds $1500 to the price of a U.S.-made car compared to Toyota's $186 per car when it manufactures cars abroad. Zakaria suggests that when China and India start making cars for sale in the U.S. their health care costs will add only $50 per car. GM has recently announced that it will be cutting 25,000 jobs over the next three years, obviously moving its work to Canada, and Toyota has announced that it is putting its new RAV4 manufacturing plant in Ontario rather than the United States!

Can any of our political leaders connect these dots??? Do they even want to, with all of the political cash flowing their way? It is quite apparent that they do not.

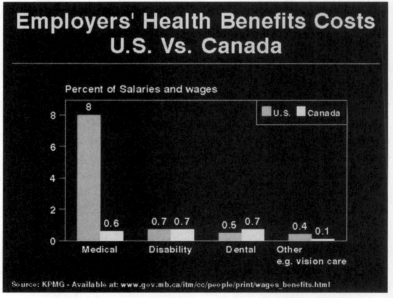

Figure 18: Why Canada looks so attractive to manufacturers. But the U.S. can do better and we will do better. Courtesy www.pnhp.org

Part of GM's U.S. problem is that it pays for current employee medical costs and must, by union contract, continue paying even after retirement; whereas Canada's manufacturers were never saddled with medical costs in the first place. That provides a strong competitive advantage that U.S. companies can only dream of, unless of course they too move their operations northward, which some have. Whether businesses are competing globally or against imports, their foreign competitors need not include health care costs in their product prices.

For those free marketeers who support market-driven medicine, our costly and inefficient for-profit medical system actually blocks America's free market capabilities of this nation's manufacturers, who must include health care in their prices and compete globally and against imports that don't carry this burden. The health care lobby is killing U.S. businesses, with profits and jobs going abroad as a result. We must find a better way to pay for medical costs.

Why are we talking about health care in a book on campaign finance reform?

The point of this chapter is to demonstrate that there is a better and cheaper way to provide health care, but our moneyed political system is blocking its progress at every turn. Our politicians *can* fix the system if they want to, and our business leaders must demand that they do it immediately. A universal health care, single-payer program, *National Health Insurance* (NHI) is the way to do it, and the business community must battle the health care interests to make it happen. In our world of moneyed politics that means that they must send more campaign cash than the health care interests send, and in this case it will incidentally benefit the public (though not as much as would eliminating the moneyed political system altogether).

It is by historical accident that employers have given health insurance to employees, and this practice is now driving jobs out of the country. The practice started in the Roosevelt era during World War II, when wages were frozen and unions could only bargain for additional benefits, and companies bought it because they were offered tax breaks for their additional personnel expenses. Now it's a terrible business and labor burden that must be eliminated.

Unfortunately, if health care expenses were turned over to individual responsibility, as some would like to see, many people would simply forego insurance until they needed care so badly that the rest of us would have to foot their bill in the emergency room. Already, according to the *Annals of Emergency Medicine*, about 500,000 patients per year are diverted from one emergency room to another because of ER overflow, and the patient's chance of survival is reduced. So some form of paying for universal care through increased payroll deductions (above a certain wage level) and/or taxes on luxury items such as tobacco and alcohol products is the best way to fund such a system (though using punitive awards will also be discussed). No matter how, it shouldn't be an employer burden.

According to a study at **Johns Hopkins University**[6], in 2002 U.S. health care costs were $5,267 per capita (compared to Canada's $2,931, France's $2,736, Australia's $2,504, the U.K.'s $2,160 and Japan's $2,077). The average cost per day of a hospital stay was $2,434 in the U.S. compared to Canada's $870. The U.S. spends 14.6% of its GDP for health care compared to Canada's 10%, and the authors note that "Americans have access to fewer health care resources than people in most other [industrialized] countries when looking at per-capita hospital beds, physicians and nurses. Source: http://content.healthaffairs.org/cgi/content/abstract/24/4/903

Gilbert M. Gaul of *The Washington Post* (July 24, 2005) sites a Dartmouth Medical School study showing that **one-third of Medicare dollars are wasted on unnecessary and inappropriate care.** But that's also true of our private health care system. Neither system is cost efficient because they include the same for-profit motivation. Gaul also cites Medicare data that ranks Louisiana 50th in quality but highest in per capita spending and New Hampshire first in quality and 47th in spending.

And as noted previously, our high costs are still not helping us live any longer, and our health is not getting better no matter how much we spend, even though employer health insurance premiums have jumped an average of 11.2 percent in 2004, more than five times the rate of inflation. I write about why those costs are increasing, and I'll cover some things nobody seems to want to talk about in Chap.6

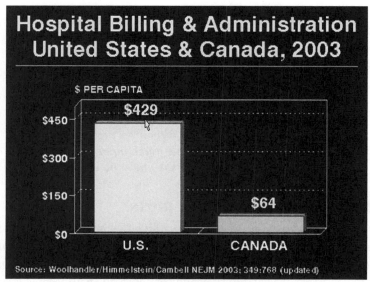

Figure 19: Courtesy: www.pnhp.org

As much as corporations hate government intervention in their own industry, over 40% of America's small business owners — the ones that can't easily outsource their products to other countries — support a single-payer system like that in Canada. Our free market approach turns out not to be very free at all, and that's because it's a for-profit system and people are unfairly making a lot of money on it. If we want jobs and profits to remain in the United States and our economy to grow, we have no other option but to eliminate the inefficiencies and fraud in our medical system and find a better way of funding it. Canada's system is not necessarily the gold standard, but it has many aspects that we should include in our own system. In fact, we can better their system and eliminate the wait times, and for much the same costs as we have today and while even paying our physicians better. We'll still be the most expensive system in the world but we'll be doing it right and for everybody!

Also note that Canada's physicians and hospitals are as independent as ours, as is the patient's right to selection. They do not work for the government and that independence will not be sacrificed in our system. There is a middle ground, and we must find it and use it!

We absolutely must cut the excesses. Leonard Abraham, a U.S. Healthcare CEO, reportedly took home $20 million in a single year and owns company stock worth $782 million. Tenet's CEO took home $117 million in salary and stock options in 2002. This is a clear sign of a free-market system run amok, and importantly, every excess of this type takes health care away from thousands of patients in need; patients who have prepaid for the care. When do these CEOs themselves say enough is enough? How much money will it take to finally make them satisfied? Do they have no upper limit?

How did we get into this mess?

More importantly, how do we get out of it? The answer lies in an area far removed from the hospital or doctor's office: *We must eliminate our moneyed political system at both the state and federal level.* That is the only way we can return health care costs to an affordable level. Political money got us into this mess, and only the elimination of political money will get us out of it. In fact, virtually every problem in our health care system can be linked to politicians who have turned a blind eye or altered the rules to allow conflicts to proliferate.

The U.S. health care system started going downhill fast when Congress decided that, because it works so well in business, the free-market for-profit system would work well in medicine too. (Actually, a little cash transferred on the side helped our political leaders reach that conclusion. Can you imagine that?)

But the pursuit of excessive profit and wealth is not appropriate here. The new rules allowed hospitals and clinics to switch from being non-profit humanitarian centers to becoming profit-making businesses instead, with clinic administrators and hospital CEOs being paid on the basis of profits and growth rather than quality of care. Physicians essentially lost control of their own medical practices, and to be sure, some doctors liked putting the management of their practices into the hands of others. But most are not happy with the current "business" side of medicine.

We now have a system that instead of restraining costs, as the politicians had promised, is restraining care.

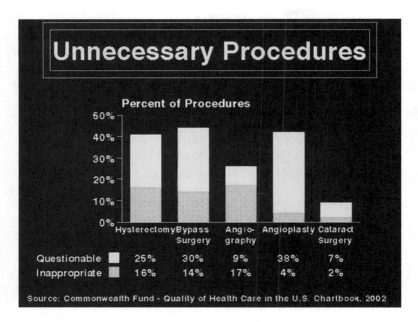

Figure 20: Courtesy: www.pnhp.org

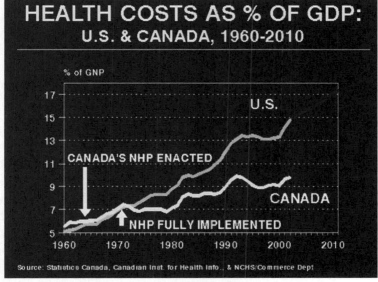

Figure 21: Courtesy: www.pnhp.org

According to reporters **Donald L. Barlett** and **James B. Steele** in their must-read book *Critical Condition*, "Much of the turmoil is a direct result of a national policy to run health care like a business, a misguided notion promoted by Washington over the last two decades that the free market and for-profit health care would restrain costs and bring high-quality care to all. On both counts, the experiment has failed miserably. In the meantime, tens of billions of dollars — money that could have gone into patient care — has been drained from consumers and corporate subscribers and transferred to investors, executives, and others who have a stake in perpetuating this myth.

"The result is a chaotic system that has shifted its focus from saving lives to saving dollars, one that discourages preventative medicine and rewards overtesting and overmedicating; a system that allows insurers to reject those most likely to require medical attention and keep only the healthiest; a system where six times as many people die from medical mistakes as from HIV/AIDS; a system that forces doctors to spend as much time negotiating with insurers over referrals and fees as they do treating patients.

"At the same time, the system has made it possible for unscrupulous practitioners to victimize elderly patients by performing painful, dangerous procedures that are unnecessary but highly profitable."[5]

The authors feel, and it is unquestionably the case, that we have some of the most brilliant scientists and physicians in the world working with the most advanced technology. It's because of the moneyed focus that we also have far from the best health care in the world. But give us this: ours *is* the most profitable!

Remember that for-profit hospitals and HMOs can legally pay their executives as much money as their board of directors will allow, but the IRS limits excessive salaries for non-profit entities. And the hospital CEO hand-picks the board, and the board's salaries can also increase wildly with their sweetheart deal, all without any incentive to improve patient care. It should therefore surprise no one that the health care interests prefer the for-profit U.S. model over all others. The last thing in the world they want is an efficient Canadian-style system, but the American business lobby must demand it.

Enter the MBAs – The beginning of the end

Astute hospital and clinic administrators learned their biggest lesson in business — that their pooled campaign contributions would give them the tremendous political clout needed to get Congress and state leaders to change the rules to their financial advantage — and it has been downhill for the health care system in this country ever since.

Not long ago in our state and others, a Certificate of Need (CON) was required for all major hospital purchases and new construction. This had to be approved by a state review and planning board. But our hospital administrators didn't like having their spending habits limited, and they lobbied the CON out of existence. They discovered in the process that campaign contributions could convince the state's politicians to eliminate this inconvenient impediment to health care and profit growth, the CON, and they started writing campaign checks. This has cost the public and business leaders dearly, and even some smaller hospitals are now wishing that the CON would be reinstated. For them it has backfired because the big hospitals are now free to trounce on them, much like Wal-mart takes over small towns.

Medicare rules established in 1989 even *encourage* physicians to purchase their own money-making equipment, thanks to the extensive lobbying of one now-defunct equipment manufacturer with dollar signs in its eyes. But Medicare (read: the taxpayers) lost hundreds of millions of dollars in the process as many physicians quit using independent labs for testing their patients and instead bought their own equipment and performed such tests themselves. That turned those medical tests into cash cows, and many of their test volumes increased by ten times and more.

Mishaps like this at the federal level would have been headed off by a properly run CON, but unfortunately, our state's policy requiring a CON went AWOL at a time of dire need. The savings if the policy were still in place would not be just in the elimination of the occasional $3 million expenditure for an unneeded MRI, but mainly the $50 or $100 million worth of tests generated by each MRI — all charged to the consumer and much of which will be unnecessary but profitable procedures. Multiply that by hundreds of unnecessary MRIs and thousands of other high-tech devices and millions of unnecessary tests and you're talking about billions of dollars in real money. Of course we'll not have wait times under that scenario.

FIX: The Certificate of Need (CON) must be reinstated and operated by a nonpartisan health care commission that is isolated from political money.

Payments for poor medical care?

Gilbert Gaul also wrote in *Newsweek* that "in Medicare's upside-down reimbursement system, hospitals and doctors who order unnecessary tests, provide poor care, or even injure patients, often receive higher payments than those who provide efficient, high-quality medicine." **Mary Brainerd,** CEO of Minnesota's *HealthPartners*, a non-profit HMO, said "It's the exact opposite of what you would expect. The way Medicare is set up it actually punishes you for being good."

This occurs when patients contract infectious diseases from a first hospital visit and must be readmitted. The hospital gets paid for the second admission as well. "When reimbursing hospitals, Medicare does not distinguish between new cases and problems that result from medical errors or poor care" Gaul reports, and blames the powerful lobby of hospitals, doctors and nursing homes for corrupting the system. (Read that: political cash!)

FIX: Hospitals should be paid a fixed yearly budget for operating expenses and another for capital expenditures, but they should have to absorb the costs of their mistakes themselves. (Actually, they do, when they get sued for malpractice; but then they add their malpractice costs to their prices and the consumers pick up the tab anyway.)

Hospital-based medical practices

What was once illegal became the norm when politicians allowed hospitals to buy up medical clinics and physician practices. The physicians, who once referred patients to multiple hospitals based on the best quality of care, now have an unwritten obligation to refer patients to their own hospital — even if it is not as well equipped to serve their patient's disease as is a competitive hospital down the street. After all, physicians are human, and they receive salaries and, get this, production incentives as well as lucrative rights to interpret lab tests, all of which are controlled by the hospital that now employs them. They do not receive these production incentives from competitive hospitals they do not work for, so it seems unlikely that a doctor would ever choose differently.

In Minneapolis, one hospital conglomerate (*Allina Hospitals and Clinics*) bought a multi-physician cardiology practice seemingly because they wanted exclusive access to those cardiologist's patient referrals, and they were willing to pay dearly for them. Salary guarantees averaging $586,000 and yearly perks of $143,000 and a lighter workload made this an easy decision by the doctors. (Star Tribune, July 17, 2005) The salary is not offensive, because good cardiologists are worth that and more. It's that they are now employed by the hospital which can create a conflict of interest if the patients of those doctors experience less hospital selection than before.

Hospital-employed physicians and physician-owned hospitals also create an atmosphere in which doctors that see poor medical practices in their hospital can be gagged. Their opposition to unsanitary conditions or inadequate staffing will not be as strident as that of independent physicians who can withhold their patients when dissatisfied with the quality of care. But when that hospital controls their salary and incentive bonuses they can tend to walk softly.

FIX: Hospitals must be prohibited from employing their own physicians (except for administrative functions). Production Incentives, whether at hospitals or clinics, must be prohibited.

Pouncing on the little guy

Our community has a health care conglomerate that owns dozens of hospitals and clinics in the area. It is now lobbying to build a new hospital near, and to "compete with" — their words, not mine — an established small-town hospital that has a 60% occupancy rate and 40% of its beds underused. The conglomerate tried but failed to buy the existing hospital, so instead, they purchased the major clinic in town — the very clinic that provided the majority of patient referrals. Now that they own most of the area's referring physician base, they now want to build a second hospital to "compete with" the first. If this occurs, hospital beds will double in the area while the patient population remains essentially the same, and the per-patient cost will increase. This is the kind of competition that will increase costs, not decrease them. We will all pay the price for what is essentially a business move driven by the profit potential.

> *FIX: Hospitals must be prohibited from building in areas already adequately served, a situation that would not be allowed with a CON.*

Physician-owned hospitals

Once considered a major conflict of interest, at one time even fraudulent, physicians can now own up to 49% of the hospital to which they refer patients. Medical groups and astute business investors who liked the idea of a locked-in referral base successfully lobbied (read: paid dollars to) congressmen to get the rules changed, and the public and employers are now paying the inevitable heavy price that resulted.

In my community, despite the existence of several well-equipped cardiac hospitals, a new heart hospital was built and is 51%-owned by private investors and cardiologists who once sent patients to other hospitals, but they will no more. The remaining 49% of the new facility is owned by another local hospital that obviously felt that getting 49% of the profit was better than getting nothing. This over-building will have significant cost consequences to the public, despite claims to the contrary.

When 51% of the ownership is in the hands of a company under shareholder demands for higher profits, it makes health matters worse and can jeopardize the quality of patient care — and the nurse-to-patient ratio is the first place the damage can be measured. A strategic decision by an independent review board — like our befallen CON program — would have stopped these profit-oriented efforts at first base, but lobbying and campaign contributions won over the public interest.

There is generally nothing wrong with specialty hospitals, and indeed, this one has attracted some of the best cardiologists in the city.

But did we need it? A CON review board should have made that determination, not the investors. And as to whether physicians should have ownership in a hospital to which they refer patients, critics unequivocally say no, citing the likelihood of physician-owners keeping the more lucrative patients and procedures and admitting the less profitable patients to another hospital. That's called cherry-picking and cost shifting, and the taxpayers usually pick up the resulting tab. But unnecessary admissions, surgeries and testing are also potential abuses of such a system — one driven by profit and not by good health care or patient need.

FIX: Physicians should be prohibited from having any ownership in hospitals to which they refer patients.

Think about it

No, this kind of competition will not decrease costs. In cases of investment-driven decisions in the health care realm, costs almost always increase. This is not really "competition" in the sense that we know it. Patients rarely select their hospital on the basis of value because either their insurance company or the government is paying the bill. They don't price shop. They select a hospital at the recommendation of their physician and the hospital's local image, which the hospitals often create themselves by advertising and passing those costs on to the public. Even if the patient's physician is employed by the hospital or has ownership in this or another hospital, it is still likely that the patient will select an option based on the physician's recommendation.

Most patient's cannot intelligently shop medical services on the basis of quality, thus proposals for transparency and disclosure of statistics and prices so patients can assess the quality of care by a given facility are essentially worthless. As well, they may cause physicians and hospitals to turn down patients with complicated diseases because the higher risk of failure will harm their statistics.

Independent laboratories

One category of health service provider that the public knows little about is the Independent Diagnostic Testing Facility (IDTF) that provides services like mobile echo, MRI, ultrasound and cardiac monitoring. IDTFs play a vital role in the health care system because they are independent from the physicians and cannot order patient tests themselves. They can only provide services upon a physician's request and they cannot self refer. They actually compete with hospitals, which tends to keep them both on their toes, and for this reason Medicare and other insurers should embrace them.

Importantly, by time-sharing their equipment and personnel, IDTFs obviate the need for hospitals and clinics to purchase expensive equipment and hire staff that cannot be justified because the machines are not used enough to justify them. When clinics purchase their own equipment you can be sure that their volumes (and unnecessary testing) will increase to pay for the investment and to create greater profits for the facility or physician.

There are often several IDTFs competing with each other in an area, but usually on the basis of quality of service rather than price (because they usually bill the insurance company rather than the ordering physician). But these companies are not without faults. Though they cannot order unnecessary tests themselves, they can inappropriately charge for the procedures they do perform, and they should be closely monitored by the physicians using the service.

In the cardiac field there is a 30-day monitoring procedure that captures episodes of heart arrhythmia over the 30-day period. It is an excellent procedure, and though the procedure has one reimbursement code for the one 30-day test, one less-than-reputable IDTF was billing private insurers 30 times for the same procedure, and they got away with it because these insurers were ignorant about the correct billing procedure. What the heck; 30 units for a 30-day test seemed reasonable. Trouble is, they ended up paying ten times what they should have paid. Smartly, the IDTF stayed clear of billing Medicare in this fraudulent manner (though it is now out of business because the Feds ultimately stepped in). Most IDTFs avoid these kinds of shenanigans because they can get turned in by their competitors, but this type of billing practice is not necessarily isolated to IDTFs and could also exist in clinic and hospital billing as well.

One problem IDTFs face is that many HMOs and PPOs refuse to allow more than one or two IDTFs into their plan as providers of certain tests, thus the older and sometimes less up-to-date IDTFs get entrenched with contracts and the newer companies with newer technology and a stronger will to provide higher quality services are locked out. This may reduce the number of contractors an insurer has to deal with, but it can also reduce the quality of service to the patient and usually ends up increasing costs for the insurer and patient because the locked-in company knows they are locked in. This is very counter-productive, but that's what "free market" is all about. Get used to it.

In order to insure the best service for the best price, states should pass "any willing provider" laws that open the market to competition by allowing any qualified IDTF to be selected by the ordering physician who has evaluated what is in the best interest of the patient, and obligates the insurer to reimburse the company at the equivalent rate it has contracted with the older IDTF. Of course, a universal health care system would fix this problem.

FIX: States must pass "any willing provider" laws to eliminate the stranglehold certain IDTFs can have on the system and to open the market to other qualified IDTFs.

Nursing shortages

In the true spirit of American ingenuity, private companies have latched onto the nurse shortage by hiring nursing staffs away from hospitals, paying them 25% more, and then renting the nurses back to the same hospitals at 50% more than they were paid when they were on staff. Business people like to call that entrepreneurship and Congress likes to call it free-market. But the practice is helping to increase staffing shortages and health care costs. In effect, hospitals are now paying the price for three nurses to get two, a 50% increase in nursing personnel costs. The justification has been that these nurses can be hired only as needed, but in fact, they are always needed because of the nurse shortage. Another problem this creates is that it removes nurse continuity with both the medical staff and patients, because it's sort of like hiring a new employee when a nurse comes in for a day. The most obvious resolution is for the government to fund more and perhaps even free nurse training to qualified students, but with Bush's tax breaks and reduced tax revenues, that prospect seems pretty bleak at the moment.

> *FIX: Expand nursing education and make it free, or at least more affordable. Retrain the best of the displaced workers and make immigration easier for trained nurses.*

Build it and they will come!

Elsewhere in our state, the lack of a CON approval process has allowed unlimited hospital and clinic spending and expansion, both in beds and equipment. Whenever a hospital purchases a new technology $3 million scanner, every other hospital in the area tends to follow suit (so they can keep their current physicians happy and on staff). Equipment salesmen love this competitiveness and actually play multiple facilities against each other. But once purchased, the hospital must then ensure that the expensive systems are used to their fullest in order to pay for them, which becomes easier as they employ more of their own referring physicians and offer them production incentives. The total diagnostic imaging market is over $100 billion per year and, if 30% of these tests are unneeded, $30 billion per year is being wasted and not going to other patients in need.

Why do we allow this? Because our politicians are paid to allow it. It's called "$100 million per year in political contributions given by our health care and pharmaceutical industries." As mentioned earlier, political money got us into this mess and eliminating political money is the only way of getting us out of it. One would think that the businessmen who must pay exorbitant insurance costs and the politicians who can fix the system would surely piece together this perverse logic, but it doesn't seem to have sunk in yet.

Most certainly, with all of our overbuilding and overpurchasing and excess capacity, we are not going to suffer from the wait lists Canada is criticized as having. Can there be any doubt in that?

> *FIX: CON and proper health care planning must limit the number of high-tech scanners in a geographical area.*

And the list goes on!

In addition to hospitals, individual physicians and clinics are also allowed to spend unlimited dollars on high tech scanners that duplicate the nearby hospital's service, and they prefer directing their patients to the tests done internally. They will not send an MRI, CT scan or echocardiogram patient to a hospital when they can log the profits themselves, thus in the future, if we are to effectively control costs, all physician and clinic purchases must be subject to the same CON planning board approval as is required of hospitals.

When there are too many pieces of the same equipment in town, or the technology is in the wrong hands, overutilization and increased costs will result without fail. These added costs are also prompting insurance and government approval of unjustified fee increases, which lobbying with cash in hand also facilitates.

FIX: CON and health care planning approvals must also apply to physicians and clinics. They must prevent physicians and clinics from duplicating hospital services. If a service is not available at an area hospital or through an independent lab, the new service might be allowed but closely monitored.

Physicians frequently complain about the massive paperwork required of Medicare, Medicaid and managed care systems, but much of that is due to the insurer's attempt to make sure the doctor is not unnecessarily ordering tests he would directly profit from. In many cases their fears are justified. One 1999 **Kaiser Family Foundation** survey found that half of physicians admitted to manipulating patient symptoms to justify the care needed by the patient. But how much of that manipulation was really due to the profitability of the procedures? If all diagnostic tests were performed by an independent hospital or independent lab, these fears would subside and I suspect so would the mandated paperwork and justifications.

One note on hospital and insurance company price increases; these are in part necessitated by the increasing number of uninsured people whose health care services must be written off or otherwise offset by those of us with insurance, and by those people driven into bankruptcy. A universal health plan would eliminate those instances and appropriately spread the costs. But these cost increases are also necessitated by inappropriate increases in utilization because such services are profitable and they can only make money when they are used. This is another case for "follow the money!"

Mode of payment

Physicians often receive extra payments for providing a medical interpretation of the lab tests they order, which can provide an incentive both to purchase unnecessary high-tech equipment and to artificially increase patient testing.

> *FIX: Physicians should be paid extremely well, far more than CEOs and far more than attorneys, but not on the basis of the number of tests they order or interpret, which the current system promotes. Over 56% of physicians prefer a straight salary system, and that salary must be high enough to attract the best and most qualified students into the field.*

To be fair, physicians aren't perfect. They sometimes don't know whether or not a test they want to order is necessary until the results come back. If the results are positive the physician can mark one up for being correct in his assessment, but if negative he can be accused of ordering an unnecessary test. His effort could have been a stab in the dark or motivated by profits. Some will claim it is defensive medicine. In any event, if he were not getting the whole or a piece of the profits, as physicians are today, inappropriate ordering for profit-making purposes would cease. Only then will unnecessary test volumes go down.

And please hear this loudly and clearly. The 80-20 rule works here too. Eighty percent of physicians are irreplaceable humanitarians that work hard and make their money by seeing higher volumes of patients and properly ordering only needed tests. My own cardiologist ordered an inexpensive test by a second cardiologist to prove I didn't need an expensive and more risky procedure that he would have been paid to perform. That was in my best interest, not his, and most physicians would have done the same.

However, 20% (or some unfortunate number) of physicians see fewer patients and make their money, and a lot of it, by ordering unnecessary and expensive tests, even if at higher risk to the patient.

They are in it to get rich, and they are the exception rather than the rule that is helping to drive the cost of medicine out of sight. This group of bad apples in medicine is no better than the greedy and disreputable CEOs discussed elsewhere. We must eliminate both.

Dr. Michael Rachlis, in his book *Prescription for Excellence*, describes a conversation with a taxi driver that vehemently argued "We don't have to spend more money, just stop wasting money! I took my wife to the doctor four days ago. She had a cold. The doctor ordered an X-ray and prescribed her antibiotics. The medicine cost us over fifty dollars. Then he asked her to come back today. She's feeling fine, so I phone the office to find out about the X-ray, but the secretary says she has to come in to get the result. So I have to get off work and drive her. It costs us more money. Then he tells her the X-ray is fine and she should finish the medication. I don't think she needed the X-ray. I don't think she needed medicine. And I don't think she needed to come back to see him."

> *Does this sound all too familiar? Did we have to hear it from a taxi driver to believe it?*

The games people play

Most doctors are rightfully very tired of the silly games HMOs and other insurers use to cheat them out of their fair payment, all to increase the insurer's own profits. The practice is called "down coding" (paying on a code that is related but reimbursed at a lower dollar amount) — and bundling (merging two or more codes and paying on the least expensive). Physicians are also tired of using valuable telephone time fighting with some low-level clerk who is following orders from a computer program designed specifically to increase profits for the insurer. And doctors are tired of fighting the for-profit insurers to keep critical patients in the hospital longer than the prescribed amount of time. It is a physician's duty to treat the patient appropriately, and they want to be the one making the tough decisions — not some untrained clerk, nurse or administrator. Of course, this down-coding allows insurance company executives to increase their own salaries at the expense of the doctors', so it's the market-driven system playing out again.

Are there cases in which a doctor would leave the patient in the hospital longer than needed so he can collect his daily visit charge? Probably, but that again is the exception rather than the rule, and the possibility of that happening is also why hospitals have medical directors who can intervene when such abuses occur. If it's a Medicare patient being reimbursed on a flat-rate basis for the hospital stay — called a DRG, for Diagnostic Related Group — the hospital wants that patient out as soon as possible. If it is a private-pay patient paying on a daily basis they want them in as long as possible. How about that? That's the way the market-driven system works.

A universal single-payer system doesn't totally resolve these conflicts, but it does eliminate the for-profit insurer from trying to second-guess medical decisions. That said, if physicians were salaried as they should be and many would prefer, there would be no financial incentive for them to keep patients in hospitals longer than necessary.

Not to be ignored are the cases in which doctors, hospitals, and independent laboratories "up code," that is, use a reimbursement code with higher payment than is appropriate for the test. Call it what you will, but Medicare calls the practice false billing (i.e. fraud), and it should be treated as such. Too bad the reverse isn't true.

Physician Conflicts of Interest

There are many situations where physicians receive large sums of money -- sometimes an extra $100,000 to $200,000 per year is added to their income -- from pharmaceutical companies and medical device manufacturers for relatively little work; maybe only a day's worth. Sometimes they act as opinion givers, giving speeches and touting that a drug is good when it might not be as good as its competitor. Or worse, even dangerous. In other cases they may actually implant pacemakers or other medical devices when the device is not as good as another one on the market, but their side-money comes from the manufacturer for which they consult. These conflicts must be totally prohibited. If I need a pacemaker, I want my cardiologist's loyalty pointed at me, not the pacemaker company he gets paid by.

Hospital advertising

On the advertising front, hospitals are now doing heavy advertising to fill empty (and added) beds, to increase technology utilization, and to support the physician staff they've now hired or purchased. These advertising costs must ultimately be reflected in their patient charges and of course would not be necessary had they not overbuilt in the first place. These marketing costs are unnecessary because patients usually do (and should) follow the advice of their physicians anyway.

FIX: Hospital advertising must be prohibited, though the media might not like that because of the loss of advertising revenue. Remember that both the media have lobbyists and make campaign contributions too.

Medical malpractice

Yes, the malpractice insurance system needs significant overhauling, but it is not the monster driving the system. The legal liability issues represent only a fraction of our medical costs; actually less than one half of one percent (<0.5%), but they are often used to hide the real culprit, runaway profits. Malpractice premiums have been driven by an insurance industry running unchecked through the marketplace; allowed by law to (a) offset losses due to poor investments elsewhere and (b) to increase profits due to the demands of its own CEO and shareholders. You can bet that Hurricane Katrina losses show up as an increase in malpractice premiums.

A study commissioned by the **Center for Justice and Democracy** (which appears to be supported by the legal profession) and released by **Public Citizen** et al, claims that the leading malpractice insurers took in approximately three times as much in premiums as they paid out in claims, and several insurers substantially increased their premiums even though their claims payments substantially decreased. Several paid out only 10% to 15% of their premiums in claims. Other horror stories describe malpractice awards as driving physician premiums to $200,000 per year and physicians out of a state. In our free-for-all market (sorry, free market) system I can believe the wildness on both sides of the issue. But with all of the organizing of the medical industry, it is puzzling that no health care group has seen fit to create a national self-insurance system to eliminate the manipulation of malpractice fees. Canada has done this with its Canadian Medical Protective Association (CMPA), and it seems to work. (Oh, I forgot. We don't do things that Canada does).

As well, the **John's Hopkins** study found that malpractice payments represented less than 0.5% of our total health care spending, but the costs of defensive medicine that resulted was as much as 9% of our total costs.[6] Others peg the overuse at 30%.

> *FIX: Peer review panels staffed by three retired physicians must be allowed to disqualify incompetent physicians without the threat of lawsuit (though an adequate appeal system should be available). However, the physicians who take on the toughest cases should not be lost to regulation, and leeway should be given where appropriate.*

According to **Dr. Bernard Sussman**, a professor of neuro-surgery at *Howard University,* an estimated 80,000 patients per year die in the U.S. as a result of malpractice, and many more are egregiously maimed. But the vast majority of cases are settled out of court because doctors won't testify against other doctors out of fear of retaliation. (It's easy to see, then, how the *World Health Organization* lists the U.S. at 37th in the world.) Some states have put a $250,000 limit on punitive damages to victims, but this cap does not limit economic damages when harm or deformities result from mal-practice, such as a lifetime in a wheelchair. In the cases where claims are legitimate, fair lifetime support of the victim is not objectionable to most of us. But giving juries a blank check on punitive damages has proven to be an extremely unfair burden to the public that must pay the bill when a few unscrupulous attorneys and patients want to get rich quick.

Punitive awards are designed to "punish" the offender, to fire a shot over the bow of other potential offenders and to protect the rest of the public, and in many cases they are indeed be justified. But if they were used instead to help fund a universal health care system rather than going to the plaintiffs and their attorneys, perhaps they would be easier to stomach by the public. But they aren't, at least not yet, so caps on punishment are being sought across the nation (but again, leaving the economic damages to the patient to fluctuate with the severity of the case).

FIX: Punitive awards should be used to help fund a universal health care system rather than going to the plaintiff who has already been awarded economic damages.

To be fair, some unnecessary ordering of tests is indeed the result of defensive medicine by physicians covering themselves to prevent a frivolous patient lawsuit. While the jury awards have remained steady for the last five years — at about 0.5% of total health care costs even as malpractice insurance rates have increased by 120% over the last two years — the resulting "over ordering" can increase total costs anywhere from 20% to 30%.

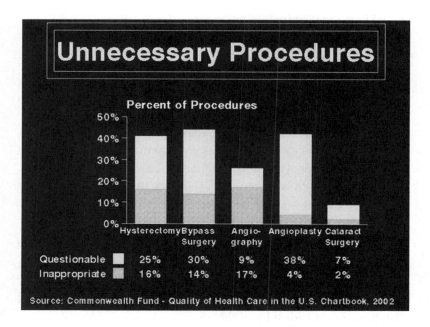

Figure 22: Unnecessary medical procedures easily add 20% to the cost of our health care services, and these must be held in check. Source: www.pnhp.org

However, over-ordering is often just an excuse. The fact that physicians also get payments for performing and interpreting the tests they order, and because the profits nonetheless accrue to the bottom line, makes any unnecessary ordering quite palatable to the health care industry. For example, a 30-minute echocardiogram with a gross profit margin of $1200 is not hard to take regardless of the reason for doing the test. Potential malpractice issues or not, many of these tests are cash cows and need strict oversight, but under our current moneyed political system the chances of that happening are slim.

It should also be noted that if health care costs are rising at double-digit rates — and malpractice claims have remained at 0.5% of the total health care costs — that automatically means that malpractice awards and attorney income is also rising at double-digit rates! I am relieved that the attorneys will not starve.

The real malpractice

As much as it is needed, reforming the legal system will not occur until we stop the money that flows from the trial attorneys to (mainly) the Democrats where they use the filibuster in the senate to block any meaningful changes. Despite the massive contributions from business groups to Republicans, the filibuster kills meaningful tort reform every time, and most certainly the nearly $50 million in campaign contributions from attorneys in 2004 gets the attention of most members of Congress. The real malpractice is that public laws can be manipulated by private campaign contributions.

The filibuster strategy is not bad in and of itself, and I support it because it prevents a minor majority from driving the country down the wrong path. But what's really bad is that legislation results (or doesn't) because of the political money that drives the system, and that happens on both sides of the isle.

I chuckle every time I hear **President Bush** declare that his judicial nominees deserve "an up or down vote." He knows full well that he controls over 51% of the senate and his choice would then be virtually guaranteed. The last thing in the world he wants is to have to meet the 60 vote criteria of a filibuster. Getting 60% is tougher than getting 50%. Would he feel the same way about an up-or-down vote if the situation were reversed? Of course not; the Republicans also used it to their advantage when they were out of power. The 60 vote requirement must be retained for all critical policy decisions, regardless of which party is in power, and the Republicans should be ashamed of themselves for trying to eliminate it on their watch.

But really, if Bush is so hot on up-or-down votes, why doesn't he force the Republicans to allow the six health care reform votes put forth by the Democrats? Or the full public funding of campaigns (2003 H.R.3641) put forth by **Rep. John Tierney** (D-MA)? Could it be because he doesn't want a negative result to be used against the Republicans in the 2006 elections when they use their majority to kill these bills — or because the health care and Fat Cat lobbies have a way of getting to his campaign coffers? Of course the answer is *both*.

A new tort reform law moves certain class action suits from state to federal courts, where they must meet tougher standards. This seems a good change because class action lawsuits driven by the trial lawyers have run amok and must be reeled in, but I wish the reform had passed without political money changing hands (most of which occurred on the Republican side of the isle).

FIX: Lawyers and patients must be held financially accountable for frivolous lawsuits, and we must establish a 3-person binding medical review board (using retired judges, physicians, attorneys and nurses) to adjudicate medical malpractice suits and to determine awards, if any.

Another approach to determining awards, once guilt is determined by the panel, would be "final offer arbitration," which seeks from both sides their bottom line offer or demand. The panel could not make any changes, but must select the more reasonable of the two proposals, which becomes the final settlement. This discourages either side from making outrageous offers because that would then exclude their offer from being the one selected.

And as well, if the 3-person panel determines that the losing side frivolously charged or defended a claim, that is, there was no reasonableness in their position, the loser's attorneys must be made to absorb the legal expenses of the winner. This will reduce the number of unreasonable cases brought forth, like the hot coffee case of the McDonald's customer. Stupidity should not be profitable. The 12-man jury system should be restricted to criminal trials, and as well a three-strike system must threaten bad lawyers, bad doctors, bad hospitals and habitually litigious patients (though allowances must be made for physicians taking the more difficult cases, or extremely sick people will not be able to find a doctor to treat them).

Break the financial link

According to **Carolyn Castore,** Program Director at *Wisconsin Citizen Action,* 75% of the cases that reach Wisconsin's state Supreme Court involve a campaign contributor on one side or the other. Of course, the judges should recuse themselves in these cases of conflict, which effectively means that they should bow out of 75% of the very cases they are being paid to adjudicate! Why not just stop the private money flowing to judges???

Such restrictions should also extend to Supreme Court justices, like **Clarence Thomas,** who accepted $42,200 in gifts since the beginning of his term. Why are gifts to judges allowed in the first place? These are not generally given by disinterested parties, but by people who know the power of money! Can you imagine that transfer of cash being allowed at the Olympics or any other sporting event?

This is an unconscionable judicial intrusion by special interests that must be stopped immediately. The practice should result in jail time for both participants because this is just graft and influence peddling by another name.

> *FIX: Lawyers should be prohibited from investing in the election campaigns of state judges, which they are now allowed to do, or giving gifts to Supreme Court Justices. And in fact, if judges are elected they should receive full public financing of their campaigns using the Clean Money system described later in this book. Alternatively, judges could be appointed by the governor and confirmed by the state senate, as they are at the federal level.*

Pharmaceutical Costs

Fighting to legalize the purchase of drugs from Canada is a smokescreen and a political diversion that obscures the real issue. The U.S. represents 5% of the world population and 33% of the world prescription drug market, yet drugs cost Americans nearly $500 per capita per year compared to Canada's $310 (at just 1.5% of the world market). The big difference between the two countries is their political systems. In ours, politicians are not at all bashful about transferring taxpayer health and wealth to the drug companies and the executives who helped fund their elections. Nor are they bashful about passing laws to protect the companies from declining prices and profits. Unfortunately, most seniors and poor people do not make campaign contributions, so their concerns will not rise to the top of any politician's list.

Fareed Zakaria also reported that "The most recent steps to change things have made the situation worse. The new Medicare prescription-drug benefit took the fastest-growing segment of the American population (the elderly) and gave them a free ride on the fastest-growing item on medical bills (prescription drugs). The result is going to be a fiscal black hole, estimated to be a bigger drain on the federal treasury than the entire Social Security system."

This new Medicare drug plan promises to put over $700 billion into the pockets of the pharmaceutical giants over the next decade. Price increases in the last couple of years have already eaten up any savings promised under the new program. You can be sure that the industry would eventually have found a way to negate the discounts, and they did. Their profits will remain but the payment will now come from the U.S. government as well.

Dr. Marcia Angell, in *The Truth about Drug Companies*, predicts that the drug benefit could lead to Medicare's dismantling and also points fingers at the lobbying and campaign contributions of the drug companies. She blames two very meaningful changes in law that gave drug companies the moon, starting in the 1980s with the Bayh-Dole Act, named after its senate sponsors **Birch Bayh** (D-IN) and **Robert Dole** (R-KS), which gave away the patent rights and exclusive licenses on drugs developed under taxpayer funds through the National Institutes of Health (NIH). Then in 1984 the Hatch-Waxman Act, after its senate sponsors **Orin Hatch** (R-UT) and **Henry Waxman** (D-CA), extended the patent rights via the U.S. Patent Office and the FDA, giving the pharmaceutical industry billions of dollars in additional protection from low cost generics. These often cost 80% less than the original product and perform just as well, and in some cases better.

Would these protections have been given if political money had not changed hands? Of course not. Without political contributions, good laws will be passed, but *with* political money bad laws are virtually the only thing the taxpayers can expect. The political duos named above also demonstrate that both the Republicans and Democrats can be bought and are equally willing to serve as industry puppets. That's called true bipartisanship.

Angell also reports that 77% of all new drugs are not new at all, but are me-too drugs based on formulas of drugs whose patents have run out. This is the best way to compete against the generics that are sure to enter the market at lower prices. The remakes are not necessarily better, and indeed may be worse than the earlier versions. But because they are tested against placebos (sugar pills), instead of the original drug, they are sure to pass muster the second time around. Were the FDA to require them to be tested against the earlier version they might not be allowed on the market at all. Angell points to the four years beginning in 2000 when just 32 out of 314 drugs passing FDA approvals were truly innovative and the rest were me-too formulas. Pfizer, Lilly and Schering-Plough were not even on the list of 32 innovators, though they are quick to claim that high-profits are needed to innovate. We know that to be false anyway; they just want new profits from any source.

But those extra profits come from the public; the sick, the poor and the elderly. If physicians would prescribe the equally effective but lower priced generics, these kinds of costly games would cease. They could prescribe diuretics rather than the more expensive calcium channel blockers that are newer, not necessarily better, may be worse, and cost nineteen times as much. As well, the running of old drugs through the approval process a second time takes up precious FDA resources. But this is what our politicians allow.

FIX: Repeal the Bayh-Dole and Hatch-Waxman Acts; require remakes to be tested against their predecessors and to be clearly labeled as a remake of an older product.

Advertising

Drug companies spend more money on marketing than they do on research and development (R&D), and their profits often exceed their R&D costs. Pfizer made 22% profits on sales of $53 billion in 2004, yet spent 32% of the $53 billion on sales, marketing and administration and only 15% of it on R&D. The broadcast media and drug companies lobbied heavily to get permission to air television ads for prescription drugs. The media, of course, reaped millions in newfound revenues, while the pharmaceutical industry can now influence the patient and add their advertising costs to the drug prices. This can easily add 5-10% to the cost of prescription drugs.

These ads are designed solely to sway patients despite their physician's advice, and they unnecessarily add to the cost of medicine

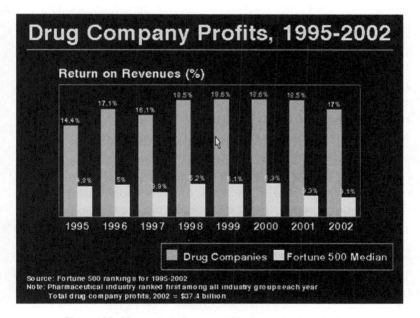

Figure 23: Note that these profits are calculated after deducting for administrative, R&D and advertising costs. Courtesy of: www.pnhp.org

both directly and by putting an upward pressure on physicians to prescribe them when over-the-counter drugs work just as well.

FIX: Like tobacco companies, drug companies should be prohibited from advertising prescription drugs.

R&D Funding

One third of all new drug research and development is already funded by the taxpayers via grants from the National Institutes of Health (NIH). Like all other costs, the public is paying for industry research in the price of the product anyway. Frankly, it would be cheaper for the public to have 100% of pharmaceutical research funded by the NIH and made available to all qualified manufacturers so they could sell them in the competitive marketplace. You know; the market-driven system that Bush and the right wing so strongly support. Drug costs could then be cut by 50-70%, though that would mean increasing the involvement of government to the dismay of those on the right. Ouch!

Drug companies would still be able to develop drugs, if they wanted to, and test them on animals as they do today. But when it comes time to test them on people they would turn them over to the NIH system and if approved, the company could receive a flat 5% royalty from all industry sales. That would stimulate private innovation, still reimburse the innovating company and maybe even more than they'd get if they had a market exclusive. Drugs developed outside the US would have to go through the same approval process.

FIX: Fund all medical research through the National Institutes of Health and license qualified drug manufacturers to market the drugs. Multiple licensees would create a competitive market, and the public and private sectors would both benefit. A royalty would be paid to NIH but that would transfer to the innovating company if one were involved. Even without this, at the very least all research funded by the NIH should remain the property of the funders (the taxpayers).

Drug patents

Today, drugs that result from NIH funding are not licensed, but thanks to Congress and the Bayh-Dole Act, the intellectual property — that is, the patents — are *given* to the drug companies so they can lock out cheaper generics for 17 to 20 years. Ironically, while America's patent laws protect new drugs against less-costly generics, the U.S. recently coerced Guatemala into repealing an important Guatemalan law to lower the price of pharmaceuticals and allow U.S. generic competition. Why doesn't Congress do this to protect Americans??? Why this double-standard?

The answer is simple: U.S. laws prevent our politicians from receiving lobbying money from foreign drug companies, but American companies can freely write the checks! It should be illegal to receive money from American manufacturers as well. And as pointed out elsewhere, most drug research is not done on new drugs, but on old drugs that are nearing the end of their patent protection. By changing just one molecule and releasing the new version they can market the dug as "new and improved."

Reader Resource: Generic Drug cross-references

This is a moving target, but a Google search on "generic drug cross-reference" either with or without the quotes will yield many results. But never switch from a prescription to a generic drug without your physician's approval.

> **www.health.gov.on.ca/english/providers/program/dr ugs/limited_use_mn.html**

> **www.inshealth.org/Formulary/trdNm-generic.htm**

Addicted to profits

The pharmaceutical industry is the most profitable in the world, at 15% to 25% even *after* deducting its legitimate R&D and high television advertising costs. Don't let them mislead you into believing that those profits are needed to develop more drugs — that 15-25% profit is calculated after the research money and advertising costs have been spent and high executive salaries are paid. Lowering drug company profits would not, by itself, take one dime away from drug development research, as industry apologists' claim.

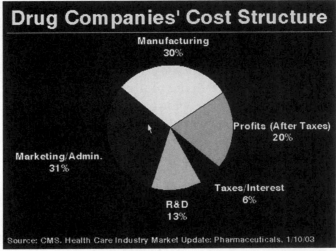

Figure 24: Courtesy of: www.pnhp.org

Instead of those profits going into R&D, Dr. Angell points to the compensation of former *Bristol-Meyers Squibb* chairman and CEO **Charles A. Heimfold, Jr**, at $74.8 million in 2001 with an additional $76 million worth of unexercised stock options. Not bad at all. The chairman of *Wyeth* also made a paltry $80 million. And keep in mind that the other high level executives also get million-dollar-per-year salaries, so the sick and elderly simply have to accept that if they want to get healthier they will have to help support these kings.

Of course, the one slice missing from the pie chart in Figure 24 is the one for fraud. In 2001, *TAP Pharmaceutical Products* paid $875 million to settle criminal charges. The company was charged with manipulating its price structure so physicians could buy a drug product at $207 and in turn sell it to Medicare patients for $475, in which case the doctors could pocket another $50,000 per year in 1996 dollars. Other settlements included $49 million from *Pfizer, $88 million from GlaxoSmithKline*, $257 million from *Bayer, $355 million from AstraZaneca, and $430 million to settle claims against the Warner-Lambert* division of *Pfizer.*[5] Oh, and there's another slice missing, the one for the $50 million per year the industry spends on lobbying and campaign contributions to make sure that government doesn't get in its way.

With extra income from sleazy business practices like these, it is easy to see why the pharmaceutical industry is the most profitable in the world; but worse, it is also apparent why patients often have to scrimp for critical drug therapy (or even go without) to fill the pockets of these drug lords. And don't you fret for a moment that these settlements have eaten into their profits — the drug companies just add their penalties to the price of their product and consumers pay for them at the cash register.

Pricing

As it is today, the pharmaceutical patent holder can charge the public whatever the market will bear — with price having nothing to do with the cost to develop or manufacture the product, especially if it is a remake of an older drug. As a result, critical drugs for seniors and the seriously ill have the highest markup, and drugs that U.S. drug companies sell for pennies in Africa are sold for dollars in the U.S.

> *Why? Because they can! Politicians have written the laws to allow it.*

The costly cancer drug Taxol and the AIDS drug AZT are two examples, but there are hundreds more. The markup on these drugs is astronomical, even though they were both developed with taxpayer funds. Taxol, for example, accounts for a $1 billion per year market for *Bristol-Myers. See The Great Taxol Giveaway* at:
www.MultiNationalMonitor.org/hyper/issues/1992/05/mm0592_08.html.
Of certain interest is that Bristol-Myers' company executives alone gave $2 million to George Bush in 2000, which indeed keeps the lines of communication open.

The high profit margins have also encouraged counterfeiting that jeopardize not only patient safety but also efforts to purchase drugs from Canada. Counterfeiting thrives on high profits, thus it is more likely to occur with America's exorbitant prices than with the lower prices found in other countries. And those who argue that the Canadian system encourages their citizens to come to the U.S. for health care ought to look at the Americans who are going to Canada for prescription drugs. Whose system is better?

FIX: Drug companies must be prohibited from charging higher prices in the U.S. than they do in other countries. They must guarantee any government plan their best price.

Why do dumping laws affect one industry and not another? Only your congressman knows for sure. But by charging all countries the same it would remove the unfair burden that currently rests on the shoulders of American seniors and the sick that are disproportionately unable to pay the bill.

Medical research

At one time, all clinical trials on new drugs were performed exclusively by independent medical research scientists and physicians working for independent universities. For these researchers, it was a matter of pride and professional recognition to be published in an international journal. And of course they received financial grants for their work that helped fund their university. Today it is not uncommon for the pharmaceutical company to use its own employees or subcontractors (contract research organizations, or CROs) under their own control to run their clinical trials. Then they simply pay a university physician to review and sign off on it as though it were his or her own unbiased work.

As well, all too many physicians are on the payroll of drug and medical technology companies and let their salaries and stock options get in the way of good patient care.

Why? *Because they can!* And it gives them more control over the output of the study, and even whether they want to release the results to the public. The obvious fallout from this is that corners can be cut that an independent scientist would not cut, and too often a blind eye is turned toward potentially hazardous medicines in order to get the product to market fast. The drug companies like to retain control of the process in part because independent physicians are more likely to ask more questions of the patient than required. Product recalls are more common today, but unfortunately, they occur after many more lives have been lost or egregiously harmed. And if tort reform provides protections to the pharmaceutical industry, there is not much reason for them to make this research process safer.

FIX: Require all FDA-approved drugs to undergo unbiased patient clinical trials through a qualified medical university (as described above). Prohibit physicians from owning stock in or receiving fees from drug or technology companies.

Medicare extravagance

To the dismay of many, Congress prohibits Medicare from negotiating lower prices from the drug industry under the new Medicare plan (unlike the Canadian government and our own Veterans and armed forces health care systems, which all mandate negotiation for the lowest prices). This extravagance on the part of Medicare is obviously the result of the moneyed pharmaceutical and insurance industries and their massive lobbying force, all of whom are very generous with their favorite congressmen. As well, why else would politicians create a whole new *private* industry to administer its Medicare pharmaceutical plan, rather than using what was already in place: Medicare administrators and local drugstores? Following the money from the insurance and pharmaceutical companies makes it clear that this plan was designed to serve the industries rather than Medicare patients -- and at a cost of over $700 billion in the next decade, one of the biggest government giveaways in history.

FIX: Medicare must be required to negotiate prices, and drug companies must sell to Medicare at the lowest price charged to other countries (the most-favored-nation concept).

Life enhancement drugs – Just say No!

It has been found that in the Medicaid system (read: the public) the government has even paid for sexual enhancement drugs like Viagra and Cialis, it would appear thanks to campaign contributions from the companies that manufacture these drugs! (However, at this writing, congress is planning to exclude criminal sexual predators from getting these drugs at public expense. Whew! But while that was a no-brainer, all reimbursement for these drugs should be prohibited by all government programs. These drugs absolutely must not be funded by taxpayers, nor should we pay for cosmetic surgery, breast implants or other non-essential drugs or medical procedures.)

FIX: Life enhancement drugs and medical procedures such as elective cosmetic surgery like breast implants should not be paid for by the taxpayers. They can be purchased outside of the plan, if desired.

FDA conflicts of interest

According to *USA Today*, another issue of great concern is the fact that 54% of scientific advisors to the FDA have financial ties to pharmaceutical companies whose drugs they are reviewing for safety and effectiveness, which is not terribly unlike the Bush administration's appointment of energy executives to develop the nation's energy policies, or logging industry executives to design the "Healthy Forests Initiative" (read more on that later). Note the following FDA info (reprinted from **www.mercola.com**):

A *USA TODAY* analysis of financial conflicts at 159 FDA advisory committee meetings from Jan. 1, 1998, through June 30, 1999 [18 months] found:

➢ At 92% of the meetings, at least one member had a financial conflict of interest.

➢ At 55% of all meetings, half or more of the FDA advisers had conflicts of interest.

➢ Conflicts were most frequent at the 57 meetings when broader issues were discussed: 92% of members had conflicts.

➢ At the 102 meetings dealing with the fate of a specific drug, 33% of the experts had a financial conflict.

Conflicts are most common on the committees that consider heart drugs (48% of experts had financial conflicts when considering the worthiness of specific heart medicines). So much for unbiased public servants.

FIX: All FDA conflicts of interest must be strictly prohibited. Pay them well if you must, but use only independent scientists.

If you have ever wondered why an increase in drug recalls has occurred, look no further than the campaign coffers of your favorite congressman. In 1992, Congress approved legislation that reduced the number of clinical trials needed for new drug approval, speeded up the approval process, and allowed the drug companies to promote their product for diseases they were not tested for. Source: **www.PubliCampaign.org**

Even if the NIH were to fund all future drug development, as I have earlier suggested, Dr. Angell adds that the FDA should replace the industry-controlled clinical trial system with a taxpayer-paid and FDA-sponsored *Institute for Prescription Drug Trials* (IPDT). I agree. The drug companies (or the NIH) would submit their product to the IPDT which would contract with independent university scientists to conduct the clinical trials. The results, good or bad, would be made public so other scientists could learn from the successes and failures. Today the failures never see the light of day.

Angell points to the 1999 advisory committee that approved Vioxx and found that four of the six members had conflicts of interest that were waived so they could remain on the evaluating board. Conflicts usually mean they are shareholders or paid consultants of the submitting company (sort of like insider trading on steroids). And the 2005 panel that declared COX-2 inhibitors safe enough to stay on the market had nine members with financial ties to the industry, and those nine conflicts were enough to put the vote over the top for *Vioxx* and *Bextra*. You've seen the result.

It just doesn't get any better than that. Is there any wonder that more prescription drugs are causing more patient deaths today than ever before? Is there any wonder why pharmaceutical and other companies are seeking greater protection from class action lawsuits by the public they've harmed? Is there any wonder why drug companies are so willing to share their profits with the politicians who regulate their industry? And that those politicians are so willing to take the cash? Have these politicians no shame; no family to answer to or to protect? Where are the new morals and values we were promised by George Bush in the 2000 elections?

NIH Conflicts of Interest

As well, many NIH research scientists — who are already in the highest paid government jobs — can receive an extra hundred thousand dollars (or two) annually from consulting agreements with private-sector pharmaceutical companies they do official business with. This can interfere with their obligation to serve their employer, the taxpayers, when assessing potential government contracts with their second source of income.

FIX: All NIH conflicts of interest must be strictly prohibited. Pay them well but use only independent scientists.

Not all is bad with Big PhRMA

Industry supporters abound, most notably their trade organization Pharmaceutical Research and Manufacturers Association (PhRMA) which provides much of the industry's political cover with its assorted PACs and political contributions.

Do a Google search on "big phrma" and also see the web site
www.stealthpacs.org/documents/092004Phrma.pdf

As much as we may dislike the materialism of drug manufacturers, there is indeed much good that results from prescription drugs and they have most certainly helped reduce costly hospitalizations and mortality rates. Sometimes they work in reverse, but on balance we are better off because of them.

Despite the fact that the pharmaceutical industry is gouging wherever they can, some drugs (like those for lowering cholesterol) actually reduce the need for high-cost surgeries.

In her book *Miracle Cure*, **Sally Pipes** cites *Columbia University* professor **Frank Lichtenberg**'s study that credits every $1 spent on newer pharmaceuticals as reducing other health care expenditures by an average of $7.17. Without going into the amount of money he or his university may receive from the pharmaceutical industry for performing clinical trials themselves, or even if Pipes' own *Pacific Research Institute* accepts such outside support, I seriously question that number especially given **Marcia Angell**'s definition of what constitutes a new drug (versus a me-too drug that may not even work as well as its predecessor). But very clearly the return on investment (dollars spent versus heath care dollars saved) in research is somewhat higher than 1-to-1 and very likely in the 3-to-1 range.

But none of that should mean that the industry deserves a free run on society, and it doesn't mean that the above reforms should not be carried out. The same and probably better return-on-investment could be obtained under the above NIH development scenario in which the current over-spending is eliminated. Price gouging pads salaries, not R&D expenditures.

Pipes' book was co-published by *The Fraser Institute*, a highly conservative Canadian group that appears to receive support from a number of industries, including pharmaceutical and insurance interests. She proposes faster drug approval times (which helped advance the Vioxx demise), supports moving more drugs to over-the-counter status (which bypasses critical physician scrutiny), and opposes the Canadian universal health care system. While her book certainly offers the commercial options, it is safe to say that Canadian consumer opinions will differ somewhat on her proposals.

The money trail is clear and unimpeded

All of the prescription drug issues described above have been fueled by a pharmaceutical industry that spends over $50 million annually lobbying and to fund the reelections of their favorite congressmen, an investment which of course works exactly as planned and protects the industry from needed adjustments to protect the public.

Get this loudly and clearly: these campaign contributions would not be made by any sensible CEO if the money did not buy policy that transfers taxpayer funds from you to them, thus we absolutely must get the private money out of political campaigns before any of these rip-offs can be terminated. The cheapest way is for the taxpayers to pay for the electoral process directly as outlined in chapter 11. If campaign contributions work to the benefit of the giver, they should be made by the public instead. That's Politics 101.

Corporations outside the medical industry that support our moneyed political system are now feeling the excruciating pain in the high health care premiums they must pay. Having helped create the moneyed political atmosphere, one might say they are getting exactly what they deserve. But the public is the ultimate loser as high health care costs stifle wages and drive American jobs abroad. We can and must eliminate the unnecessary costs that result from over-utilization and overcharging by the medical community, and the inefficiencies foisted upon us by health care interests. Business leaders can and must make this happen. They have the money to do it.

> *FIX: Before we can fix the health care system, though, we must get the politicians off of the health care payroll. If they are taking money from the industry, that's where their allegiances will remain; unless, of course, business leaders are willing to outbid them. Only then can we make progress.*

Fraud and abuse

The health care system is rife with overuse, misuse, abuse and fraud, in all health care sectors: public, private, for-profit and non-profit. This easily adds 20% to our health care costs though **Gilbert Gaul** of the *New York Times*, after months of study, pegs the waste at a more likely 30% of our total costs. Nursing homes have reportedly sat patients in front of a TV and then billed Medicare or Medicaid for a therapy session. "Insurers cheat patients and doctors; patients cheat doctors and insurers; doctors cheat insurers and patients; and all cheat federal and state governments."[5]

> *FIX: Every health care provider that bills the government must have all employees sign an anti-fraud declaration that describes fraud and how to report it anonymously and receive a reward for reporting legitimate and major abuses.*

Insurance companies

Up to 30% of the cost of health care is administration costs, thus a *universal single payer system* like that in Canada (with its 8% administrative costs) should be our target. According to a 2003 *New England Journal of Medicine* report, the per capita administrative cost in the U.S. is $1059 versus Canada's $307.

The trend in the U.S. is now toward outsourcing the call center functions of larger HMOs to English-speaking India to increase profits. When you dial an 800 number, you may first land in India where medically untrained clerks take your initial call, ask a preset list of medical questions, and then determine the worthiness of passing you on to a nurse who does the same thing before passing you on to the doctor in the U.S.. Their aim is to divert as many patients as possible away from doctor appointments and hospital admissions, so you must be prepared to battle if you are truly in need. (The only positive, if you can call it a positive, is that these call centers sometimes use nurses from other countries, which relieves pressure from the nurse shortage in the United States.)

Note that some professional jobs, like those of physicians who interpret radiological, echocardiographic and other tests that are easy to transmit via the Internet, are already on the way to outsourcing and the hospital CEOs love it. The overhead of doing business, in this case with normally high-priced expertise, goes down substantially. Questions of competence are not automatic because the physician is foreign-born and foreign-trained, but how much corporate oversight as regards quality can there be from thousands of miles away? And when medical records are the issue, how safe is your data?

But insurance gouging is of concern, and one red flag is a wild corporate culture, and you'd hope that our government officials would be skilled enough (or free enough) to identify the signs of such a culture when they see it. If medical providers (hospitals, HMOs, PPOs, etc) are paying their CEOs millions of dollars per year in salaries, perks and stock options, or have 11 corporate jets as did **HealthSouth** in Birmingham, this skimming and extravagance can only detract from one area: patient care. I'd find a different provider.

Insurance types

Here are some differences between the various systems.

Single-payer (or universal health care) is like our Medicare, where hospitals and physicians are independent but are restricted to the prices they can charge the administrative contractor (which gets reimbursed by the government). Medicare is our nation's most popular single-payer system. It has the lowest overhead at 3.5%, and in Wisconsin it is administered by *WPS* in Madison (in other states, companies like *Blue Cross* and *Travelers* administer Medicare). If you want to label this type of system anything, it is socialized insurance but not socialized medicine. The Medicare administrator, a private contractor, controls excessive and unnecessary testing, but in cases of need, the physician can justify and obtain extra tests or longer hospital stays. Patients may pay for uncovered procedures outside of the system, either independently or with Gap insurance. Hospitals and physicians are independently employed.

Socialized medicine is used in the U.K. and several other countries. Its hospitals are owned by, and the physicians employed by, the government, much like our Veteran's and military health care systems are in the U.S. All of which, incidentally, have some of the best care in the world, and for these systems at a cost of under $5000 per person for unlimited services (though they do have a co-pay on drugs). There's nothing wrong with socialized medicine, except for the ideological issues of wanting to limit the size of government. Otherwise, this type of system can be as good as or better than the rest if properly funded and administered. We should all be so lucky as to be in the V.A. or armed forces "socialized" system.

For those concerned about the potential of "rationing," the practice already exists in our for-profit HMO, PPO and hospital systems. And besides, what system could be worse at rationing than one that excludes 45 million people, 15% of our population, and under-insures an additional 50 million people? That's the American free-market system at work for you today!

Health Maintenance Organizations (HMO) are alternatives that some employers have chosen to reduce costs, but they have been heavily criticized for making their profits from the denial of care rather than giving the care they are being paid to provide. Obviously, the more patient income they have that is not spent on services to the patient, the higher their profits and executive salaries can be. But some patients have died or their conditions gravely worsened while waiting for the physician to succeed in convincing the HMO management that emergency care or a hospital stay is indeed necessary. The chances of this happening can increase substantially with for-profit insurance companies, HMOs and PPOs, and the others which carry the moniker of "managed care." No, we do not have the best care in the world, no matter how hard politicians try to convince us, and no matter how hard the health care industry tries to convince the politicians. It is what it is and try as we might the *World Health Organization* still places us at 37th compared to all other countries.

HMO overhead runs from 14% to 21%. Both for-profit and non-profit HMOs exist, and generally the latter are less criticized. Some are staff models, where the physicians are employed by the plan. Others are group models where the plans contract with outside physicians who may also serve multiple plans. In some cases doctors and hospitals are "capitated," meaning they get a lump sum per patient enrolled and they make more money by not treating the patients they've been paid to treat. Capitation is not good for the patient under any circumstance.

HMO Executives' Compensation, 2002

Executive	Firm	Pay	New Stock Options
John Rowe	Aetna	$3.5 mil	$5.4 mil
Ronald Williams	Aetna	$2.3 mil	$3.8 mil
Larry Glasscock	Anthem	$3.3 mil	$22.9 mil
Edward Hanway	Cigna	$1.0 mil	$6.4 mil
Jay Gellert	Health Net	$1.5 mil	$11.7 mil
William McGuire	United Hlthcr.	$7.2 mil	$72.0 mil
Stephen Hemsley	United Hlthcr.	$3.3 mil	$14.9 mil
Leonard Schaefer	Wellpoint	$6.9 mil	$12.0 mil

Source: Managed Healthcare Market Report 4/15/03

Figure 25: It is difficult to accept that any one of these guys are worth a penny over a million dollars per year. And if they want stock let them buy stock. Giving them $72 million worth of stock is ridiculous. That stock should have been sold to the public and the proceeds put into patient services. Let the CEOs purchase their own stock with their own money and let them be at risk it with everybody else when they make bad management decisions.
Courtesy www.pnhp.org

Note that even non-profit HMOs can be an offshoot of a for-profit organization that receives a substantial management fee from its non-profit entity, a fee from which high executive salaries can be paid. For example, the non-profit Tufts HMO in Massachusetts is said to have paid over $90 million to the Tufts Associated Health Plans Inc, thus the non-profit charitable status may be more of a gimmick to enjoy tax-exempt status and limits on liability than a charitable function.

Significantly, CEO compensation packages at for-profit HMOs have run as high as $75 million per year with CEO stock ownership as high as $720 million. Thus a major chunk of cash is diverted from patient services to executive wealth (clearly not the most humanitarian side of the health care industry, and perhaps this explains their propensity to be large campaign contributors).

I say again that I am not anti-high salary, only that I believe that such salaries should be decided upon by the shareholders — the owners and investors of the company — and not by a board of directors carefully selected by the greedy CEO who inevitably pads the board's pockets depending on it's generosity. The board can recommend but the shareholders should determine the need to pay high or exorbitant salaries to protect their investment. My guess is

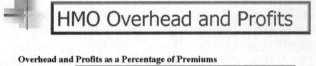

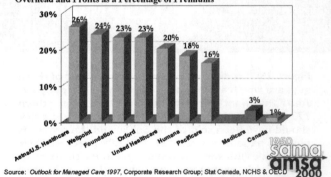

Source: *Outlook for Managed Care 1997*, Corporate Research Group; Stat Canada, NCHS & OECD

Figure 26: Insurance Company and HMO overhead negatively impacts patient care. Courtesy of: www.amsa.org

that reasonable salaries would prevail in most cases, but the CEO contributions to congressman have sufficiently tilted the *Securities and Exchange* rules to ensure that such regulations are not passed. These are usually not well-deserving CEOs. They are too often devious and greedy and ripping off unwary investors. (However, with sole proprietorships, where the CEO is the sole owner, the sky is the limit. His customers will judge whether he is getting too rich.)

But once again, excessive CEO salaries would not be an issue under a universal health care system like Medicare because the reimbursement levels would allow fair but not exorbitant salaries.

I do believe that if HMOs are going to take people's lives into their hands and deny care when it is medically indicated to save a life or limb, all to increase their profits, then such denial of care should be challengeable in a court of law. But the Supreme Court has ruled that, per the laws written by Congress, patients cannot sue their HMOs when they deny care and they are harmed, no matter how egregiously. Congress must change the law to make HMOs accountable, but when they get millions of dollars per year in contributions from HMO executives that seems an unlikely course of action.

Preferred Provider Organizations (PPOs) are insurance plans that essentially contract with certain hospitals and physicians who have agreed to discount their prices and live within the plan's rules, and then the plans are offered to employers at a discounted price. HMOs and PPOs limit the choice of physician and hospital to only those on their contracted list unless the patient agrees to pay any overcharges resulting from services outside of the plan. As well, they very often have a "gatekeeper" nurse who determines whether or not you really need medical attention. This would not be bad if the nurse was face-to-face, on site as a first-tier, but sometimes they are at an off-site location, perhaps even in India or another country.

Health and Medical savings accounts (HSAs and MSAs) sound great but have their own set of problems. They are designed to allow patients to control their cost of medicine, sort of like having them function as their own primary physician. They make out okay while they are healthy because their money is mostly saved. But when they encounter health problems their medical decisions become warped.

They get the patient involved with the management of money by offering rewards for nonuse, but that often discourages early detection and prevention. Usually only well people select them, reducing the cross-subsidy needed to support the other systems. Singapore has an MSA plan, but with serious gaps in coverage. As well, the mechanism is there for the wealthy to use MSAs as tax shelters (perhaps an indication of why the wealthy like medical savings accounts so much).

And now you see why the U.S. has 1500 health care insurers.

It's that Golden Rule again!

Many experts have studied this problem and feel that the best model is an adequately-funded Medicare-for-all program with proper oversight and where the denial of care is not the moneymaker. But the health care, insurance and pharmaceutical industries, the ones who are benefitting from our current runaway system, strongly disagree and will do everything in their power to block progress toward an efficient system. They lose profits if that happens, and it is understandable that they would prefer things just as they are.

The most effective way to block progress is, of course, to send more money to politicians than do the supporters of progress, and that is being done with vigor by these wealthy health care interests on both sides of the border. At this point, with the moneyed politics-as-usual system in place, the only strategy that can overcome the industry lock is to increase the cash coming from the corporations who are being bled to death by medical costs. Then we'll see politicians do what they are really good at; dancing to the tune of the highest bidder.

It's too bad that we must depend on a bidding war between two greedy special interests, neither of them wearing a white hat but one, the business interests, that will inadvertently better serve the public if the decision goes the right way — at least on the health care issue.

Getting rid of all private money in the political system is the best way of ensuring that, whatever health care system is finally chosen, it is in the best interest of the public and not the private sector. And don't miss this point for a single moment: it is both the Republicans and Democrats who are blocking progress.

Canada the good

The good things about the Canadian health care system, as per **www.pnhp.org**, can be easily laid out:

> ➤ Universal, comprehensive coverage
> for 100% of its citizens
> ➤ Life expectancy 2 years longer than ours
> ➤ Infant deaths 35% lower than ours
> ➤ More per-capita MD visits, longer hospital care
> ➤ 75% Less Bureaucracy
> ➤ Quality of care equivalent to that
> afforded insured Americans
> ➤ Independent physicians and hospitals
> ➤ Free choice of doctor and hospital
> ➤ And, yeah, all at 40% less cost

Dispelling the Myths

To put down a couple of myths, this comes from a survey of U.S. ambulatory providers near the border, including hospital discharges and Canadian citizens:

> ➤ 40% of U.S. ambulatory facilities near the border treated no Canadians last year; another 40% treated less than 1 patient per month.
> ➤ Michigan, New York and Washington hospitals treated a total of 909 Canadians per year (only 17% of them elective).
> ➤ Of "America's Best Hospitals" only one reported treating more than 60 Canadians per year.
> ➤ In a survey of 18,000 Canadians, 90 had received any medical care in the U.S. last year, and only 20 had gone to the U.S. seeking care.
>
> Source: Health Affairs 2002;21(3):19

Reader Resource -- An absolute must-read on the affects of money in our health care system is at: **www.publicampaign.org/ healthcarepaybacks/healthcare_paybacks_report.pdf**

Canada the bad

Could Canada's system be improved? Of course it could. All they'd have to do is spend the same amount of money the U.S. is spending (though they'd still end up covering 100% of their people versus the 85% the U.S. system covers).

Yet it is clear that virtually every private health care interest in Canada wants to see their system opened up for profit taking, just as their brethren south of the border enjoy. They are constantly lobbying Canadian officials to reduce funding of their system in an attempt to turn people off and make them more open to a privatized system. The sabotage works like this:

> ➤ Wealthy Canadians lobby for private funding and tax cuts; they resent subsidizing care for others,

> ➤ Result: government funding cuts (e.g. 30% of hospitals beds closed during the 90s) causing wait times and patient dissatisfaction,

> ➤ U.S. and Canadian firms seek profit opportunities in heath care privatization (on both sides of the border),

> ➤ Conservative foes of public services own 2/3 of Canadian newspapers, and

> ➤ Misleading waiting list surveys by right wing groups.

Courtesy: **www.pnhp.org**

Sally Pipes says in her book that "US employers want to engender the employee goodwill that comes with offering medical insurance, but they want to put an end to the relentless price increases."

I doubt that very much. It may have been true in decades past, but it is certainly not the case today. U.S. employers are increasingly leaning toward not having US employees at all and outsourcing their jobs to countries where employers do not have to pay for health care. Or they are forcing their current employees to pay higher deductibles and absorb more of the costs, exactly the opposite of what Pipes claims. Ask any sensible business owner: "Would you vote to eliminate your 15% health care burden and become more competitive with foreign imports," and he'd be a fool not to jump at the chance. Call them what you want, but they are not fools.

The solution is to create a solid universal health care system for all citizens and have it funded by the taxpayers directly. A properly funded and properly controlled Medicare-for-all system could fix the problem virtually overnight, but the right wing and the health care and pharmaceutical interests will fight to their last breath to keep the inefficient but profitable system we have. The current system is getting worse; not better, and political money ensures its longevity.

Funding

Canada's health care is mostly funded by a progressive tax on the public, and wealthy people on both sides of the border don't like that idea at all. In the U.S., employer health benefits add up to 15% of payroll, but in Canada it's just 0.6% because their taxpayers pay the rest (the same as in many countries). That's why every business leader in the U.S., especially those that compete either globally or against imports, must demand a universal single-payer plan. They should call their politicians today, especially those to whom they contribute. They must make this happen!

There is absolutely no valid reason for businesses to have to add our high medical costs to the price of their product — they lose sales and we lose jobs in the process. Cash from health care lobbyists is foisting a system upon Americans that is totally undermining the profitability of U.S. businesses and thus job growth, and our politicians are letting it happen right in front of our eyes!

As mentioned elsewhere, there is absolutely no reason why punitive damage awards in malpractice lawsuits shouldn't be directed to help fund the universal health care system, rather than go to the patient that was already awarded economic damages. This is frosting on the cake, and it should be applied to the right cake. Of course, campaign money from the trial attorneys will decide this idea's fate.

How to fix our system

The following chart compares the number of administrators and paper-pushers added to the employment roles compared to the number of physicians and reveals just how far out of hand the situation has gotten in the health care industry. Clearly the patient

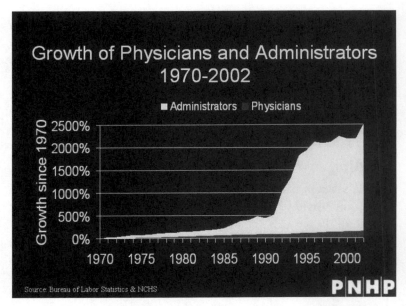

Figure 27: More administrators have not contributed to better health care, just to higher costs. Courtesy of: www.pnhp.org

population did not grow as rapidly as the administrative staff, so the massive administrative waste goes to the bottom line.

There are many ways to fix the American system, but starving it is not the best way. Eliminating the waste, abuses, excessive and unnecessary testing, exorbitant CEO salaries and predatory pharmaceutical pricing must all be at the top of the list. But beyond these measures, any new system must assure the populace the same or a higher level of patient care, avoid excessive wait times, and extend care to all U.S. citizens. That can be done today and at less dollars than we are spending on our for-profit system.

For example, starving Medicare when it is a good (but not perfect) model for a single-payer plan only adds to the myth that the for-profit system works better. That's what special interests are attempting in Canada. If Medicare were adequately funded and taken out of the hands of the moneyed politicians, it could reimburse physicians and hospitals fairly for their work and their costs. But often Medicare itself, in its current form, operates by starving its providers, expecting them to make their money from privately funded patients instead. And they do, because they must. If we had no private insurers and only a fair Medicare-for-all system with appropriate cost controls, it would be the model of choice, favored even by most physicians. (However, for-profit hospital CEOs will always oppose anything that controls their growth, spending and personal income, and the politicians they contribute to will come to their rescue.)

One claim is true: Some physicians do turn away Medicare patients, especially those without Gap insurance that pays what Medicare doesn't. But that's because the private system has no controls and is far more profitable, and their practice has become big enough that they prefer allocating all of their time to the segment of the market with higher profitability. That's human nature. But it's not necessarily because they lose money on Medicare patients. If that were the case, the over-treating and over-testing of Medicare patients would not be as frequent of a problem that it is. If you are losing money on a test, you can't usually make it up in higher volumes.

Under a properly funded universal health care system, where all physicians were reimbursed fairly, such problems would disappear.

Co-Pays and deductibles

A cardiologist friend of mine reminded me of the old adage that people will consume as much health care as someone else is willing to pay for. That's certainly true in some cases, like welfare services, though I do not think people in general like sitting in waiting rooms. Some surely will pull the trigger faster than others, especially if it is their child at risk. There are two schools of thought in this regard: (1) patients will abuse the system if they are not involved financially; and (2) co-pays and deductibles are counter-productive because they cost more to administer than is brought in and they don't reduce costs (or if they do, they also reduce preventative care and any resulting disease would cost more to treat later). You could counter that, with prepaid health insurance, people are more willing to visit a doctor when not truly needed, but in Canada and other countries that has led to better health care at less cost.

It is somewhat true that patients with maximum coverage are insensitive to the costs of medicine; and insensitive to their contribution to the costs when they do not share in them. They are naturally concerned with their health. Studies clearly need to be done in this area, if they don't already exist. An estimated 18,000 people per year die because they lack health care, and charging patients will keep at least some away from the doctor. If only one patient dies as a result, we create a moral and ethical dilemma. My friends **Drs. Gene and Linda Farley** feel strongly (and I tend to agree) that it is the physician's responsibility to recognize when patients are misusing the system and determine whether it is organic, psychological or social and then modify the patient's behavior.

Wishful thinking?

Unfortunately, few of the recommendations mentioned above are likely to occur under our current moneyed political system. Since 1990, the pharmaceutical and medical industry alone have given over $118.9 million in direct campaign contributions to members of Congress and the president.[1] Tens of millions more have been given by the trial lawyers to keep the legal system in its current chaotic state. Much to the public's chagrin, these political investments are working precisely as planned, and neither the politicians nor special interests are ashamed of it or want to change it.

People don't give money to politicians unless they provide the influence intended, and the amount of taxpayer assets executives receive in return almost always exceeds the money they paid out. That's what business investments are all about. You can be sure that if money was not changing hands many of our societal problems would have been fixed years ago. That politicians can look their children in the eye is puzzling to me. Their kids are going to pay the price too.

There are only two industrialized nations without a single-payer system: South Africa and the United States! Canada provides health care for its entire population for just 10% of its GDP. In the U.S., where 15% of the population remains uncovered, healthcare spending now represents 15% of GDP (and that is rising).

When all else fails, money works!

Lobbying is not the problem; lobbying with cash in hand is. That state and federal leaders are allowed to take money from industries they regulate is a major conflict of interest, corrupt in fact, and here we see the results in the form of runaway health care costs. But health care is just one of many industries being controlled by special interests willing to fund our elections. A classic example is the objection to medical marijuana by congressmen who happen to also own stock in drug companies that compete with pain medication or who receive tens of thousands of dollars in campaign contributions from drug companies or right wing supporters with an ideological bent against the drug. The chances are high that the medical marijuana industry does not give large amounts of campaign cash. But for patients with incurable disease or who are in the last days of their lives, cannabis can work better than drugs proffered by the pharmaceutical industry, drugs that can have major adverse and painful side effects. And while physicians can disperse high-powered Morphine when warranted, they can't prescribe marijuana. Go figure! I've never used marijuana, but I support the right of those in need to choose what is reasonably in their best interest.

How a single payer health plan works

It is also called a Universal Health Care Plan:

> ➤ A "single payer" would replace the existing 1500 different insurance plans. The administrative savings derived from eliminating the bureaucratic duplication, marketing costs and profits associated with these plans are immense — $100 billion in 1991, according to the U.S. General Accounting Office. These savings would be enough to provide coverage for all those persons currently uninsured.

> ➤ Further savings would accrue by replacing itemized billing that hospitals currently use with annual global budgets. Eliminating patient-specific cost accounting (documenting and billing for each item and/or procedure) would free resources for increased clinical care. The U.S. Congressional Budget Office estimates that these combined savings would reduce overall health care costs by $225 billion in addition to extending comprehensive care to all. No other health care plan projects such savings.

> ➢ The plan would be federally financed on an ongoing basis through personal and payroll taxes, thereby replacing insurance premium payments with a health care tax. Proposed taxes on alcohol and cigarettes would also contribute to these funds — 90-95% of Americans would pay less for health care than they do now.

> ➢ A balanced national health care budget would be negotiated yearly, with a single insurer in each state, locally controlled but subject to stringent national standards. Health care providers would negotiate a fee schedule with their state health plan yearly. Patients would receive no bills. Providers would be reimbursed directly by the insurer.

> ➢ Coverage would be the same for all, regardless of income. Risks and benefits would be shared by all.

Sources:
Good sources on heath care reform: *Wisconsin Citizen Action* **www.CitizenActionWI.org/PDFs/Aiv1.pdf** and **www.CitizenActionWI.org/ai.ppt** and *Boston University*'s site at: **http://dcc2.bumc.bu.edu/hs/ushealthreform.htm** and **www.wisconsinhealth.org/sglpay2.html** and **www.pnhp.org/facts/why_the_us_needs_a_single_payer_health_system.php**

When high health care costs contribute to the exodus of jobs, domestic employment and tax revenues are critically reduced as a result, which increases taxes for the rest of us as we now support the unemployed. The effects these deficits have on our nation's financial stability and the security of our children's future are tremendous. In all cases, the only way to stop the drain is to eliminate the transfer of cash from those who want laws written to those who write them, and that can only be done with full public funding of campaigns.

Why politicians want to live under this cloud of corruption is bewildering. That they even allow their lack of loyalty to the public to also affect their own families is a pretty strong indicator as to how important this money and power is to them. Most of us would clean up the stench and sleep well at night because of it, but our current crop of politicians seems able to ignore the negative effects their actions have on the country.

Interesting quotes about Canadian system

Here are some quotes from the much-used source **www.pnhp.org**

> Blue Cross in Massachusetts employs more people to administer coverage for about 2.5 million New Englanders than are employed in all of Canada to administer its single payer coverage for 27 million Canadians.

> Physicians in the U.S. face massive bureaucratic costs. The average office-based American doctor employs 1.5 clerical and managerial staff, spends 44% of his gross income on overhead, and devotes 134 hours of his/her own time annually to billing. Canadian physicians employ 0.7 clerical/administrative staff, spend 34% of their gross income for overhead, and trivial amounts of time on billing (there's a single half page form for all patients, or a simple electronic system).

> Canadian patients have an unrestricted choice of doctors and hospitals, and Canadian doctors have a wider choice of practice options than U.S. physicians. [We are losing such choices in the U.S.]

> Canadians (per capita) get more doctor visits and procedures, more hospital days, and even more bone marrow, liver and lung transplants than Americans.

> While patients must wait for a handful of expensive procedures, there is little or no wait for most kinds of care in Canada. An oft-cited survey that alleged huge waiting lists counted every patient with a future appointment as "in a queue."

> There are virtually no waits for emergent coronary artery surgery in Canada, though elective cases face delays, particularly with the surgeons held in highest regard.

> Surveys show that Canadian doctors are far happier with their system than we are with ours. According to a 1992 poll, 85% prefer their system to ours, 83% rate the care in Canada as very good or excellent, and most physicians would urge their children to enter the profession. Fewer than 300 out of Canada's 50,000 physicians emigrate to the U.S. each year.

> Surveys show very high patient satisfaction in Canada — 96% prefer their system to ours and 89% rate care good or excellent (up from 71% four years ago).

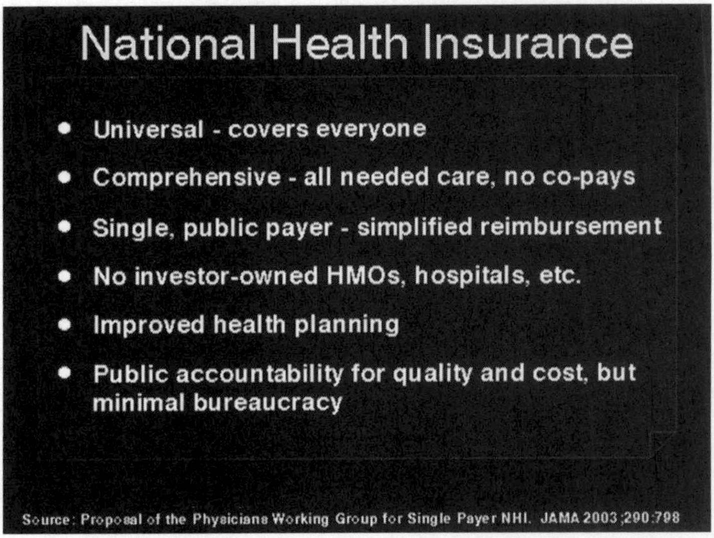

National Health Insurance

- Universal - covers everyone
- Comprehensive - all needed care, no co-pays
- Single, public payer - simplified reimbursement
- No investor-owned HMOs, hospitals, etc.
- Improved health planning
- Public accountability for quality and cost, but minimal bureaucracy

Source: Proposal of the Physicians Working Group for Single Payer NHI. JAMA 2003;290:798

Figure 28: Courtesy www.pnhp.org

Why should taxpayers pay for health care?

Because the taxpayers are already paying, and they are paying far more than they would under a universal single-payer plan where they would pay for health care up front. What we are really talking about is getting rid of the waste, inefficiencies and misuse, and paying less per patient and insuring the total population instead of 85% of it.

The issue is not whether we have the money to pay for health care, but how we collect and use the money. We are all paying for the present health care system — which costs approximately $1.7 trillion nationally each year — and 100% of this money comes from we individuals through taxes, premiums, co-pays, deductibles, tax breaks for employers, higher-priced products and any other method we use for collecting money. When we buy product, that company adds its health care costs to the price and we pay at the cash register (unless that product is made in another country). We'd still all pay for the universal health care system, but in a different way than we are today.

FIX: Rescind the Bush tax breaks for the rich and institute a value-added tax on all non-essential and luxury products sold in the U.S., even foreign products. Punitive damage awards in malpractice cases should go to the health care treasury instead of going to attorneys and patients who have already been compensated for economic damages. These will all help pay for a single-payer system.

Sounds good, but it likely won't happen under the current moneyed political system, where the health care and legal industries have a virtual lock on our politicians. A national Clean Money Clean Elections system would fix that in a hurry and allow politicians to vote for the correct solution rather than for their pocketbook. But we may have to wait for the U.S. business leaders (who would greatly benefit from this) to lobby congress to get it passed.

Universal health care is the most pro-business and pro-public benefit the government could implement. The cost to our society goes well beyond the current $1.7 trillion tab for health care when you add the gigantic costs that result from the unemployment and the dollars the unemployed do dot have to spend on products and services. But the special interests (health care, insurance and pharmaceutical) could care less about those dollars and will continue sending cash to the politicians who write the laws.

But business leaders should fight for single-payer because it will reduce employee benefit costs and protect the very market they cherish. For the people it will decrease the outsourcing of jobs, and it will increase the government's income tax revenues.

Workers will have greater choices about where they can work, eliminating company insurance coverage and pre-existing diseases as a factor in job hunting. They can work anywhere. And companies can have greater choices by hiring the best people without worrying about pre-existing diseases within their family, and they'll avoid bogging down union talks as well. A single-payer plan as outlined herein is a win-win policy, except for the highly profitable health care interests!

Japan's health care costs are 59% less than ours, but the life expectancy in that country is four years longer (even with their larger smoking population) than in the U.S.

Think about it

If taxpayers paid for our health care costs — as they are doing now but should do more directly — U.S. corporations would no longer have to add those costs to the price of their products and they would be more competitive with foreign products, both here and abroad. Medical costs would no longer be a factor when deciding whether to move their plants offshore or to Canada, though wage issues and environmental costs would remain. But fewer Americans would lose their jobs, and the U.S. would collect the employment tax revenues rather than the foreign countries that are collecting them now. In the process we'd reduce our medical costs, employ more people, and reduce our unemployment costs. And 100% of the population would have insurance coverage rather than having 15% that do not — and another 50 million underinsured would have their services upgraded to the universal coverage. What's not to like about this?

> *Why is this not a reality today? Ask your House and Senate representatives. Perhaps they'd at least be willing to give up their health care contributions and fix our system of medical care to benefit the country. If our government were truly "compassionate conservative," this would be a no-brainer.*

How do you keep big government out of it?

By establishing a quasi governmental entity called the *U.S. Council on Health Care* (USCHC)[5] modeled after the Federal Reserve Board where members serve staggered 14-year terms. The Fed has worked well because it keeps politicians at arm's length. The health care board would adjust coverage policy and increase funding if and when it is needed.

The only thing standing in the way of this (or any clean solution) is that the politicians will lose the $100 million per year in campaign cash they currently receive from health care interests, but that's why the business community must step up to the plate and make it happen. It is in their best interest too.

It is not possible to get a clean cup of water from a dirty swamp, so unless business demands it and stakes their campaign contributions on the outcome, it may not get done.

Should it be state or federal?

Indeed it should be a federal policy, but the political situation (and greater money flow) may delay that for some time. In the meantime, the states could implement their own single-payer plan and make hay with it. Why wait for the Feds to level the playing field when they can use lower health care costs to attract businesses and tax revenues from other states? Manufacturers that can reduce their costs by up to 15% will jump at the chance to make the move to a state that has fixed their health care system. More small businesses will start up and more will remain afloat.

However, once again, fixing the system will not be the political choice for the public sector unless it is, first, best for the private sector that funds the political campaigns.

If you haven't gotten this point by now, political money is driving the health care system, but we may nonetheless stand a better chance of fixing it at the state level. Let us just hope that the business lobby understands the competitive issues and sends more cash to the politicians than do the health care, pharmaceutical and insurance lobbies which oppose efficient medicine.

And again, it is a very sad state when we have to hope that one greedy industry outbids another greedy industry to win the hearts of the politicians to the benefit of the public. But that's the way it is. It wouldn't be required if we'd just get the money out of the political system altogether so our elected representatives can design an unfettered system rather than a mish-mash in their attempt to satisfy campaign contributors on both sides of the issue. Lofty as it is, that is this book's goal.

The health care system does not have to remain broken. We can fix it and provide coverage for 100% of the population for the same $1.7 trillion we are paying to cover 85% of the people today. The best is a Medicare-for-all system that leaves physicians and hospitals independent, and patients with the free choices they have today.

But for that to happen, we must discard and ignore the scare-mongering perpetuated by (a) the moneyed interests in the US that don't want to see our system become more efficient, and (b) by the moneyed interests in Canada that want to see their system opened to profit-taking like their brethren south of the border enjoy today.

Remember that the profits are in the inefficiencies of the system: excessive administrative costs, overuse and abuse of expensive testing procedures (the cash cows), and billing for services not provided (that's called fraud, which under a federal system means jail time). Easily 50% of these unneeded costs could be eliminated if there is a political will to do so. But whether today's crop of politicians has that will is questionable. We may indeed need a complete turnover of politicians: Vote out of all those who have been in office over five years, excepting for those who have made sincere reform efforts.

"Many in the profession are seriously concerned that some physicians are willingly violating their integrity in personal profit-making ventures at the expense of patients' welfare. These excesses are not new, but they are far more widespread than in the past, and their consequences more profound."

Jerome P. Kassirer, M.D.
Author, *On The Take*

Good sources on the single-payer can be found at:

➤ Physicians' Working Group for Single-Payer National Health Insurance – **www.physiciansproposal.org**

➤ One of the best sources for a single-payer system **www.pnhp.org**

➤ Dr. Michael Rachlis, an expert on Canadian Health Care, has written two books on their system. A free download of his latest book can be made at **www.MichaelRachlis.com**

➤ The Coalition for Wisconsin Health **www.WisconsinHealth.org**

➤ American Medical Student Association **www.amsa.org**

➤ Everybody In Nobody Out **www.everybodyinnobodyout.org**

➤ Commission on the Future of Health Care in Canada **www.HealthCareCommission.ca**

➤ Friends of Medicare **www.keepmedicarepublic.ca**

➤ Benefits of a single-payer system: **www.pnhp.org/facts/why_the_us_needs_a_single_payer_health_system.php**

➤ Excellent PowerPoint presentation: **www.amsa.org/hp/sppres.ppt**

➤ PowerPoint slides with some duplication: **www.pnhp.org/slideshow/pnhp2003/ PNHPNovember2003.ppt**

➤ Wisconsin Citizen Action **www.citizenactionwi.org/PDFs/Aiv.1.pdf www.citizenactionwi.org/ai.ppt**

"An honest politician is one who, when bought, stays bought."
Sen. Simon Cameron (R-PA)
Quoted to *Time*, Aug. 7, 1978

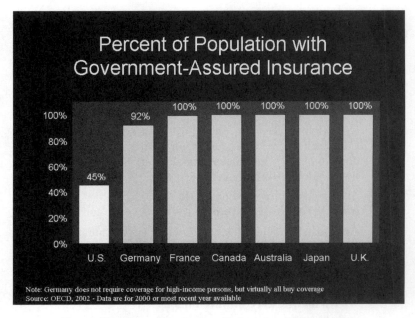

Figure 29: Courtesy: Emory University, Henry Kahn, MD, FACP, Department of Social Medicine

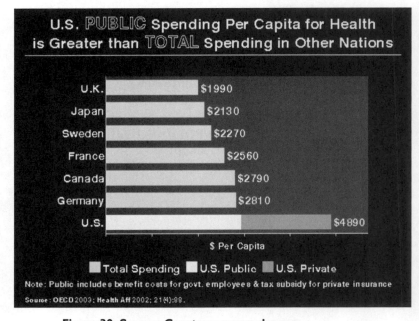

Figure 30: Source: Courtesy www.pnhp.org

7
It doesn't stop there

Campaign finance abuses affect every walk of life. If there is money to be made by a government decision, the potential beneficiary of that decision is most assuredly on the giving end. Whatever your issue, it is strongly affected by the passing of dollar bills from hand to hand, and you can see just how much money has changed hands by looking at the *Center for Responsive Politics* alphabetical list at **www.crp.org/industries/alphalist.asp**.

The late **Marty Jezer**, one of the early architects of *Clean Money Campaign Reform*, described it well: "Money determines which candidates will be able to run effective campaigns and influences which candidates win elective office. Money also defines the parameters of political debate: which issues get raised, how issues are framed, and how legislation is drafted. Money enables rich and powerful interest groups to influence elections and dominate the legislative process."

In their 1995 article *People or Corporations* that appeared in *Social Policy Magazine,* Jezer and **Randy Kehler** ask several pertinent questions:

> ➢ Why are essential public institutions like schools and parks always underfunded when wealth abounds in the unaccountable corporate sector?

> ➢ Why are programs for the poor being defunded while welfare for the rich is being increased?

> ➢ Why are food stamps being cut while tobacco subsidies are maintained?

> ➢ Why can't congressional proponents of single-payer health care get their proposals on the table while corporate opponents of environmental protection are actually writing the bills that Congress is passing?

> ➢ And why are there so many millionaires in Congress, so many qualified individuals choosing not to run for office, and so many ordinary citizens of modest means feeling shut out of the political process altogether?

One can only respond to each with "follow the money."

Illegal immigrants and border control

This should be a no-brainer. At a time when we should be scrutinizing every person coming across the border for security reasons, you would think that every red-blooded American would want the borders closed to all except those who have legally applied and received a U.S. visa.

If you thought that the case, you would be terribly wrong. The more illegal immigrants that cross the border and take American jobs, the more our American business leaders like it — and politicians like what business leaders like. Agricultural mega-farmers and meat packers absolutely love the current hands-off approach of the Bush administration. Rather than paying fair wages to Americans to do their farming and meat packing, they can pay extraordinarily low wages to Latinos who have crossed the borders and need a job — any job — to survive. That Americans usually command fair wages is not convenient for them and goes against their corporate culture.

The more our U.S. wages become depressed, the higher are corporate profits and CEO salaries. Even non-offending companies benefit from the labor glut, so don't expect them to come running to our rescue.

Okay, so that's corporate greed — nothing new about that. But then you'd think that our U.S. Congress or the president would block this dangerous greed by passing (or enforcing) laws that penalize companies who hire illegal immigrants.

You'd think that would be their reaction, but you'd be wrong again. CEOs that make a lot of money because of bad laws are very generous with politicians. Members of Congress and the president of the United States collect millions of dollars per year in campaign contributions from these fellows, and to stop any such flow of immigrants would also stop any such flow of campaign money. It isn't going to happen, at least not under the current system.

So, to make acceptance of this corporate abuse seem to be a plausible humanitarian struggle, the Bush administration came up with a game called "matching willing workers with willing employers," which President Bush gushes at every opportunity.

But that is the biggest pile of hogwash ever put out by any president of the United States. Pure and simple, this was a way of appeasing corporate campaign contributors, and so far, this claim has kept at least some of the public off the president's back.

That political money has trumped national security is unconscionable, but even beyond security issues, these untoward practices threaten our very democracy. We are becoming a plutocracy, a government by the wealthy and for the wealthy, and some day we will not even need elections. The corporations will control us.

Congressman **F. James Sensenbrenner** (R-WI) deserves praise for his fight to eliminate the issuing of driver's licenses to illegal immigrants. Over 90% of the public supports his position, but in 2004 he found it impossible to get his very logical amendment attached to the proposed national intelligence bill precisely because the moneyed interests won over political reason and public safety.

The people who won this battle are the corporate CEOs who prefer lax border control over national security, and these businessmen are willing to share their profits with the politicians who made it all possible.

However, having opposed campaign finance reform for many years, Sensenbrenner carries a share of the blame for this situation, though hopefully he will have a different perspective the next time the campaign reform issue is debated. He is one of the more principled members of Congress, and I usually support his positions, but he has his limits. His principles and convictions have not been strong enough to drive a sincere challenge against our corrupt political system. After all, he benefits from that system when his party is in power and thus he has a propensity to defend the status quo.

Sensenbrenner is also the epitome of another congressional shenanigan: grandstanding when it doesn't really harm his party. During his town hall meetings he criticized the CAFTA bill as a job loser. Even voted against NAFTA for that very reason. But because it was a close vote and his was needed by the party, he cast his in favor of the Bush administration. His was one of two Republican votes that put CAFTA over the top, though his vote wasn't needed for NAFTA to pass. Yet when the pork-laden highway funding bill was in front of him, his was one of only 8 votes (out of 435) that were cast against this egregious spending bill! That's called political showmanship. Senator **Russ Feingold** (D-WI) did the same when he grandstanded as the only vote (one out of 100) to oppose the U.S. PATRIOT Act.

Another common ploy is for politicians to spend money drafting and introducing bills that they know don't have a chance in hell of passing, but nonetheless satisfies a generous contributor. And of course that starts money flowing from both sides so it benefits all politicians. These are costly playthings that wouldn't occur under a Clean Money system, but what is hurtful to the taxpayers are when a few of these bills eventually do get greased through the system.

Back to the immigration issue, this process of allowing employment to illegals has a rippling effect up the chain of companies and depresses wages in other industries as well. We actually do have a law in place that makes it illegal to hire undocumented workers, but the enforcement of that law has been ignored by President Bush, thanks clearly to the money flowing from corporations to politicians. This problem could be solved virtually overnight if employers were heavily fined for hiring undocumented workers, as they were before the Republicans came into power.

Certainly, the corporations whose executives are paid tons of money and give tons of campaign contributions are not complaining, but noise does come from the non-influential Americans who do not contribute substantial sums to campaigns. Be assured that the guys with the Big Bucks will win this and other political/economic battles.

Incidentally, it is hard to criticize the millions of Mexicans who feel depressed by their own government and seek a livelihood elsewhere. But they must understand that our porous border with their country will attract terrorists from all over the world to Mexico seeking the opportunity to slip into the United States. Some terrorists will make it through and some will remain south of the border. Don't be surprised if, just prior to the 2006 election, we have a breakout of terrorism resulting from five years of open borders under George W. Bush. And then he'll wonder what we could have done to stop it.

Terrorism in America will have disastrous effects on the lives of Mexicans and their families, and they must help us stop it at all costs. Mexicans must play by the same rules as do Americans, and if they don't like the rules or corruption in Mexico, they should fight for changes. But that fight should start in their own country, where their families would be direct beneficiaries. And American companies hell-bent on outsourcing should give preference to Mexico. If we help them succeed, we can build a strong neighbor and help stop the games we are playing at the border. These people want to work, and we can help them achieve that goal on their own soil.

Outsourcing of jobs

While the influx of millions of illegal immigrants does great financial harm to lower-income households, the outsourcing of technical jobs to China and India has a serious impact on higher paid white collar workers. Internet technology allows the transfer of data around the world almost instantaneously, thus making outsourcing of jobs that deal with information a snap. In short, it is no longer just manual labor positions that are at risk. We are getting hit on both ends of the scale: software programming, engineering, accounting, banking, legal research, technical support, call centers, transcription, and even foreign services that provide physicians to read wire-transferred radiological studies have all fallen prey to the ingenuity of the selfish businessman. However, issues such as patient privacy and consumer fraud promise to be a major flaw in this system as credit card and personal information as well as social security numbers are transferred overseas. Identity theft is on the rise already, and these outsourcing practices certainly won't help combat it.

One thing that doesn't seem not real bright is the transfer of American technology to countries like China, which does little to protect the intellectual property rights held by U.S. companies. *Callaway Golf Clubs*, as just one example, transferred some manufacturing of its products to China, and not long after, Chinese copies showed up on the U.S. market. My gut tells me that they rue the day they off-shored their products, as these things cannot easily be reversed. It's sort of like un-ringing the bell. Many people, me included, think the company got what they deserved.

Trend of male median income

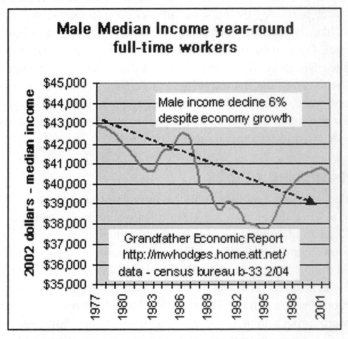

Figure 31: Trend of male median U.S. income
Source: http://mwhodges.home.att.net

The benefactors of these ploys are the corporations who get cheap labor, which in turn increases profits, CEO salaries and — you know the drill by now — campaign contributions. But the shareholders of these companies will end up the losers if product designs are hijacked by a low-balling country.

According to *United for a Fair Economy*, the top executives at the 50 largest outsourcers of service jobs make, on average, $10.4 million per year. The average pay of the leading outsourcing CEO is 3,300 times the pay of an average Indian call center employee and 1,300 times that of an Indian computer programmer. These same 50 companies gave over $10 million to members of Congress during the 2004 electoral cycle. I wonder why. **www.faireconomy.org**

To see the complete story download Executive Excess 2005 at **www.FairEconomy.org/press/2005/EE2005.pdf**. It's not a pretty story. They point out that CEOs of military contractors received a 200% raise since 9/11. One body armor profiteer, **David H. Brooks** of *DHB Industries*, went from compensation of $525,000 in 2001 to $70 million in 2004, a 13,349% increase. It would take an Air Force airman 3,634 years to make the $88 million that *United Technologies* paid its CEO **George David** in 2004.

Yeah, war is hell.

I suppose that it is not fair to criticize these CEOs for putting the profits into their own pockets rather than reinvesting them in new product development. After all, that would provide shareholder and job growth for the future, and the CEOS may not plan on sticking around for the future. The politicians who made this all possible, of course, always get their share in campaign contributions. Other sources have shown that these factors have driven average American wages down by $4000 per year since 2000 (which of course includes the now unemployed).

I blame the political pressure that has been placed on our "kinder, gentler SEC" to allow CEOs to hire and control corporate board members under a sweetheart deal that bypasses the legal owners of the company: the shareholders. You can be sure that worker wages went down while CEO wages at these above referenced 50 companies went up. Depressed wages is exactly what the corporate fat cats want, so even John Kerry backed away from the issue during his presidential bid. Making it illegal for companies to hire undocumented workers would end this travesty overnight, but neither political party will go there, not even the Democrats who would have championed the little guy's cause once upon a time. What is puzzling is why the U.S. Government is giving tax breaks to companies that outsource jobs to other countries. (Forget I asked.)

One must wonder how many of the wealthy — who just received one of the largest tax cuts in American history and enjoy the largest wealth gap ever, who have promoted conditions that destroy jobs for Americans through illegal immigration and outsourcing to China and India — have the unmitigated gall to oppose fair wages, welfare, health care and unemployment benefits for the very people they put out of work! Somehow I'm missing the compassion in this.

Tobacco

Can you imagine the tobacco industry getting taxpayer handouts at the same time we are suing them in federal court? As of this writing, the Bush administration is backing down from Bill Clinton's $130 billion suit against the industry — Bush proposes to settle for only $10 billion. That Philip Morris, the world's largest cigarette manufacturer, is the Republican Party's largest campaign contributor certainly should not be lost in the discussion.

But the biggest destruction of all was at the state level when the tobacco giant lobbied state legislatures behind the scenes to make sure that the tobacco settlement money was used for anything other than for what it was intended: educating kids on the risks of smoking. And their lobbying money paid off. Most states used the money instead to offset budget shortfalls, often compounding the problem (but pleasing Philip Morris immensely, which paid only **30 cents on the dollar** when it provided a lump sum settlement up front).

It's an intriguing relationship between tobacco companies and politicians. Whenever there is, say, a tobacco tax that needs defeating, congressmen like Sen. **Mitch McConnell** (R-KY) will in essence say "Okay, I'll take your money and I'll vote your way. But I need cover.

You must heavily advertise in my district encouraging my constituents to demand that I vote against this bill as yet another tax on the public. I'll then take an anti-tax stand and we'll both get what we want." And of course this manipulation of the public plays out the same in many other policy votes.

Sugar

Between 1985 and 1990, the total contributions to House and Senate members from sugar interests exceeded $3.9 million. In 1985, both the House and Senate voted against reducing price supports and import restrictions after 17 sugar PACs contributed more than $900,000 to congressional campaign coffers over a 3 year period. The price supports, quotas, and import restrictions that the sugar industry received as payback added $3 billion annually to the cost American consumers pay for sugar. For an average of $780,000 per year in contributions, the revenues of the sugar industry have increased by $3 billion — an ROI of 3846:1. That's not at all hard to take for any "investor."

Farm

Subsidies to the family farmer may be justified, but most of the current subsidies are going to industrialized and mega-farmers that are squeezing out the little guys. Think about the Wal-Marts and Home Depots squeezing out the family-owned hardware store and you have a valid comparison. We are helping the big guy crush the little guy to the point that he just wants out, and is willing to sell his farm at nearly any price.

Subsidies should be limited to the smaller farmers whose taxable income is less than, say, $200,000 per year. But the little guys are not the ones giving the campaign contributions, so they'll continue to see agribusiness laws slanted against them. Subsidies should also be given only to those agricultural entities that take steps to protect their crops from bioterrorism. Fences aren't a practical solution, but video surveillance and product testing is (and testing should be mandated for all imported foods as well, as long as we are touching on the subject of food and terrorism). While Japan tests 100% of its beef for Mad Cow Disease, only 2% or so is tested in the U.S.

In March 2005, **Wisconsin Democracy Campaign** reported:

➤ Loans to these [farms] to buy cows are being funded with community development block grant money intended to help low and moderate income people get good-paying jobs

➤ The review also showed 48 of the state's 135 corporate farms received $6.4 million of the $16.6 million in state aid awarded to more than 600 farmers and dairy operations. Commerce Department documents also showed, like large corporations, at least some of these recipients did not appear to need state aid.

➤ One Winnebago County operation whose owner lives in Ireland received a $337,500 low-interest loan from the state even though documents described him as an individual "with significant net worth."

➤ Another problem with helping these operations buy hundreds more cows is that it ultimately results in an increase in milk production, which lowers milk prices. That phenomenon hurts smaller family farms, which have fewer resources to weather low milk prices.

➤ The winners are large corporate farms, 86 of which also received about $27 million in federal farm subsidies, and large cheese producers like Kraft Foods because lower milk prices help them cut their production costs and increase profits from cheese sales.

➤ Executives of Kraft and its parent company have contributed nearly $27,000 to Thompson, McCallum and Doyle, whose administrations have generously helped corporate farmers.

Source: **www.wisdc.org/pr031605.html**

For details on farm subsidies on a state by state basis, see **www.endgame.org/farm**. *Endgame* has documented $131 billion in government subsidies between 1995 and 2003, with most of the money going not to family farmers but to the mega-farmers who control the campaign contributions.

The *Environmental Working Group* has also documented that 72% of the subsidy payments went to just 10% of the recipients. According to EWG, "Taxpayers may not realize it, but the money they send to Washington is hastening the demise of family farms through the agricultural subsidy programs that purport to save them." Source: **www.ewg.org/reports/greenacres/exec.html** Money changing hands? Over $348.3 million has made its way to campaign funds from agribusiness since 1990. Source: **www.opensecrets.org**

Public Campaign **www.Publicampaign.org**, headed by **Nick Nyhart**, also reported that $249.6 million changed hands between agribusiness and politicians nationwide, which in turn won $180 billion in subsidies over a ten year period. Do the math! That's an outstanding return-on-investment. The consumer pays the bill in the form of higher prices for sugar, peanuts, milk, beef and dairy products, while the manufacturers share part of their booty with the politicians to win future windfalls funded by taxpayers — thus the losses for the public regenerate many times over. (I just priced a prime tenderloin at my local market: $29.99 per pound. That's what happens when congress allows the elimination of competition. I walked.)

Subsidies

Tax breaks result in lower taxes paid by an individual or corporation. Subsides and grants are checks from the U.S. Treasury made out to the lucky company. This is like getting a refund check for excessive taxes paid, but many of these companies, even the most profitable, pay no taxes at all. So Congress has decided to write them a check (no, you and I are writing the check, they are just mailing it).

Gun rights and gun control[1]

Gun Rights groups, like the National Rifle Association — which is funded mostly by gun manufacturers, not gun owners — have given over $17 million to political campaigns since 1990 (86% to Republicans and 14% to key Democrats), as compared to Gun Control groups giving only 1.6 million, 96% to Democrats. So, what has the NRA given us for their dollars? For one, laws that allow even suspected terrorists to buy guns in the U.S., simultaneously tying the hands of officials seeking to protect the public. Were there not a 10-to-1 ratio in the amount of dollars given to congressmen, we'd probably see a reasonable compromise between the rights of

Americans to own guns and the ability of authorities to ensure that they are not getting into the wrong hands. (I favor concealed carry laws, part of my right wing bent, but not Florida's shoot-first-and-ask-questions-later law, or the legalizing of assault weapons.)

Broadcast media[1]

In addition to swaying Congress on the pharmaceutical advertising issue, the media's campaign dollars won them $70 billion worth of high resolution digital broadcast frequencies — at no cost to them but costing taxpayers about $700 each. They also won the lifting of restrictions on how many stations they can own, plus the killing of a proposed rule to make a certain amount of time on the public airwaves available for free during political campaigns. Though the public owns the airwaves, we do not own our Congressmen. The media owns most of them. According to The Center for Public Integrity, more than $222 million in media money given to members of Congress between 1998 and 2004 made that relationship work!
www.publicintegrity.org/telecom/report.aspx?aid=406

As of this writing, the House has promised to overhaul the 1996 Telecommunications Act, and the only thing we can be assured of is that the special interests on all sides of the issue are going to start the campaign contributions flowing. It's the telecom utilities versus the Internet companies versus the cable companies versus satellite companies versus the corporate broadcasters, and that will ensure that the money flows promptly and continuously and in all directions.

> *"We always prefer to give the money directly to the guy, or the woman, that you're going to support. You like to walk in, you like to give them the check, you like to look in their eye and say 'I'm here to help you.' You always do."*
> **Rodney Smith, SBC Communications**

If these high-dollar issues didn't regularly bubble to the surface, just how would the electoral process ever get funded?

Banking, securities and insurance industries[1]

According to the *Center for Responsive Politics*, these industries gave $576 million to members of Congress since 1989, 58% to

Republicans and 42% to Democrats. These contributions won them new regulations that permitted financial institutions to merge into mega-banks that can speculate in risky stocks even while being protected by government (read: taxpayers) insurance against bad investments. (Does that sound like another Savings and Loan fiasco?) They also won the right to compile and use private financial and credit information from their customers. (Money can work wonders.)

Credit card and banking companies[1]

These industries have given more than $151 million to members of Congress since 1990, with 61% going to Republicans and 39% to Democrats. Their persistence paid off. These contributions finally won them limits on bankruptcy procedures and the amount of relief a person is entitled to under the new law signed by President Bush. As one of the taxpayers who are paying the bill for those who abuse the bankruptcy system, I support certain protections. But it is hard not to be critical of the banks who hand out unsolicited credit cards with no effort to reign in misuse, banks that put forth too little effort to fend off fraud, even refusing to require simple PIN numbers, especially at gas pumps, to prevent misuse of credit cards.

The technology exists to record a digital signature and a digital photograph at the point of sale and to make this information available to the card holder on their Internet account to see who actually made the charge. But card companies refuse to do this because the losses do not yet exceed the costs to implement such technology. The real card owner's picture, taken at the time of application or uploaded later, could also be downloaded and displayed both on the credit card and to the clerk at the time of sale. And if the card is stolen it should display STOLEN (rather than a simple "declined.") and automatically page security personnel. What part of "security" do they not understand?

The smartest of the credit card companies will be the first to introduce these security measures and capture the bulk of the public's business. Most certainly mine. Even today they should ask for photo I.D. on every point-of-sale card usage! This extra security would save the public billions of dollars per year, yet may need to be mandated by congress. Credit card companies have their own interests in mind, not the public's. They just charge the losses to the merchant.

According to **Jonathan Alter** in *Newsweek* (April 25, 2005), about half of those filing for personal bankruptcy had themselves been abused by exorbitant health care costs (remember Chapter 6?). Senate amendments in the Bush bankruptcy bill that would have protected those who went bankrupt because of high medical costs, and another which capped interest rates at 30%, failed! "Although the bible clearly bars usury, the big congressional Bible Thumpers sided with their corporate contributors," Alter said. It is hard to argue that, if this legislation was needed, it would have been better for the public if money hadn't changed hands at the political level. It would have then gotten passed into law.

Big corporations[1]

This group as a whole gave $150.1 million from 1991 to 2001, 66% to Republicans and 34% to Democrats, and won $55 billion in tax breaks from 1996 to 1988[1] (that doesn't count the latest Bush tax giveaways to the wealthiest in our midst).

Has this gracious giving had any effect on legislation? The folks at Gallo Wine believe in this system a lot. They gave candidates $463,000 for the 1992-1994 election cycle and in return received more than $5 million of taxpayer money to promote their wine products overseas, a return on investment greater than 10-to-1, thanks to the federal Market Access Program (MAP).

Telecommunications[1]

These companies have given $255.8 million to members of Congress since 1989, 59% to Democrats and 41% to Republicans, if you can imagine that, and in return they received the deregulation of rates and a green light for phone, cable and broadcast companies to merge. Thus, cable rates have risen three times faster than inflation and we've seen immeasurable cost to the public as the industry consolidates from hundreds of small stations into ten or fewer giant media conglomerates that will control virtually all public news and political coverage. Over time, Congress eliminated the anti-monopoly laws for the telecom sector, and the U.S. now has the 13th slowest cable system in the world. Japan's is seven times faster (up to 40mps) and operates at half the cost. Ours is not a political system the Japanese will want to copy either.

Petroleum[1]

American oil producers are drooling at the thought of drilling in Alaska's Arctic National Wildlife Refuge (ANWR). They've tried for years to get congressional approval, and although rivers of cash flowed from their corporate accounts to Congress over the decades, it has been to no avail until Bush II. But now oil prices are skyrocketing and President Bush is withholding the one tool available to help stabilize the rising prices: releasing some of the U.S. oil reserves into the market. This is another way of starving the system and pressuring Congress to open ANWR to domestic companies, and a natural remedy for a former oil man. Hurricane Katrina did force the issue and reserves were released to the market.

Another issue is conveniently being glossed over: thanks to the moneyed political system, Congress turned a blind eye as 10-15 major competitive oil companies merged into four biggies (ExxonMobile, ConocoPhillips, ChevronTexaco, Royal Dutch/ Shell), thus giving control of the industry to fewer businessmen and substantially reducing the competition among oil companies. True competition can only occur when there are more companies, not fewer, and only true competition will temper the gouging of the public. In the 1980s, the Federal Trade Commission would have pounced on the big oil companies, but corporate leaders have found the way to the politicians' hearts — through their pocketbooks.

I personally support drilling in ANWR, though I would demand one restriction: that the extra production is only available to the U.S. market. The oil industry wants to lay a pipeline between Alaska and Japan and export the ANWR oil, which would reduce Japan's gas prices but not ours. The government should also contract with an oil producer, even a foreign one if necessary, to explore and drill where American companies will not, and move that oil into the reserves or market to help control prices. Or buy Unocal, which is up for sale, and compete with the biggies that are limiting output to escalate prices. Yes, that's government intervention where the private sector should prevail. But some strategic resources (like defense and medicine) must be nudged when the private sector fails to fill the need.

Americans could have confidence that the right decisions are being made if oil company money was not changing hands at the political level, but that's not the case. The *Center for Responsive Politics* reports that $178.5 million in campaign contributions has flowed to politicians since 1990 ($18 million to Republicans alone in 2004). According to The Center, the big players who will benefit from ANWR drilling are *ChevronTexaco* and *ExxonMobile*. Source: **www.opensecrets.org**.

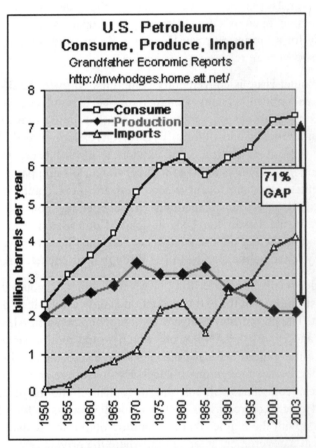

Figure 32: Demonstrates that U.S. production is going down and imports and consumption are going up. Source: http://mwhodges.home.att.net

Campaign money has also bought these companies seats at the White House table, and the claims that our energy policies are being written by the energy lobbyists (read, the oil corporations) are unfortunate but all too true. Just as the "Healthy Forests Initiative" was written by the logging industry lobbyists, which allows their industry to "clear cut" our forests on the premise that fewer trees would reduce forest fires! As I write this the courts have just blocked President Bush's bid to allow 100-year-old trees to be cut down in 2000 acres of the Sequoia National Forest. Though Congress passed the law in 2000 allowing this cut to "protect against fires," the work did not begin until this summer when timber prices were high. How convenient.

Selling our national treasures for campaign dollars is an absolute disgrace that only politicians could stomach. The government employees we are paying to establish these policies on behalf of the public have given their seats at the table to the private sector representatives (read: the industry lobbyists). Have they no shame? Source: **www.tompaine.com/articles/mapping_the_oil_motive.php**

Resource extracting industries[1]

The oil and gas companies, mining concerns, electric utilities, chemical manufacturers and timber companies have given $318.7 million in campaign contributions since 1989 and in return received $33 billion in tax breaks, a weakening of Superfund cleanup laws (with toxic waste sites remaining on the list that may never get cleaned up), and the freedom to "top" mountains and deposit the waste in valleys. So we pay with dirtier air and water as well as millions of dollars in price gouging. Aren't we lucky folks?

Look at all the extra arsenic we get in our water (and without even having to pay extra for it!). According to **Paul Begala**[4], a liberal pundit, Clinton ruled to lower the allowable parts per billion of arsenic in water from 50 parts to 10, but Bush overturned the rule. Arsenic is not a real healthy additive — it is responsible for cancer in kids and adults alike. The Environmental News Network (**www.enn.com**) thought that was a little suspect after Bush received $5 million from the mining industry, but what do they know?

And don't even think about updating the 1872 Mining Act, which allows a few select companies to extract billions of dollars in gold and silver resources per year without paying a penny in royalties to the land's owners — the citizens of the U.S.. Moreover, mercury from the extraction process is winding up in our water resources, where it is not only killing off bird and fish species but going into the bodies of our children and expectant mothers. The industries dumping mercury into the air and water got a free walk, and people are growing sick and dying as a result.

It doesn't matter whether you are Republican or Democrat, there is absolutely no need for companies to disperse dangerous chemicals into our air or water. They are not doing it because they have no other choice, but because it is cheaper than disposing of the waste appropriately. And our politicians are bending to their whims. If Congress wants to start cash flowing, all they need do is start talking about restrictions or royalties.

Got milk?

Another interesting issue was the *Bovine Growth Hormone* fiasco. BGH is manufactured by chemical giant *Monsanto* and injected into cows to increase milk production by 15% to 25%. The issue wasn't just whether cows should or should not be injected (they shouldn't be), but **whether consumers had the right to know what they were drinking** (they *should* have that right). Product labeling seemed like a no-brainer — let the public decide what they want to drink and what they want to avoid. But this information has been suppressed from the public. Monsanto didn't like the idea of disclosure, and they lobbied, sent cash, and I think even stomped their feet.

Monsanto even sued one dairy farmer in Maine who had the gall to advertise that his milk did *not* contain BGH! They argued that the *exclusion* ads cast a negative light on BGH, and they won! The FDA, with several ex-Monsanto employees on its panel, had ruled earlier that labeling was *not* required in spite of the fact that, since 1994, every other industrialized country in the world, except the U.S., has banned the BGH drug altogether! The medical journal Lancet has also reported a potential link to cancer. BGH can also cause cows a painful udder infection that must be treated with antibiotics, which of course, are transferred to humans who drink the spiked milk (who then can build an immunity to them and render the antibiotics ineffective when they really needed them).

Nearly $4 million in contributions since 1990 certainly hasn't hurt Monsanto's goals. Our moneyed political system has allowed the usurping of public health. That story would be weird enough, but in an ironic twist of fate, BGH was so successful at increasing production that dairy farmers in Wisconsin experienced a glut of milk on the market that drove prices down. Got that? BGH caused them to produce too much milk and prices plummeted! They got very upset and demonstrated in the streets for higher milk price controls and even dumped cans of excess milk into the sewers to show their ire. Taking their cows off of BGH and returning production and costs to normal (and safer) levels never occurred to them. Only in America!

Churning

You've heard about "churning" mostly in the insurance world, but it happens in politics as well. If politicians aren't writing legislation, they aren't generating cash, even if they know their bill doesn't stand a chance of passing. A good example involves the tobacco industry. Just mention the possibility of increasing the tobacco tax or implementing workplace smoking restrictions, and the tobacco giants come out of the woodwork and cash immediately begins to flow.

Another example involves the makers of the latest technology to attempt to find a home in the hearts of politicians — global positioning systems to track the number of miles drivers travel in their cars so they can be taxed accordingly.

Pay no attention to whether this scheme makes any sense at all, because it doesn't. Look first at which legislator is pushing the idea and whether he received cash from the manufacturer. The product doesn't make sense because we already have a mechanism in place — it's called gasoline taxes. The more you drive the more you pay. We don't need another state or federal bureaucracy to monitor vehicles or to give gas guzzlers an advantage over those who conserve. But this silly idea is being proposed anyway; because some legislator has a special reason to propose it.

Virtually every piece of major legislation has special interests behind it, and they almost always come with cash in hand. Legislators can pass laws because they are needed, but most often they pass laws because they are paid to pass the laws. Again, they are not paid by you and me, at least not sufficiently to warrant their attention, but by the special interests who want to push their products or services. If cash were not changing hands, not only would fewer laws be written but those that were would be in the best interest of the public rather than the private sector.

Savings & loan taxpayer rip-off

You've heard of the Keating Five, which included my favorite Senators, **John McCain** (R-AZ) and **John Glenn** (D-OH). Following contributions of over $300,000 from S&L director **Charles Keating,** a series of accounting rule changes prompted by the five senators' interventions with the banking commission allowed the S&L industry to make risky investments. These ultimately caused an S&L failure that will cost taxpayers $500 billion over the next 30 years. The logical question here is "who has this S&L money now?" Money like this doesn't just disappear. It goes into someone's pocket or foreign bank account, and someone is living very high on the hog thanks to the taxpayers who continue to fund this fraud. Perhaps Keating would like to tell us where the money went, and how he's being supported.

The only positive that came out of the S&L scandal is that it seems to have been the turning point for Senator McCain. He saw the massive destruction money in politics had on the system and began pushing for campaign reform. If we are extremely lucky, he will be our next president. But his Republican colleagues are not likely to let an effective reform bill get to his desk.

Stock ownership by congressmen

Now picture this: Your U.S. Representative or Senator is considering a bill on whether or not to allow drug companies to extend their patent rights on drugs from the standard 17 years to an unprecedented 20 years, adding three more years to the company's monopoly and locking out any efforts by generic drug manufacturers to provide lower cost products to those in need. Of importance is the fact that your politician happens to own $250,000 of Bristol-Myers stock — the company that makes the highly profitable drug Taxol — and this patent extension would add three more years of record-breaking profits. His choice is between protecting the public by allowing competition into the marketplace earlier rather than later or increasing his personal wealth. How do you think he is going to vote? You can be assured that you didn't elect a dummy.

Take **Dr. Bill Frist,** for example, the majority leader of the U.S. Senate. He and his wife owned upwards of $27 million of stock in what was once the Hospital Corporation of America, the infamous hospital conglomerate. According to *The Senator from HCA* by **Wayne M. O'Leary:** "Accusations against Columbia/HCA included overcharging, improper billing, denying emergency care, bribing physicians, defrauding the Medicare program, avoiding taxes, and (shades of Enron!) disseminating inaccurate financial data to investors. The company eventually acknowledged guilt, paid $1.7 billion in fines, and reorganized under another, less infamous, name". The company is now known as HCA — The Healthcare Company, and First is currently being investigated for insider trading after unloading his HCA stock just prior to its crashing. (That's interesting in itself. All of his stocks were supposedly in a blind trust and he wasn't supposed to even know he owned them! Must be secret vision.)

Not to be ignored are the campaign contributions the Republican party has received since 1990 from health care professionals ($180 million) and the pharmaceutical industry ($80.8 million). None of this, mind you, had anything to do with Frist's blocking of a strong patient's bill of rights proposal (allowing patients to sue their HMOs for denying care, the very action HCA was charged with) and negotiating the Medicare prescription drug plan, which promises to put over $700 billion into the pockets of the pharmaceutical giants over the next decade.

These conflicts of interest occurs every day congress is in session, yet it was comical to see the senate criticize **Judge Samuel Alito** for his investments in a mutual fund. Members are allowed to own stock in every industry they regulate or deregulate. That's insider trading at its worst, and **Ivan Boesky** and **Michael Milken** went to jail for less. Congressmen should be held to the same standards.

Consider this from **www.mercola.com**:

> ➢ Rep. **Robin Hayes**, R-N.C., one of the wealthiest members of Congress, owned more than $11 million in drug stocks on Dec. 31, 1999, the *Washington Bureau of McClatchy Newspaper* found in reviewing 180 members' latest financial disclosure statements. The reports showed that 36 members or congressmen's families owned drug stocks — including a number who sit on committees with jurisdiction over the industry.

> ➢ Rep. **Jim Sensenbrenner** of Wisconsin owned shares worth $2.2 million to $7.1 million in five drug makers. He [was] the ranking Republican on a Judiciary subcommittee that often reviews patent legislation that can deliver windfalls to name-brand drug companies. [His wife also owned over $250,000 in Philip Morris stock and he has shunned calls to curtail the industry.]

> ➢ Although Sen. **John Kerry**, D-Mass., sits on the Senate Commerce Committee that likely will have a role in shaping any Medicare drug package, his wife Teresa, a Heinz family heiress, owned shares in eight drug companies worth $2.1 million to $4.2 million.

> ➢ The year-end pharmaceutical shareholder lists also include Republican presidential nominee **George W. Bush** and his family with between $62,000 to $234,000 in drug stocks; his running mate, **Dick Cheney** ($150,000 to $350,000), and the wife of Sen. Joe Lieberman, the Democratic vice presidential nominee ($15,000 to $50,000).

Sources: **www.mercola.com/2000/oct/15/congress_conflicts.htm**
www.mercola.com/2000/oct/8/moneyed_interests.htm

U.S. Representative **Bernie Sanders** (I-VT) submitted a bill to require all congressional members to put their personal holdings into a blind trust where they would be managed competently without conflicting with the political votes made by the member. But his proposal did not see the light of day as it was blocked in committee by members that it would have restricted from playing the insider game themselves. (At least one U.S. Senator, **Herb Kohl** (D-WI), has voluntarily put all assets except his ownership in the Milwaukee Bucks into a blind trust.)

Reader Resource: To find the financial holdings and potential conflicts of interest of your representatives, point your browser to **www.crp.org/politicians/index.asp**, enter his name and click GO! Under Campaign Finance Profiles, click the year of interest, and on the left sidebar click "Personal Finances," and then click the latest year. Note that these are usually rather large .pdf files so have patience as they download.

Is there a double standard?

Consider **Martha Stewart,** who was prosecuted and spent six months in jail for selling stock based on hearsay knowledge that it was going to tank. But **George W. Bush**, as an insider board member of Harken Energy Corporation, was allowed to sell over $800,000 worth of restricted Harken stock after being advised in board meetings and written memos that the company needed a $38 million influx of money just to stay afloat. The SEC has yet to investigate, and it likely never will.

The energy crisis in California is an excellent example of privatization gone awry, coupled with the ownership of politicians by special interests. Money bought political votes to privatize the energy system in California, and Enron was right in the thick of things when energy prices tripled for the public sector (and local CEO salaries tripled for the private sector). When the state appealed to **President Bush** and **Dick Cheney** to intervene with price controls, they refused to get involved and chose to let the rip-offs continue. How convenient it was to back away from state issues in their moment of need.

Of particular interest is that **Kenneth La**y was the largest single contributor to George Bush's many political campaigns, and though Bush later claimed that he didn't know Lay very well, he knew him well enough to nickname him **Kenny Boy.** Cheney, too, continues to receive $194,000 yearly in deferred earnings from energy giant Halliburton.

Let us hope for good health for Dick Cheney.
If anything happens to him George Bush would
automatically become president. (Author unknown)

Pork and the Pig Book

If you haven't already, you must get your personal copy of The Pig Book published by Citizens Against Government Waste (**www.cagw.org**). With an estimated 13,000 pork-barrel projects in 2005, this book describes "How Government Wastes Your Money," but even more so, it speaks volumes about how your trusted elected officials grovel at the feet of their local campaign supporters. They have followed the infamous $436 hammer and $640 toilet seat to their 2005 heights with expenditures in:

> ➢ $102 million for Screwworm Research

> ➢ $7.4 million for peanut research

> ➢ $7.25 million for grasshopper research

> ➢ $3.2 million for cranberry and blueberry research.

> ➢ $44.6 million for Alaskan salmon restoration

> ➢ $60.5 million for East-West Center in Honolulu

> ➢ $24.5 million for the Asia Foundation and $1.25 million for the Irish Institute at Boston College

> ➢ $50,000 for a tattoo removal program in San Luis Obispo, CA

> ➢ $10 million for Brown Tree Snake research (which is only found in Guam)

> ➢ $28.7 million to the National Automotive Center in Michigan involving "smart truck" technology

> ➢ $1.1 million for the Shakespeare Theatre

> ➢ $7.75 million for the Gridley Rice Straw project

> ➢ $12 million for the Vermont Gasification project

> ➢ $50 million for an indoor rainforest in Iowa

> ➢ $290 million for the International Fund for Ireland

Let's not forget the infamous **Big Dig** tunnel in Boston, which earned over $16 billion of taxpayer assets ($12B over budget) for a host of world-class campaign supporters. The *Pig Book* doesn't pull punches — **www.cagw.org** provides a searchable database and lists the "Pork per capita by state" with Alaska leading the pack at $984 while Minnesotans got just $17.47 per citizen. This demonstrates the value of having your congressman on the Appropriations Committee.

Take Alaska, for example, where **Rep. Don Young** is that state's lone congressional Representative and also chairman of the *House Transportation and Infrastructure Committee.* He managed to wrangle more than $1 billion out of the recent highway bill to fund two pork projects, widely criticized as being "bridges to nowhere:"

> ➢ $200 million for the Knik Arm Bridge in Anchorage, the bill's largest earmark, and
>
> ➢ $175 million for the Gravina Bridge in Ketchikan, and island with 50 people and 350 deer.

These bridges came under heated debate after Katrina: why spend this money on waste when it would help rebuild New Orleans? Young refused to budge but public pressure won over (partially). The bridges will not be built, at least not from that allotment of money. But Young made sure that Alaska will nonetheless get to keep the money and will most certainly spend it elsewhere. In the end, these bridges will be built or his name isn't Mr. Pork.

Why we continue two elect yokels like this is totally baffling.

As well, Alaska received $2.3 million for a study of the Bradfield Canal Road. In a 1997 study on the Bradfield Road, the *Alaska Department of Transportation* concluded that "we have no compelling reasons to spend more public money on more detailed corridor studies. The project won't work." But don't tell Don Young who has different ideas and some very happy road builders.

Of the "earmarked" projects Washingtonians received $84 per capita compared with $1,448 for each Alaskan.

As of this writing earmarks have come under intense scrutiny, but because they benefit the vast majority of congress members they are not likely to be eliminated. Bush wants the line-item veto to eliminate them, but the only ones likely to be eliminated are those of the Democrats. They must be eliminated totally.

From a 2004 Zogby poll:

33% listed greed and materialism as the nation's
*   most urgent moral crisis*

31% listed poverty and economic justice

16% listed abortion

12% listed gay marriage

Source: **www.zogby.com/soundbites/ReadClips.dbm?ID=10389**

The state of the state

8

In my state, *Wisconsin Democracy Campaign* (WDC), run by **Mike McCabe**, **www.wisdc.org** is our leading public advocacy group that tracks legislative overspending and abuses, including the most recent federal indictments of six powerful state political leaders from both sides of the aisle, including the former senate majority leader, **Chuck Chvala** (D) whom you simply couldn't see to discuss an issue without a $500 contribution to his campaign.

Two state senators have already been convicted, one is in prison and serving time, one is in appeal and the rest are under indictment and still going through the legal system at the time of this writing. That's Wisconsin politics. According to WDC, "The common thread running through almost all of the criminal charges is the chase for campaign money." The following is from its March 2005 report, "*Have-Mores' Clean Up at Corporate Welfare Trough — Campaign donors get substantially more help than non-contributors:*"

WDC reviewed more than 5,100 state Commerce Department grants, low-interest loans and tax credits awarded between 1999 and September 2004 and found:

> Those who made campaign contributions received grants, cheap loans and tax breaks eight times greater per capita than non-contributors

> Among the corporations deemed in need of state help were Fortune 500 companies and household names including Wal-Mart, General Motors, Kohler Company, Procter & Gamble and Home Depot

> The state did not follow the original intent of some of these aid programs, namely to create jobs in distressed areas whose populations need work and an economic boost. Instead, it gave money to large companies for projects in affluent areas whose populations also generate large amounts of campaign contributions

> The department doled out $16.6 million to dairies and farmers, much of which went to four dozen large farms commonly known as corporate farms or livestock factories. Agriculture industry recipients who had a history of making campaign contributions received awards nearly 10 times larger, per capita, than non-contributors

> One program handed out about $344,000 between 1999 and mid-2004 to help companies pay for sending employees on trade junkets around the world

WDC found that recipients of state aid who did not make campaign contributions received awards averaging $129,990 while those who made contributions received awards averaging $1.04 million.

"If it's a coincidence that campaign donors get so much more help than non-contributors, then it's one hell of a coincidence," WDC executive director Mike McCabe said.

Wal-Mart, the world's largest retailer, which turned a $9 billion profit in 2003, has received $2.2 million in state commerce and transportation aid and $7.8 million in local aid and tax breaks since 1999 to open facilities in Tomah and Beaver Dam.

"The Arkansas-based Walton family, which owns Wal-Mart, and company executives made $17,600 in contributions during the first six months of 2004, coinciding with a $500,000 Commerce Department award for its Beaver Dam distribution center." Source: **www.wisdc.org**

The state once known for its squeaky clean political system has now become the disgrace of the country, with a half dozen Democrats and Republicans being indicted, some already in jail, and with both Democrats and Republicans playing a cynical game of "catch me if you can" when it comes to supporting the campaign finance reform that over 80% of Wisconsin voters approved in a 2000 non-binding referendum. Just prior to the 2002 elections the state legislature did create and pass a so-called campaign reform bill, but they planted a time bomb in it that they knew would get thrown out by the courts after the election. They purposely spiked it with unconstitutional clauses, and their trick worked. It tricked the voters who thought we now had a clean system, but it was thrown out by the courts after the elections and both political parties went back to their sleazy ways.

At the time of this writing, politicians are proposing campaign reform without providing funds for it. They absolutely refuse to propose a meaningful bill that can get signed into law, though they "talk" like they support it. Your state might not be all that different, unless you live in Maine or Arizona, which both enjoy the Clean Money Clean Elections system of financing elections.

WDC also charges that "This corruption of the state's campaign finance system has produced an epidemic of uncontested state legislative races. In 1970, there were no uncontested races for the Assembly or Senate.... In 2004, more than 2 million voters will have no choice of who represents them in the Senate or Assembly because there is only one name on the November ballot." (It's called the "Wealth Primary" See chapter 10).

Contrast that with Arizona (**www.azclean.org**) (in chapter 12), which saw a 110% increase in the number of contested senate seats, up from 10 in 1998 to 21 in 2002, all because special interest campaign money was removed as an entry barrier. And Maine, where 78% of the current legislature won as "Clean" candidates.

Road builders

One of the most active lobby efforts on the political front consists of road building contractors, who not only have won tons of no-bid road contracts but, when the state was jumping through hoops to cut spending to balance the budget, the contractors won a $70 million increase in road contracts! Not just "the same" $70 million they would have made anyway, but $70 million more than they got the year before. In one case, a simple repaving job was turned into a complete rebuilding of the freeway, moving a left lane exit to the right lane but ending up with the same number of lanes that the road had in the first place! The taxpayers lost tens of millions of dollars in that deal, while the road builders liked it just fine. WDC reported an increase in road construction costs of 34.1% between 1996 and 2001, and over the last 16 years, the list has included eight projects worth $824 million that were not requested by state transportation officials but instead by legislators who received money from the industry.

At the federal level, road building is the single biggest pork barrel project, and Bush's new budget will increase their current $218 billion by an *additional* $284 billion! And this increase is being handed out when we are cutting vital public services to the poor. It is unconscionable, but that's the way politicians play the game while the taxpayers look on as spectators.

Realtors

How in the world would a million dollars in campaign contributions from Realtors cost the taxpayers of Wisconsin? Or any other state? Simply by redirecting costs from their own building projects to the public. WDC points to:

➢ Shifting the cost of streets, curbs, gutters and sidewalks in new developments from real estate developers to taxpayers;

➢ Eliminating a requirement that certain subdivisions comply with local master plans as a requirement for plat approval;

➢ Exempting seasonal homes from shoreland zoning laws;

> ➤ Requiring local governments to conduct more assessments, provide extra notice to homeowners, and pay more legal fees in connection with zoning changes and disputes. Each of these put a greater burden and more costs on local governments. The result — higher taxes.

Property tax exemptions

If you own a home, you pay taxes at the end of the year to support your schools and other community costs. If you own a business, you often do not have to pay taxes on your personal property, the equipment used within the business, which costs the state of Wisconsin about $717 million in lost taxes (which of course must be offset by citizen taxpayers). There are good reasons to reduce taxes for businesses in an attempt to get them to either stay in or relocate to your state, but political money should not need to change hands in the process. Legislation ought to happen because it is good, without the politicians being bought with campaign contributions.

Ethanol subsidies

For a mere $50,000 in campaign contributions, agriculture interests whittled a $3 million per year subsidy out of taxpayers. Perhaps it was justified, perhaps not. But would it have happened if cash had not been given to political campaigns? It's doubtful.

Prison expenditures

Crime has gone down in many places, and perhaps because we are locking up more criminals for longer periods of time. The state of Wisconsin contracts with prison operators like the *Corrections Corporation of America*, which has made its share of contributions to the governor and politicians who approve the prison contracts.

There is no question that major crimes should be dealt with harshly. Capital crimes and those involving murder, child seduction, rapes, violence and selling drugs should carry rigid and sometimes life sentences without parole. But the cost of housing a marijuana or drug user who harms no one but himself seems a bit impractical. Steps should be taken to rehabilitate minor offenders and keep them out of a costly prison. The $30,000 per year it costs to incarcerate drug addicts would go a long way toward anti-drug therapy and employment training. Where are our heads?

Prisons have a tendency to convert soft criminals to hardened criminals who are more costly to society down the road. If anything, we should release the marijuana users to make room for identity theft criminals who are presently rising to stardom,. And the child molesters whose first offense should get them 25 years and their second offence life without parole. These people really need to be taken off the streets, and fast.

State pork projects

In its September 24, 2001 report, "Hey Bidder, Bidder....", WDC described the process as follows:

"New-pork budget items affected dozens of special interests — some big, some small — and they cost state taxpayers anywhere from a few thousand dollars to tens of millions of dollars. In addition, the budget was packed with non-spending items that provided undetermined benefits to narrow interests. The total value of the tax breaks, exemptions and other items that benefitted special interests that were approved by legislators and for which the Legislative Fiscal Bureau could determine a dollar value was about $819 million — the equivalent of $211 for each of Wisconsin's 3.9 million income tax filers. The total value of such items that were proposed or given final approval by the governor was about $573 million — the equivalent of $148 for each state income tax filer."

It's not a pretty sight.

Money coming from unions representing state employees and teachers are indeed contributing to the loss of integrity of our state leaders, and even the integrity of those giving the money, but the amount of dollars they give comes no where near that given by the state's business associations, Wisconsin Manufacturers Commerce (WMC) members, and other chambers of commerce and corporate executives.

TABOR

Would a *Taxpayers Bill of Rights* (TABOR) law even be needed if politicians were not overspending to satisfy their special interest friends? My guess would be No. Such a mechanism will only tie the hands of the people closest to the voters, the local politicians.

However, some activists, rightfully distraught with government spending, have proposed a TABOR bill, and it is easy to understand their frustrations. I have them too. But while we all would like to see lower taxes, a better first step is getting the special interest portion of our taxes eliminated. TABOR should be the second step, if needed.

Don't freeze the pie; just ensure that the campaign funders don't get a piece of it.

Only when we stop the cash that flows between those who want laws written and those who write them will we see reduced taxes and a balanced state and federal budget. After this is accomplished, TABOR likely will not be needed at all.

Our current governor, **Jim Doyle**, campaigned on the issue of election reform, but now that he is in office it is the last thing on his mind. He likes the moneyed system just as it is, thank you. While the Clean Money system is fair and levels the playing field, incumbent politicians don't like fair and level playing fields. Even as Doyle's scandals mount with favors to state contractors, he has not changed his tune. We are seeing cuts in state revenue sharing dollars for a number of services at the local level, and though some may be appropriate, wouldn't it be nice to know that these cuts were not protecting the special interest giveaways at the state level? If money were not changing hands at the political level, these local cuts would have been the last cuts made, or rendered unnecessary altogether, rather than being first on the list.

The winners in TABOR will be the likes of **Grover Norquist** of *Americans for Tax Justice* and **Dick Armey** of *Citizens for a Sound Economy* (Armey was one of our most "creative" congressmen). Both are very "public interest" sounding organizations, but they are funded by the wealthy folks whose goals are more aimed at their own economic well being than yours and mine. That should immediately send up a red flag, I distrust friends like these.

The first question we must ask is: Do we want our elected officials bought and sold by special interests, even those we agree with? Of course, Norquist and Armey would say, Yes! Then they can simply buy the legislation they want.

My answer would be No! We must take steps to correct this problem. The public cannot continue diverting money and resources from their own families and local security to support politicians and the special interests who own them.

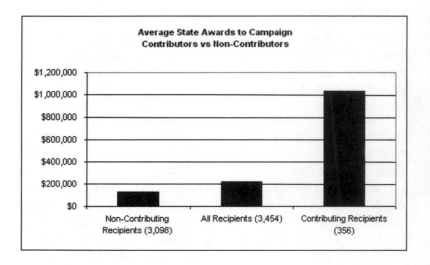

Figure 33: Of the $771.3 million in state grants to businesses, the 10% who made campaign contributions averaged over $1,000,000 each in grants, while the 90% who were non-contributors averaged less than $130,000 each. Source: Wisconsin Democracy Campaign, www.wisdc.com

Electoral reform measures

Voter turnout provides a strong indication of where our own democracy stands. While we seek democracy in other countries, by force in a few infamous cases, the numbers here are not encouraging. With only a 59.6% turnout in the contentious 2004 U.S. elections compared to an estimated 72% of Iraqis who faced threats of bombings at the ballot box, it would seem that we have a long way to go to catch up with their enthusiasm.

This is a direct result of American voters being fed up with our system, seeing it controlled by private interests no matter who they vote for, and being left with a vote for the lesser of two evils. Clean Money Campaign Reform can change that, as will be explained later. In the meantime, major changes are needed in:

- ➢ Campaign finance reform
- ➢ Instant runoff voting
- ➢ Voting machines with paper trails
- ➢ Electoral College
- ➢ Unicameral state legislatures
- ➢ Voter integrity and voting integrity
- ➢ National I.D. or voter registry cards
- ➢ Term limits
- ➢ None-of-the-above ballot option

> ➤ Full and prompt disclosure of contributions
> ➤ Presidential debates
> ➤ Independent redistricting
> ➤ Independent ethics investigations
> ➤ Initiatives and referendums

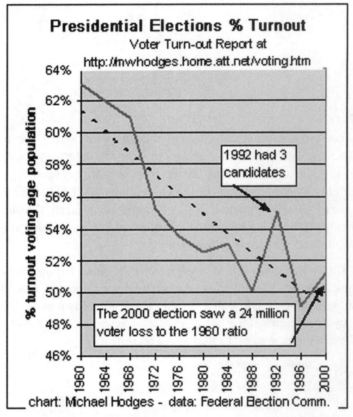

Figure 34: The trend on voter turnout is not good. Though it reached 59.6% in the 2004 elections, two factors drew voters to the polls: the Iraq war and the 13 states that had referendums to ban gay marriages. The upturn is not likely to have been caused by a spike in voter confidence in politicians, though voter dislike for both candidates cannot be ignored as a potential magnet. Source: http://mwhodges.home.att.net

Citizen Trust in Government

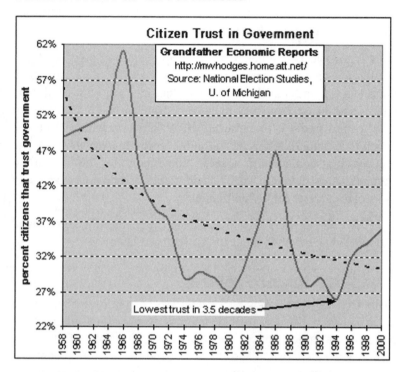

Figure 35: The trend on voter trust is not good, though in 1994 we turned our trust towards Republicans and Newt Gingrich's Contract with America. Unfortunately, as campaign contributions rose, so did distrust, government spending and our national debt.
Source: http://mwhodges.home.att.net

Steve Perry, in "Dime's Worth of Difference," explained voters this way: "Start with the people: they are tired, overworked, and scared — about their own livelihoods and threats from without. More important, they are woefully ignorant, and easily worn down, concerning the details of any political subject. They are acclimated to political races in which the main differences revolve around personality, and comfortable making almost entirely emotional decisions about candidates. This is an over-generalization, but to date a viable one. Presidential elections are mass-culture phenomena, and the majority of voters in any election know very little of substance about the candidates or issues involved."

Perry projects that "80% of the people get their political digest from TV," which of course is why money for TV ads is so vitally important to the politicians. What the average viewer doesn't understand is that the money must come from special interests rather than getting free TV time during the 60 days preceding elections, which they should. After all, the public owns the airwaves and the broadcasters should return at least "something" for the $70 billion Congress gave them in 1996. Then politicians would not be beholden to special interests for TV ad financing.

However, the cash that flows from the media to congressmen, $27 million since 1990, blocked this logical adaptation.

Campaign finance reform

Years from now we'll look back on today's corrupt campaign system in total dismay. That a great democracy would allow this massive political corruption that, in effect, robs its people of the very democracy we cherish is absolutely astounding. That our country is interfering with other countries to bring our kind of democracy to their people, but in turn allows our own wealthy interests to corrupt our own democracy, is hypocrisy at its most villainous.

We punish U.S. corporations for bribing foreign politicians and contributing to their political campaigns, but virtually unlimited amounts of money can be given to American politicians and their political parties with total immunity. Where are our morals, our integrity? Where is the right wing, the supposed defenders of our national virtue, when you really need them?

But the voter finds few politicians that want to change things. Even though they may have campaigned with promises to clean up the system, when they are voted in and see the personal benefits to the political system and their re-election odds, they flip to that side of the spectrum. It is shameful, but that's the way it is. If you want to change it review the electoral proposal I discuss in Chapter 11.

Instant runoff voting (IRV)

Our winner-take-all electoral system resulted in the Florida fiasco in 2000 and promises to plague us many times over. We should switch to a system called Instant Runoff Voting, or preferential voting, as proposed by **www.FairVote.org**. Australia has used the system for years, and several U.S. cities are now switching to IRV, which is also called "majority voting" because the winner must get a majority.

Each ballot contains check boxes for your first, second, third and subsequent choices. It is simple, fair and easy to administer with optical card reading systems, which have proven to be the most reliable and easily accommodate both computer counting and hand counting verification. My friend **Daniel McGuire** (Candidate for Utah State Senate) offers this example:

There are three candidates, Satan, Saint, and Angel. Most people (60%) prefer Angel or Saint over Satan, but their votes are split — 35% for Angel and 25% for Saint. Nonetheless, Satan wins with 40%, well short of a majority, and proceeds to advance the cause of evil over the period of his term. That's the current system!

Instant runoff voting solves this "spoiler" dilemma by eliminating the person with the least votes (Saint), and holding an immediate 2nd computerized round in the election, dividing Saint's votes amongst their 2nd choices so that voters elect a candidate that the majority (>51%) prefers over the loser. In this case, assuming all of Saint's supporters would prefer Angel over Satan, Angel would win with 60% to Satan's 40%.

This is easily done with a simple matrix ballot and immediate computerized totaling. If the voter is confused about the ballot and makes an error, it is automatically rejected and he can immediately recast his vote (you simply cannot put two or more marks in the same column or row).

Only one election is held. Vote for Saint, but if Saint fails to get 51%, your vote is automatically applied to Angel, and Angel wins on the 2nd count.

Candidates	1st Choice	2nd Choice	3rd Choice	1st Count	2nd Count
Angel		X		35%	60%
Saint	X			25%	0
Satan			X	40%	40%

Too confusing? Then vote for one person the old fashioned way. You are not obligated to mark a second choice, but those who have a second choice may mark that candidate too.

The advantage to incumbents and challengers alike is that they only need to run one campaign, the general election. Primaries would no longer be needed. And because challengers will not want to alienate voters who may give them their "second choice" on the card, they are not as likely to sling mud and incumbents are not as likely to have their reputations trashed (deserving as that sometimes may be).

This system gives third-party candidates a chance to demonstrate their real support, and we'd really know where Democrat and Republican support is lacking. But that's also why the current duopoly will oppose it. They'd rather keep third-party support to its absolute minimum, and the current system forces the Green, Reform and Libertarian voters to cast their precious vote for the lesser of the two evils. (If they vote their conscience they in effect throw their vote away completely. I've done that too many times.)

So under the current system the positions proffered by the R's and D's appear to be the most popular by the public, even though there are in fact many independents with very popular positions as well — they simply are thrown out after the primary and thus not heard from again until the next election cycle. But since the R's and the D's are calling the shots, our only chance to change the current system will require extreme public pressure.

Other electoral approaches that should be considered are the parliamentary system and proportional representation, but when you have congressmen who currently enjoy a 90% reelection advantage fostered by our moneyed political system, their priorities are naturally aimed more at self interest than public interest.

IRV makes total sense and will benefit the public, but perhaps nothing will change until we have a complete turnover in our elected officials. (Now, there's a thought!)

This system is fair, and that may be its biggest downfall. The last thing in the world today's politicians want is "fair." They like their 90% reelection advantage just as it is.

Voting machines

The most accurate approach to collecting votes is marking cards that can be optically read by computer, reread when necessary, stacked or sorted and hand counted when doubts arise. A reasonable paper trail is critical and totally missing with other technologies, such as touch screens, the results from which can be manipulated internally and by computer hackers. We've clearly learned our lessons on punch cards and butterfly ballots, and no one would seriously suggest a return to the lever machines. Optical cards also lend themselves to the IRV system suggested above, as they can be immediately rejected if more than one row or column is marked, giving the voter another chance to get it right.

The Electoral College

My gut tells me that I'd rather see a direct popular vote for the president, though there are arguments on both sides of this issue. My concern is that most people don't even know who their state electors are or how they were chosen and who chose them. And further, I doubt that most voters know that this system was put into place to protect us from ourselves, a cynical invention if ever there was one. But before we attempt to pass a constitutional amendment forcing all states to switch to the popular vote, we should allow individual states to decide whether or not they want that system. If the popular vote works in the states, it can be expanded nationally. States currently do have the option of dividing their electoral votes amongst candidates, as Maine and Nebraska have already done, but Colorado put it to a vote of the people in 2004 and it was defeated.

Unicameral state legislatures

Most states use a bicameral legislature consisting of both a senate and an assembly. Bills can originate in either house, filter through committees, and if ultimately passed by the whole, move to the other house; and if they are passed there as well, the bills move on to the governor for signature or veto.

Nebraska employs a unicameral legislature with only one house, and each member is elected on a nonpartisan ballot. They are all called senators and may represent a party, but that party is not listed on the ballot. The unicameral system employs fewer staff (Nebraska has part-time legislators who receive about $12,000 per year, though that automatically means that their other job may pose a conflict of interest, unless only retirees are allowed to serve, which is not likely).

For more debate on this see:
www.house.leg.state.m n.us/hrd/pubs/nebunic.htm

Given the gridlock and partisanship and trading that can occur with the bicameral system, it seems that Nebraska's unicameral system has a leg up on the rest of the country. Or at least so it appears. Some would argue that the gridlock with the bicameral system serves as an important check against laws being forced through the system with too little debate. I'd argue that limiting the special interest's control of the system to only one house is dangerous, and I'd prefer the bicameral system, at least until we get rid of the private-money problem.

Voter integrity and voting integrity

It is hard to argue against the concept of ensuring the right to vote for every U.S. citizen, and the charges fly on both sides of the issue. The argument really boils down to whether we can find a system to prevent people from voting multiple times or when they are illegal immigrants. It seems like the civil libertarians would like to remove all responsibility from the voter and allow same-day registration with or without positive identification or proof of citizenship. To believe that fraud does not exist in this setting would be naive; as some districts reported more votes than they had voters, so we do know that voter fraud exists.

Ours is a sloppy and inconsistent voting system. It not only allows fraud, but that fraud can be driven by the party that happens to have the most cash on hand at the time. Today, the system might benefit the Democrats, tomorrow the Republicans, but never the public.

Fraud should not be permitted at all and should be of deep concern to every citizen that treasures democracy, regardless of their party. Should we trust the driver's license or birth certificate or the electric bill? All can be fraudulently produced. Should we allow people to just show up at the polls with a "trust me" button on their shirt, or should we require that they show some responsibility and obtain the necessary registration documents in advance of voting day? After all, even the poorest can make a trip downtown to register for food stamps, why would they resist applying for a voter registration card?

Perhaps we should require purpled fingers, as they did in Iraq, but we can find acceptable ways to have those without transportation to be registered, even if it requires putting some of the unemployed to work serving as drivers for a mobile voter registration service. We can kill two birds with the same stone. It can be done if we want it to be done.

National I.D. card

There is legitimate concern that even voting records can be lost or misplaced, and it could take months or years to resolve voting issues under such circumstances. For these eventualities and a lot of other reasons we need a national bar-coded and electronic I.D. card that includes picture, proof of citizenship, fingerprints and even iris scans and other biometric information for the individual. Such cards might include DNA as well, given the needed safety for our children and even adults. These cards would be incredibly useful when cashing checks, boarding aircraft, crossing borders, applying for credit, collecting welfare checks and food stamps, applying for employment and even eliminating voter fraud and the massive identification theft problem, especially now that credit card companies are processing everything in India and other cheap-labor countries.

When used for voting, I.D. cards can be scanned and immediately validated with an online connection. What could be simpler? What could be safer? What could be more democratic? Civil libertarians will choke on this, but I am not willing to give up national security to satisfy the qualms of the purists. We do not live in a perfect society, and there are people out there who want to bury America. Yielding to the purists will hasten that day.

The ACLU and civil libertarians

Though I agree with some actions on the Left, sometimes Liberals go way too far. One suggestion I've heard is a dual airline security system: one requiring a national I.D. card and rigid airport screening to board one plane, and the other with no I.D. and no screening to board a different plane. Then the ACLU backers and civil libertarians can take the easier way, providing they can find a flight crew to go with them. (The ACLU is a prime example of the wacko left wing, and we certainly have an equally wacko right wing. Both opinions must be heard, but my choice is the moderate center with a bit of reasonableness sprinkled on the top.)

We should not violate the safety of the masses who want reasonable protection because of a few nut cases. We must remember that flying is a privilege and a choice. Voter identification or national I.D. cards will be the preferred mechanism by many. The rest can drive or take a bus if they are not happy with that system.

Term limits

This is one of the most difficult reforms to justify. On the one side is the fact that the longer a politician is in office the greater are their spending abuses. Senior elected congressmen sign 8 times more spending bills than do newly elected Representatives. They are willing to give away more taxpayer assets to get to a powerful leadership position than are junior congressmen, and they deserve to be ousted as quickly as possible. A close look at Senator **Robert Byrd** (D-WV) and his massive pork giveaways should convince even the most skeptical among us. The arrogance of this and other congressional members rises with their years in office. This guy should have been history a long time ago.

On the other hand, term limits would also require the ouster of the good guys, like Wisconsin's former Senator **William Proxmire,** the originator of the *Golden Fleece Award* and a fellow that, during his last terms of office, spent less than $500 to get re-elected. He simply shook a lot of hands and voted his conscience. Ousting guys like him to get rid of the bad ones doesn't make much sense.

But the real constitutional issue is whether your right to vote for someone should be eliminated simply because they have overstayed their two- or three-term limit.

There are stronger arguments for solving the over-spending problems by eliminating the root cause (special interest money), and leaving the right to vote to the people.

None-of-the-Above ballot option

The NOTA option for each office would give voters the opportunity to turn away all candidates on the ballot. If NOTA gets more votes than the others, a new election must be held with none of the rejected candidates on the new ballot. Even when an incumbent is the only one on the ballot, he could be ousted from office in this manner. If he is he clearly deserves to go.

Full and prompt disclosure of contributions

You'd think this would be a no-brainer with today's technology, but it doesn't agree with today's ethos. When you consider that the same politicians who would have to do the disclosing must also pass this type of bill, it is obvious why we presently do not have such a mechanism in place. It's easy to implement, but legislators like things hidden until after the elections, and prompt disclosure allows the press and advocacy groups to hold them accountable for interest group support before the election. They don't like that a bit. Politicians feebly argue that disclosure infringes on free speech, but it doesn't and they know it. Disclosure is just more visible speech and allows voters to see which special interests are supporting which politicians — by this skewed definition who's speaking and who is not — and whether or not that "speech" is buying favors from that politician.

Presidential debates

Remember when the *League of Women Voters* ran nonpartisan multi-party presidential debates? Then, we heard arguments not only from the two major parties but also third-party candidates like Ralph Nader, Ross Perot, John Anderson, Howard Phillips and others. Those were the days. But that process has been hijacked by the Republican and Democratic duopoly, and they have successfully frozen out all other parties. Only candidates who rank high in the major media polls (which often involve only 600 participants) will be allowed into the debates. This is very unfortunate because, even if they stand no chance of winning, the mavericks nonetheless bring to the debate issues that the other two parties would rather avoid.

Have you ever wondered why campaign finance reform was not a topic of discussion in 2000 or 2004? Had Ralph Nader been in the debates the issue would have been front and center in the political discourse, but the Big Two froze him out. The last thing either of them wanted to discuss is where they got their money.

Independent redistricting

Have you ever wondered why your representative's district runs all over the place, through hill and dale with no rhyme or reason? It's called "gerrymandering," and politicians do it because they are selecting the voters for their district rather than the voters selecting them as their representative. If a zip code voted for the Republicans last time, that zip code is added to a Republican's district to protect his incumbency. It's called stacking the deck against the voters.

Why would the two parties allow this? Because they both benefit and the third-parties lose; they are not even part of the discussion. The two parties are protected, and the only seats up for grab are those recently vacated. In a word, there is a vast legal agreement (like it or not, they call it a conspiracy) between the two political parties to guarantee the status quo, eliminate competition, and ensure their reelection chances. Such unbalanced redistricting is another way that incumbent politicians can ensure that the voters don't count and that incumbents have a 95% chance of being re-elected. That's our Democracy, like it or not.

Most importantly, this practice eliminates the politician's need to be responsive to the voters because they are now in a "safe" district. Complain as you may, they are locked in! Most recently, Republican House Whip **Tom Delay** shoved gerrymandering down the throats of Texas voters and won four new Republican seats in congress.

But DeLay paid a heavy price when a grand jury indicted him in 2005 for conspiracy and money laundering. Texas legislators are not allowed to take money from corporations, so DeLay was charged with arranging for the corporations to send $190,000 to a Washington PAC, which in itself was legal. And coincidentally the PAC shipped the money back to the Texas lawmakers, which in itself is also legal. But two rights make a wrong when it is "arranged," and DeLay was accused of being the arranger. The $190,000 helped the Republicans take over the Texas legislature, which then redrew the federal election maps to give DeLay an additional four republicans in the House and himself a guaranteed position as majority whip (though he later had to resign from because of his contribution to the 2005-2006 congressional scandals). This is a good demonstration of why and how federal officeholders can become so involved with the local power structure.

Actually, anything with Tom Delay involved will not favor the voters, so why didn't his voting constituents throw him out? Because his cash constituents kept him in! Money buys elections. The following trend of reelection rates shows why politicians like the corrupt system just as it is and are not likely to change it to their disadvantage (Source: **www.crp.org** Center for Responsive Politics).

US House Reelection Rates, 1964-2002

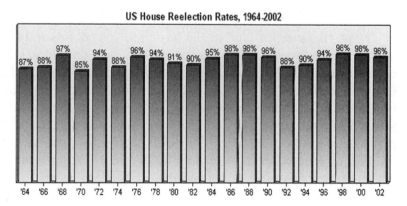

Independent ethics and elections boards

In a word, the fox should not guard the henhouse. State and federal election boards and ethics committees should be elected by and report to the state supreme court or federal judicial system, not be appointed by the politicians they are to oversee.

Members should serve 14 year staggered terms, like they do on the Federal Reserve Board to avoid political pressure. Having these committees stacked with partisan players is sort of like appointing your own umpire to oversee the ballgame. Nice work if you can get it.

But the last thing in the world politicians want is to have to an independent board overseeing their political actions and campaign contributions. When they can control the funding of the ethics board it is easier to control their investigations.

Free Media Time

Congress gave the new digital spectrum, which would have drawn $70 billion at auction, to the media giants for absolutely free. So, it would not be asking too much that all state and national candidates who agree to spending limits and personal appearances (rather than employing attack ads) be given a fixed number of free minutes per week on both broadcast TV and radio to air their political views during the 60 days preceding each national election.

In the 2000 election cycle, these stations took in $1 billion from political advertising, and once again, in return for a free package from the taxpayers worth $70 billion. It would not be asking too much if they contributed that $1 billion to the public elections.

Why? "Because it's fair" should be a good enough reason, but more importantly, it would mean $1 billion less in campaign contributions that politicians would NOT need to collect from special interests. We know by experience that such contributions end up costing taxpayers hundreds of billions of dollars per year in the government giveaways that result, all of which result in higher product and service prices charged by the special interests to cover this cost of dong business, in addition to the roughly $300 billion dollars per year they extract from government (taxpayer) assets..

Initiatives and referendums (IRs)

Sometimes IRs are good and sometimes terrible. A look at events in California are enough to turn anyone off, as their IRs are often put forth by special interests that are prepared to fund them well. But raising the bar from 51% acceptance by the people to 60% may check the impact of the moneyed folks. Still, some special interests will outright lie, as did the tobacco interests when they tried to get rid of California's law banning smoking in restaurants by twisting the language of the bill. On the good side, IRs won public funding of campaigns in Maine and Arizona, and they worked for the best interest of the people of these states. A very comprehensive list of state reform suggestions can be found on either of these two sites:

Wisconsin Democracy Campaign at **www.wisdc.org/powertothevoter.html**

The Reform Institute at **www.reforminstitute.org** or more specifically the document at **www.reforminstitute.org/resources/enhancing_values.pdf**

To find out what is going on in your state visit:
www.publiccampaign.org/states/statecontacts.htm

Where are Clean Money laws now?

Legislatures and statewide offices with CMCE, Cities with CMCE	AZ, ME, and NJ in 2007 VT, Gov and Lt Gov only CT All state candidates Portland, Albuquerque
Judicial and other offices with CMCE	NC, Judicial system NM, Pub Reg Commission
CMCE in both judicial and Legislature	None

Voter Initiative or Referendum	AZ, ME, Port. & Albuquerque
Passed by Legislature	CT, NC, NM, NC, NJ

Clean Money State by State Successes

Maine: Voter Initiative won in 1996
Covers: Legislature and Governor
Comments: 78% of current Legislature ran under CMCE

Vermont: Passed by state legislature in 1997
Covers: Governor and Lt. Governor
Comments: Not in extensive use because of challenges on stringent private spending caps

Arizona: Voter Initiative won in 1998
Covers: State Legislature, Governor and all Corporate Commissioners
Comments: * 58% of House, 23% of senate, and 10 of 11 statewide offices elected under CMCE
* Has withstood 7 court challenges

New Mexico: Passed legislature in 2003
Covers: Public funding for Public Regulatory Commission
Comments: Goes into effect in 2006 (efforts to expand)

North Carolina: Passed Legislature in 2003
Covers: State Supreme Court, Court of Appeals candidates
Comments: * 12 of 16 candidates for 5 seats ran under CMCE
* CMCE candidates won each of the two Supreme Court races and two of the three Court of Appeals seats (100% and 66% CMCE success rate)

New Jersey: Passed by legislature in 2004
Covers: Two pilot legislative seats
Comments: Expands to all Legislative districts in 2007

Connecticut: Passed by Legislature and Republican Governor
Covers: All legislative and statewide candidates
Comments: First leg. to adopt reform that applies to its own races. Passage follows scandals which sent former governor, state treasurer, state senator, and two big-city mayors to prison.

The cities of **Portland OR** and **Albuquerque NM** have also adopted CMCE for mayor, auditor and city commissioners

Wealth primary

Have you voted yet?

C'mon now. Of course there's an election going on. You just haven't been invited to it. It's called the *Wealth Primary* and was originally described by **John Bonifaz** and **Jamin R. Raskin** in the book of the same name. A synopsis is here, but details can be found at:

www.opensecrets.org/pubs/law_wp/wealthindex.htm and
www.nvri.org/about/wealth.shtml

The authors describe the phenomenon as the political process that quietly goes on during the two years that precede every primary and November election. A group of wealthy political players — corporate executives, special interest groups, lobbyists and Political Action Committees (PACs) — are hard at work selecting our future candidates. You may not like it, but there's a 90% chance that their special-interest candidate will win. The 2000 Wealth Primary selected **George W. Bush** well ahead of time by giving him massive campaign contributions that other candidates could only dream of. These moneyed interests literally drowned out every other, perhaps even more, qualified candidate like **John McCain, Elizabeth Dole** and **John Kasich.** They knew who would be the easiest to control.

Do not mistake for a moment the nearly $200 million that Bush raised as being "public support." It was private support, clear and simple, and it has undermined democracy for every voter and taxpayer in the United States, even the Republicans who supported him. These are wealthy special interests that have thrown their financial support behind the candidate they believe is going to be more supportive of their causes (read: easier to control). If they spend enough money in the primaries, while getting their favorite politician elected, their future contributions can go to those other politicians who are in the middle and are easily swayed. These practices also send a message that if their support doesn't yield favors it will go to the opposition candidate the next time around.

In the case of George Bush, the strategy worked very well. He won the hearts of the money men and has performed as expected.

The authors also charge that the contributors favor the political power brokers who chair legislative committees, as they have the authority to bring legislation to the floor for a vote or to bottle it up in committee. They also target their cash to members of legislative committees. Agribusiness interests give money to legislators who sit on agricultural committees; the energy industry gives money to legislators dealing with energy issues; bankers, credit card companies and financiers give money to members of the House Banking and the Senate Finance committees.

In the case of George Bush, the strategy was superb and the contributions paid off in two ways: first by getting their candidate elected and secondly by buying themselves seats at the policy table. Oil interests sat with Vice President **Dick Cheney** as they designed our energy policy to fit their own needs, and logging companies designed the *Healthy Forests Initiative* giving them carte blanche on clear cutting our forests. It proves that virtually every politician is for sale at the right price, and that these special interests have no minimum level to which they will not stoop.

The Wealth Primary allows corporate executives to pass a small piece of their profits to members of Congress, all to maximize and ensure their bigger piece of the economic pie. Campaign contributions are important to both the givers and the takers — that's why you hear neither complaining. For politicians, the money buys television time, and for contributors, campaign contributions are a business expense that provides a substantial return on investment (and, incidentally, they add their contributions to the price of their products as they stick their customers with their political costs).

The payoff is usually in the form of legislation favorable to their product, service, or industry, and to the disfavor of the public. A return on investment (ROI) of 100:1 — and even 1000:1 — is not uncommon, and is magnitudes greater than what they can expect to earn in the legitimate marketplace. This is clearly a far distance from the "free market" the president promises.

In every game, there is a loser....

In this one, it's the people. The authors describe the Wealth Primary as devastating in two significant ways:

> ➤ It robs non-wealthy citizens of their Fourteenth Amendment right to equal protection under the law — with regard to running for office themselves and in fielding candidates who will represent them in Washington. The idea of representative government is being systematically disassembled. The one-person-one-vote philosophy has been replaced by a system where dollars mean more than ballots and where politicians represent their contributors instead of their voting constituents.

> ➤ Special interest money not only buys elections, but also the loyalty of the politicians it puts into office. The billions of dollars spent in political payoffs to large campaign contributors is a major factor in the rapid rise of the federal debt, which if not checked soon, will sink the U.S. economy. The ultimate cost of the Wealth Primary — estimated at $200 billion annually in tax breaks, subsidies, bailouts, regulatory exemptions, and other forms of "corporate welfare" — is hundreds of times greater than if we were to toss out the current moneyed system and fund the elections through public financing using taxpayer dollars. Worse are the hundreds of billions more spent on biased government spending and local pork barrel projects. It is not a pretty sight.

Does the Wealth Primary really work?

Indeed it does — at least for the wealthy players. And that's why the politicians don't want to eliminate it. If you are one of those who believe that members of Congress would not allow an unfair, corrupt and biased system to exist, review these facts. The *National Voting Rights Institute* listed the earmarks of a wealth primary as:

> ➤ Less than 1% of the population provides over 80% of all money in federal elections. (Poverty & Race Research Action Council 1999)

> ➤ Over 60 percent of contributions to winning congressional candidates came in amounts over $1000. (US PIRG Report 1/3/01)

> ➤ Only one-ninth of one percent of the voting-age population — nearly 232,000 people — gave $1000 or more to federal candidates in 1999-2000. (Public Campaign 2/01 analysis)

> ➤ Less than two percent of Americans give candidate contributions over $200. (US PIRG Report 1/3/01)

> ➤ A 1997 national survey of major congressional campaign contributors (i.e., those who give $200 or more) revealed that 95% of such donors are white and that 81% have annual incomes of $100,000 or more. (Green, Herrnson, Powell, and Wilcox "Individual Congressional Campaign Contributors: Wealthy, Conservative — and Reform Minded" Joyce Foundation 1998)

> ➤ In 2000, winners of seats in the U.S. House out-raised and out-spent their opponents by almost 3-to-1, as winners raised an average of $916,629 and losers on average raised $309,213. In the Senate, winners raised $7,307,402 while losers raised $3,594,447. (**www.opensecrets.org**)

> ➤ Candidates who raised the most money won 93 percent of the seats up for election in Congress in 2000. (USPIRG Report 1/3/01)

> ➤ The funding of political campaigns is now increasing at roughly four times the annual inflation rate. (BNA Money and Politics Report ½4/01).

The bottom line: those who spend the most money in the Wealth Primary almost always get elected; those who do not almost always lose. The money makes the difference, and that's why private money must be eliminated. Those who make the largest contributions almost always get a major return-on-investment. Get used to it!

Just politics?

While this is easily excused as "politics as usual," the end result is a serious violation of the U.S. Constitution's 14th Amendment, our right to equal protection under the law. By allowing private money to control elections, legislators essentially permit another form of poll tax. Not only does this cost citizens their right to run for office, Raskin and Bonifaz write, it also narrows the field of candidates to a select few, thus restricting the people's right to vote for a candidate of their choice. To see how that phenomenon care be reversed, see **www.azclean.org/documents/8-9-042002SuccessStats.doc**

Voters who give lots of money to candidates have more political influence than voters who give little or nothing. One could also argue that allowing the wealth of special interests and their massive contributions to override your minimal (or no) financial contribution, you have essentially been robbed of your First Amendment free speech rights as well. Who cares? Certainly none on the giving or receiving end of this process.

The Wealth Primary *is* real. As evidence, consider the fact that there were 82 uncontested House and Senate races in 1992 and 1994, thanks to those who put their money up front. Challengers were excluded in virtually all of these races because they couldn't qualify for the Wealth Primary. Qualified — and in many cases more qualified — candidates with integrity were excluded because of a lack of money. This represents a severe political loss to the public.

You, reader, were robbed of the opportunity to vote for and have a representative chosen by the majority because a wealthy minority selected the candidates before the electoral process even began.

"The Supreme Court has already struck down poll taxes and high filing fees as being financial barriers for voting and running for office. Like poll taxes and filing fees, the Wealth Primary restricts those without wealth (or access to wealth) from participating in or influencing the outcome of American elections."

The right to equal protection

In their book, *The Wealth Primary,* Jamin R. Raskin and John Bonifaz write:

"The effective exclusion of candidates lacking personal or political access to wealth leaves poorer citizens without a natural rallying point in the electoral process. Less affluent groups are left without candidates who appeal to them.

"Just as the Wealth Primary eliminates candidates who might speak to the needs of the poor, it also denies voters the opportunity to affect the political programs and positions of candidates in the race. Citizens without money to give are totally excluded from participation in the Wealth Primary. Like African-Americans [who were] closed out of the 'white primaries,' the poor are systematically excluded from an integral part of the electoral process and thus silenced by its operation.

"Those people who can give $15 each to a House or Senate candidate — but for whom $200 or $1000 apiece is unthinkable — are at a great relative disadvantage and are thus denied equal participation in the wealth primary. In reality, the wealth primary operates today by completely bypassing tens of millions of non-affluent citizens and focusing on groups of wealthy individuals and PACs who are organized for the purpose of influencing candidates with large contributions. In practice, the political dominance of the rich means that non-affluent segments of the population are not only unable to put forward and sustain their own candidates, but they are also frozen out of the crucial fundraising process which determines the viability, success, and, perhaps most importantly, the politics of the candidates who do have the financial wherewithal to mount serious campaigns.

"When citizens of modest means go to the polls, they vote for candidates whose political seriousness has been determined by a money-gathering process which systematically disregards their interests."

Not a pretty sight, but that's the democracy we want to export to other countries.

A free copy of *The Wealth Primary* (1994) can be downloaded from The Center for Responsive Politics at **www.opensecrets.org/pubs/law_wp/wealthindex.htm**.

Also, in **Martin Schram's** book *Speaking Freely,* legislators refer to their corporate constituents as "clients." In the business world, a client is someone who pays money for services provided. That seems to be the case in the political world as well. This book provides excellent insights into the heads of congressmen and can be ordered from the Center for Responsive Politics at: **www.opensecrets.org/pressreleases/2003/SpeakingFreely.asp**

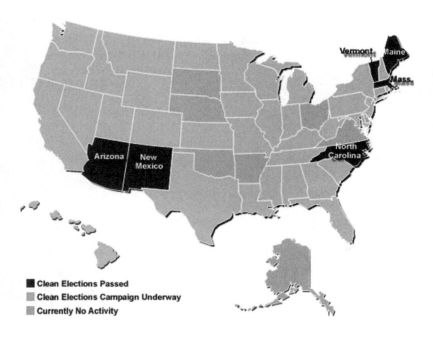

■ Clean Elections Passed
▒ Clean Elections Campaign Underway
▒ Currently No Activity

**Figure 36 - State Activities -- Courtesy:
Public Campaign www.publicampaign.org/states**

"Few men have virtue to withstand the highest bidder."
George Washington

"Politics is supposed to be the second-oldest profession. I have come to realize that it bears a very close resemblance to the first."
Ronald Reagan

How to fix it

If politicians are to be beholden to their funders, those funders should be the taxpayers. If anybody is going to own government is should be the citizens and taxpayers, not corporations.

Absolutely none of today's critical issues will be fixed as long as private money is funding the electoral system. The best, proven system is the **Clean Money Clean Elections** reform that was voted in by the citizens of Maine and Arizona (a Republican state). The system works, and it works well. So well, in fact, that the special interests and a few of their legislative puppets in the Arizona legislature chose to sue the state to have it repealed. They lost and Clean Money Clean Elections are still in place in that state.

Opponents claimed it violated _their_ First Amendment right to free speech. It doesn't, of course, because it is a voluntary system and therefore passes constitutional muster. What they really didn't like was being forced to pit politicians-on-the-take against the "clean" candidates that promised to represent the citizens instead of the fat cats. How can the moneyed candidates win in a situation like that?

The only way to effectively ensure responsible government spending is to eliminate our moneyed political system. Not reduce it, eliminate it. Totally!

The public doesn't want a partially clean system, and most are willing to pay the $5 per year needed to fund total public financing of state campaigns. But we must fund it all — not just half of it. All of it. We don't want our half to subsidize the special interest's half and leave them still in control. If we're involved, we want them uninvolved. And it bears repeating: when the public understands how it works, 80% support it and are willing to pay their $5 to fund it.

It would not be right to continue this chapter without recognizing the small group of advocates, which included the late **Marty Jezer, Randy Kehler, Ben Senturia, Gwen Patton,** and **Nacho Gonzales.** They first organized as the *Working Group on Electoral Democracy*, and for 11 years, from 1986 to 1997, put together the whole structure of Clean Elections.

That concept is being furthered today by *Public Campaign* and is supported by virtually all public interest groups (*Center for Responsive Politics, Center for Public Integrity, Common Cause, U.S. Public Interest Group* and many others.) Source:

www.publicampaign.org/publications/studies/ PCCleanMoneyComparisons.pdf

How Clean Money Elections work

First and foremost, the system's success is due to the fact that it is totally *voluntary*! Candidates not wanting to participate can continue taking money from private individuals, special interests or PACs. Period! And if you want to give money to that private candidate, you can. Period! No ifs, ands or buts.

You'd think that opting out would be just fine with the private candidate, but it isn't. As mentioned above, they don't want to have to compete with "clean" candidates and are making every attempt, using every excuse possible, to obstruct that process.

But so far, they've lost in the courts and they've lost to the people.

Clean Money Candidates must first qualify by showing community support. Money received in this process (private or grant) can only be spent on authorized campaign expenses, and they must agree not to spend private money — even their own — beyond the primary.

> **Qualifying:** Candidates must collect a prescribed number of signatures with minimum $5 qualifying contributions from registered voters in their district. No contribution can exceed $100 (in Arizona, the amount is indexed to inflation and thus is now $120). This is considered seed money to cover minor costs during the pre-primary qualifying period (making the contribution tax-deductible is optional).

> **Primary funding:** Candidates who meet the qualifying requirements (i.e., gather the required signatures) and agree not to raise or spend private money during the primary and general election campaign periods will receive a set amount of money (up to 1/3 of the total grant for the primary) from the Clean Money fund.*

> **General election funding:** Candidates who win their party primaries, and qualifying independent candidates who agree to the voluntary restrictions, receive a set amount of general election funding from the Clean Money fund.

> **Level playing field:** In order to maintain a financially level playing field, Clean Money candidates who are outspent by privately financed opponents, or who are targeted by independent expenditures or issue ads, are entitled to a limited amount of matching funds. (That tends to discourage such shenanigans in the first place.)

* In cases where Instant Runoff Voting is implemented and there is only a general election, all of the money could be applied to the general election.

Importantly, Clean Money Elections are alive and well in both Maine and Arizona. Again, they are working not just well, but in fact better than some legislators would like them to, and that could be why, with the exception of Connecticut, only states with binding referendums and the initiative process have managed to push through clean election systems. Politicians tend not to like reforms that work and are not as likely to voluntarily move them through the legislature, thus we must rely on the activists to get the job done.

How Clean Money has worked in Arizona

A close look at Arizona will demonstrate very quickly why the special interests and their puppets in Arizona oppose the clean system. The positive impact on the 2002 election is clear!

The following is from:
www.azclean.org/documents/8-9-042002 SuccessStats.doc

Clean Elections candidates won state's top offices:

> ➢ Clean Elections candidates won seven out of nine statewide offices: Governor, Secretary of State, Attorney General, Treasurer, Corporation Commissioner (2-year seat), Corporation Commissioner (4-year seat), Mine Inspector.

> ➢ 36% of Arizona's legislature is comprised of Clean Elections elected officials free of ties to special interests and big money donors.

> ➢ Nearly ½ of the House of Representatives (27 of 60 members) were elected via Clean Elections.

> ➢ Five Arizona State Senators were elected via Clean Elections.

> ➢ 41% of all state offices (statewide and legislative) are now held by Clean Elections candidates.

Non-partisan: Republicans and Democrats benefitted!

> ➢ Of the 39 clean candidates elected, 22 were Republicans and 17 Democrats.

Increased voter participation:

> ➢ Number of donations to political campaigns more than tripled thanks to Clean Elections, from 30,000 private donations in 1998 to more than 90,000 $5 Clean Elections qualifying contributions in 2002.

Increased voter turnout:

> ➢ Turnout increased by 25% in the primary and 22% in the general over 1998 levels.

Increased voter choice:

> ➢ 24% increase in number of candidates in the primaries, from 199 in 1998 to 247 in 2002.

> 13% increase in total number of candidates in the general election, from 150 in 1998 to 170 in 2002.
> 64% increase in number of candidates for statewide office in the general election, from 14 in 1998 to 23 in 2002. The number of minority candidates in 2002 was substantially increased.

Increased competition:

> 110% increase in contested Senate races, up from 10 in 1998 to 21 in 2002.

Decreased influence of Big-Money-Special-Interests:

> In 1998, 79% of all races were decided by money — the candidates with the largest campaign war chests won. In 2002, only 2% of all races were affected by disparate funding. In all other races, funding was comparable for all candidates.

Provided adequate funding for candidates:

> 139 candidates participated and 39 won their races. At least one candidate won despite having less than half the funding of his opponent (Tully vs. May).

Strongly supported by the public:

> 64% of Arizonans support public funding for campaigns (Arizona Republic poll, Oct. 2002) and 66% specifically support Clean Elections (KAET poll, June 2002).
> 80% of Arizonans believe that contributions influence votes on public policy (Behavior Research Center poll, December 2001).

How can one legitimately argue against such a system? It works, it is voluntary, it passes constitutional muster, it increases the number of candidates, increases voter turnout and it eliminates the conflicting connections between private funders and public employees. What else could we ask?

But they do argue. Opponents of reform will still manage every possible excuse. They don't like it one bit that a clean system undermines the moneyed system that they've worked so hard to perpetuate. They do not like any system that in any way passes control of the political system to the voters.

Here are arguments you'll hear against a fair system

I've heard virtually every argument that could possibly be concocted against the Clean Money system, and these responses are from my Wisconsin Clean Elections Coalition web page:

I don't want my tax money spent on political campaigns.

Guess what, folks? Your tax dollars *already are* being used to fund political campaigns. It's just through the back door — in hidden taxes — and at a cost hundreds of times more than if you simply paid for the elections up front. Wouldn't you rather pay a fraction of the cost, up front, and in a way that levels the playing field for all candidates, including third-party and independent candidates? And eliminates the excessive taxes needed to support the moneyed system? That's what the Clean Money system provides.

It is estimated by Wisconsin Democracy Campaign (and documented at **www.wisdc.org**) that each Wisconsin taxpayer is paying over $1300 per year to fund state giveaways to special interests, and at the federal level, that number is over $2000. A mere $15 per taxpayer per year would finance both state and federal elections.

Can we afford it? We can't afford not to fix our current pathetic system and give government back to its owners — the citizens.

Public financing of campaigns is "welfare for politicians."

There is no better system of "welfare for politicians" than our current moneyed system. Instead of being beholden to their constituents, politicians need only satisfy the few moneyed interests who fund their elections. Incumbents enjoy a 16-to-1 cash advantage and a 9-to-1 reelection advantage. That's a kind of "welfare" that simply can't be matched elsewhere else.

I don't want my tax money going to candidates I don't agree with.

Guess what again? Your dollars *already are* going to candidates you don't agree with, through this same hidden tax system. At the very least, you are funding the salaries of all incumbents [of both parties] when they are out campaigning and fundraising, while challengers must pay their own way.

With public financing of campaigns you are really funding a Clean Money electoral "system" that returns democracy to the electoral process. Unless you are one of the 1% who gives over $200 to candidates, your voice is simply not being heard. Don't waste sending them your money.

And, as noted elsewhere, when you buy product that company's campaign contributions are added to the price of their product and you reimburse them for their political expenses at the cash register. And most companies give to both parties, so like it or not you are funding the party not of your choice! If you can get over the ideological barrier you'd be further ahead with a clean money system. Then you'd know that your representative would then be on your side.

I don't want tax money spent on projects I don't agree with.

Translated, most people *don't* want their money spent on wasted projects. But such waste is happening today at incredible levels, and it will continue as long as special interests control our government spending. In truth, our taxes are always spent on one or more projects we don't agree with, but the bottom line is, we must eliminate the projects that are not in the best interest of the general public, and only full public funding of the electoral process will accomplish that goal.

45% public funding is enough for politicians.

Not really. Is it okay that the 45% public money subsidizes the 55% coming from special interests, which then turns it into a 45% discount to get legislation passed that results in even more legislative favors and higher taxes? No. We are better off paying the complete bill and having legislators totally responsible to the taxpayers. A 50% plan in Minnesota failed to reduce special interest influence, and any partial funding plan will fare no better.

Public financing of campaigns protects incumbents.

That is hogwash. What better protection do incumbents need than their re-election rate that exceeds 90% under the current moneyed system? Besides, if public financing really did protect incumbents, they'd have passed it years ago. But it does just the opposite and they know it, and that's why they oppose it (though they are not bashful about using this altruistic-sounding excuse). The Clean Money system levels the playing field for challengers, and good politicians don't mind fair competition because they vote on behalf of their constituents. The inept ones like things just as they are, thank you.

But then, we'll vote them out!

Maybe, but likely not. Most voters do not research legislative voting records, and politicians know it. People vote mostly on the basis of name recognition and party rhetoric. That's why money — and lots of it — is so important to the incumbents who don't want to spend their time with constituents. Money buys TV time and other media to get their names heard, loud and clear, thus overwhelming challengers that do not have access to wealthy contributors.

Public financing violates freedom of speech.

Not true, it does just the opposite. But that is sometimes a safe (though fictitious) argument that helps protect politicians at the polls. Actually, when reform proposals are voluntary and candidates can opt in or out, they pass constitutional muster. Clean Money, in fact, has already passed constitutional challenges in both Maine and Arizona. Further, such a system doesn't violate free speech, but instead ensures that one's megaphone (cash) does not drown out the speech of those without wealth or access to it. [When voters can hear both sides of the argument, without cash drowning out one side or the other, the public can only benefit. That's more speech; not less.]

Those who argue that their money represents their speech can still give money to the candidates who (a) want to take it, and (b) have opted out of the public grant. But without the optional public grant, only those voters with sufficient cash in the bank can sway the direction of elections — and, hence, public policy. That, in itself, violates the 14th Amendment right of equal protection for those without the cash to make political contributions. The Clean Money system actually increases speech.

Source: **www.WiCleanElections.org/opposing-arguments.html**

On McCain-Feingold

The McCain-Feingold law is not as good as Senators **John McCain** (R-AZ) and **Russ Feingold** (D-WI) wanted it to be, and it certainly isn't what the reform community would have asked for.

But it is where reform stands today because of the **Mitch McConnell**s and **Tom Delay**s of the world, each of whom are/were Republicans (Senate and House) and each of whom gutted the important measures of the original McCain-Feingold proposal. After performing their surgery, the *Bobsy Twins* are now ragging about how bad the law that they "deformed" really is.

It is not the best, thanks to them, but because it is so weak we now at least have a chance to fix it and clean up the 527 corruptions that hijacked the 2004 elections. Only time will tell whether the Bush Republicans will allow that to happen. They are currently pushing a bill to virtually eliminate all limits on contributions, which is what you might expect from the GOP.

There are a tremendous number of congressmen who rail against "out of control spending" and shout at the top of their lungs that excessive spending must stop! But then they refuse to tackle the one aspect of the political system that drives spending in its entirety — money from the special interests who like things that they can control.

The politicians who honestly attempt to clean up the system are castigated by the old-timers who have set the rules (which clearly adds fuel to the arguments for term limits).

"Every day I get up and look through the Forbes list of the richest people in America. If I'm not there, I go to work."
Robert Orben

I've made some pretty stupid investments in my lifetime, having been duped by some pretty unsavory "businessmen" to the tune of about $200,000 over time. That's money that I will never see again and will not be able to leave for my grandkids' education. But I invested and lost. It was my fault.

It boils me more to be cheated by my own state and federal representatives and senators who are giving away over $5000 per year of my tax money to these same types of crooks; all because they want to ensure their re-election. That money also will not go to my grandkids.

My kids and grandkids deserve better. Yours do too.

Selected writings

T he following editorials are by the author and include some of the ideas that lead to the writing of this book. As such there may be some repetition, so please be patient.

Public funding of campaigns would be fairer, cheaper
(Milwaukee Journal Sentinel on 6/9/03)

As a lifelong Republican I'd like to believe that President Bush's $350 billion tax cut is more than just payback for big campaign contributors, but common sense tells me otherwise. A more effective economic stimulus would result from reduced payroll and income taxes, which would benefit workers who buy products, not just those who sell them.

The chief executive officers of multi-national corporations have proven time and again that the jobs they want to create are those in countries with low wages that provide them high profits and enormous salaries. Give them a tax break and overseas investments and jobs will flourish.

Congress now even rewards them for taking their corporations offshore to avoid paying U.S. taxes, and somehow these now-foreign corporations are able to skirt campaign laws prohibiting their financial contributions to our political system.

While executive salaries go up, worker salaries remain stagnant or go down. What used to be a 40-to-1 differential between CEO salaries and their lowest paid workers has increased ten-fold to over 400-to-1. Those benefitting call it their "hard work;" I call it fraud and a recipe for future anarchy.

This is not a broad swath I paint. The offending executives know who they are, and the vast majority of legitimate business leaders are as much victims as is the public. They are faced with out-of-work buyers scrambling to stay afloat. All the while investor confidence has sopped capital needed for growth.

Are we having fun yet?

America cannot survive as a consumer-only nation. We must also manufacture to balance trade deficits. Supply-side economics is a hoax created by the rich to give politicians cover for their favored treatment. They call it trickle-down economics; I call it a ruse. If I'm going to spend an extra $1000 per year on their tax breaks, I'd rather send it to them directly and eliminate the government's participation.

Our economy will not rebound until we bring jobs back to America. And unless "fair" trade supplants free trade that will not happen until world salaries become equalized. Thanks to corporate control of Congress, political support of the World Trade Organization and free trade laws like NAFTA and GATT will lead to this nation's ultimate demise.

The basic problem is our corrupt political campaign funding system, and it affects virtually every economic and environmental policy. If I had an employee taking money from the vendors he controlled, I'd fire him. In America we re-elect them. In Mexico and Italy we call it bribery and payola; in America we call it free speech. In the criminal justice system we have insider-trading laws, but in the political system we have congressmen routinely passing laws that affect industries in which they have (or will have) an investment. Does that make any sense?

Our nation cannot survive under this moneyed political system, and it's just a matter of time before it totally destroys our democracy.

That's already happening at the state level. Wisconsin Democracy Campaign has identified over $4 billion spent each year by our state legislature to benefit those who fund their political campaigns. That's over $1100 per taxpayer per year, and coincidentally, it's also equivalent to our state budget deficit!

During the recent budget debates virtually all of the corporate welfare survived the ax, while Democrats and Republicans proposed cutting local revenue sharing (which promises to increase property taxes by 8% to 10%), increase college tuition (which deters students from attending), and cutting other needed public services like special education for autistic children. But the fat cats survived just fine, thank you.

If politicians are to be beholden to their campaign funders, wouldn't it make more sense for those funders to be the taxpayers? That's the way it is in five states that have passed Clean Money Campaign Reform laws that allow politicians to replace private donations with public grants. A qualifying process ensures the integrity of the system and allows third-party candidates, and it's optional to the candidate thus passes constitutional muster. And, it is working!

The cost? About $5 per taxpayer per year. Compared to the $1100 it's now costing each taxpayer in Wisconsin, this is a no-brainer. What are we waiting for?

Think about it. The political mentality described above simply would not exist with full public funding of political campaigns. Balanced budgets and modest taxes would be a given once the fat cats are put to pasture.

The state Legislature and Governor should accept nothing less. We don't want a partially clean system, as is currently proposed. We want 100% public financing of campaigns and we are willing to pay the $5 fee. It is because I am a conservative that I prefer making this investment in our future stability.

BRIBERY AND PAYOLA
(Editorial published, www.tompaine.com, 8/8/2000)

I have yet to understand how political conservatives can hate our bloated, inefficient government, excessive laws and high taxes — the symptoms — but still favor our cash-and-carry political system, the disease. These ideals are mutually exclusive, yet so many politicians claim to have both. This thing called freedom of speech — the one that allows special interests to give campaign contributions to legislators who write laws that transfer taxes and other taxpayer assets to them — will be the downfall of America's economy and democracy.

According to the Tax Foundation, the median two-income family now pays 40% of their income to federal, state and local taxes. A big chunk of those taxes is the $150 billion Congress doles out each year in Corporate Welfare, thanks to the cash clout of wealthy and special interest executives. That's $1500 per taxpayer per year that goes to federal grants, subsidies, tax breaks, and a host of other government giveaways.

If you believe in a trickle-down economy, we'll get some of that back, especially when the wealthy use their booty to purchase the products that you and I make. But that would happen even if we just sent our $1500 check directly to the executives, and bypassed the political process altogether. But that would mess up our political system. You see, it is necessary that the $1500 passes to the special interests as a result of laws written or tax breaks given by our political leaders. That way the executives know which politicians to fund for reelection, and the politicians know for whom to write the laws.

Cynical perhaps, but accurate. In any other country, we'd call this a corrupt system of political bribery and payola. In America we simply call it freedom of speech (although we only allow those with money to have such speech).

Translated, it is costing taxpayers about $1500 per year to allow private interests to fund our public electoral system. We pay it through the hidden tax system, and at hundreds of times more than it would cost if we simply paid for the elections up front. (And, In effect, our hidden tax money also funds politicians we don't support.)

I'm not asking for my $1500 back. I'd just rather see it spent on eliminating illiteracy, educating our children, fighting drugs and crime, and funding Medicare and Social Security ... But instead, my $1500 is being spent on Corporate Welfare and exorbitant executive salaries.

It is because I am a 44-year conservative Republican and want less government spending that I favor full public financing of campaigns. While we already have that — through the hidden tax system — I'd like to move it above board. For $5 and $10 per taxpayer per year, respectfully, we could openly fund our state and federal elections. Compared to the current $1500, that's a real bargain.

I'd like also to know that when laws are written, they benefit the citizens rather than special interest contributors. As mentioned earlier, I could even accept the occasional writing of a bad law, if I knew that cash didn't change hands in the process. Will it happen soon? Certainly not by today's incumbents. But November's election might be the right time for a major turnover of politicians. New blood might just change the system.

Clean government can be yours for $5 a year
(Editorial published in the
Wausau Daily Herald on 8/6/03)

As you listen to economists, political scientists and the media rant about the defects in government economic policy, do you ever wonder why they remain silent about the economics of the very process that drives all others?

It's the economics of our political system — where political campaigns are funded by special interests seeking favors — that drives the direction and magnitude of state spending, high taxes and budget deficits. It's what makes Republicans and Democrats what they are, who they represent, and why they vote for or against various laws.

It's also what's pulling our country apart at the seams, and it doesn't have to be that way.

Imagine a system in which neither Big Business nor Big Labor controlled the legislature or governor; in which elected officials voted for the people instead of their pocketbooks; and in which laws were passed or not passed because they were right or wrong, rather than because campaign money influenced political votes.

Imagine a system in which laws favored citizens, voters and taxpayers rather than the fat cats who fund the political campaigns.

Such a system exists in Arizona (**www.azClean.org**) and five other states. It's called public funding of campaigns, and it drastically reduces (and will ultimately replace) the corrupting influence of private money in the political system. It's the quantum leap in political reform that can restore this state's — and the nation's — economy and democracy.

Though less than four years old, it ultimately will eliminate budget deficits and the massive taxes needed to support the moneyed political system, and all at a cost of just $5 per taxpayer per year. Politicians must be beholden to their funders, and in the Clean Money electoral states, those funders are the taxpayers.

According to Madison's Wisconsin Democracy Campaign (**www.wisdc.org**), the Wisconsin Legislature currently doles out over $4 billion per year in special-interest tax breaks, subsidies, no-bid contracts and a host of other taxpayer giveaways, all to benefit their campaign contributors. That's over $1,100 per taxpayer per year that would mostly disappear under a Clean Money reform system, and it is many times higher at the federal level.

Think about it. There are only two kinds of campaign money — public and private — and our current system virtually demands private money influence.

Sure, there are the $10 contributions that are not intended to influence, and some small public campaign grants. But the big bucks come from business and labor bosses who are obligated to spend their organizations' dollars only where influence can be had.

It's an interesting phenomenon: If I had an employee who took money from the vendors he controlled, I'd fire him. In America, we re-elect them. In Mexico and Italy, we'd call this a corrupt system; in America we call it free speech.

We need a system in which the beliefs of the Republicans and Democrats are melded to protect the best interests of the public, and that requires laws that sometimes favor business and sometimes favor labor.

That can't be had with money changing hands. The only way to ensure system integrity is to eliminate the cash that flows from those who want laws written to those who write them.

There is no legitimate reason this system should remain broken, nor a reason politicians would want to continue with this dark cloud over their profession. They have the power to change it. Now they need the will.

Call your representatives today and let them know that you are willing to let $5 of your tax money be used for 100 percent public funding of campaigns.

The return on that investment will be phenomenal.

Free Market Needs Health Care Reform
(Wisconsin State Journal, July 30, 2005, Jack E. Lohman)

The good news is that the U.S. is on its way to an efficient national health-care system like that in Canada. The bad news is — because of moneyed special-interest opposition — it may take decades to get there.

Hospitals, insurance companies and the highly-profitable pharmaceutical industry are all spending millions of dollars annually trying to convince politicians that gobs of body bags will result from long wait times for medical care. But that is both false and unnecessary. Urgent procedures in Canada have virtually no wait times, but even the ones that do can be eliminated in a Wisconsin single-payer system. We can do better and we will do better.

Wait times don't exist today with Medicare, our most popular single-payer system, and we need not have them with a new system of care. Over 60 percent of U.S. physicians support a Canadian-style system, which is essentially Medicare-for-all, and a majority of them favor a salaried system versus the bureaucratic fee-for-service mess they face today.

What is puzzling is that some business leaders oppose this obvious fix, and it appears more ideological than logical. Today's "free-market medical system" is actually blocking U.S. businesses from engaging in a free market.

How can they compete globally or freely against imports when these competitors need not add health care costs to the price of their product? They can't, so many are taking their manufacturing (and jobs) abroad. If we'd pay for our health-care differently and removed this overhead cost, we'd keep those companies and jobs in the state.

It is by historical accident that employers are in the health-care business, and even today 40 percent of CEOs — those familiar with the differences — would like to eliminate these expenses and reduce their worker compensation costs by 40 percent. That can all be had with a single-payer system.

That more autos are now manufactured in Ontario than in Detroit should surprise no one. General Motors recently announced the cut of 25,000 jobs. Its costs are $6,500 per employee for U.S. health care versus $800 in Canada, which adds $1,500 per car compared to Toyota's $186 per car. What else should we expect but exodus?

Think it through. Canada's system is 40 percent less costly than ours because they've eliminated the insurance companies and the massive paperwork required. And their life expectancy is two years longer than ours, and infant mortality rate 35 percent lower. Their system works beautifully. Patients love it and their doctors love it. The special interests do not.

Who would pay for a single-payer system? The same people who are paying for it today — the taxpayers. The present health care system costs approximately $1.6 trillion each year — and 100 percent of this money comes from we the people, through taxes, premiums, co-pays, deductibles, purchases, employer tax breaks and the other methods we use for collecting money.

My advice: Think first about what is best for the public and you'll land on a system that is also best for business. The inefficient hospitals will learn by it, the displaced insurance personnel can be retrained for vital nursing jobs, and the country will gain jobs. Does this make too much sense to pass?

Universal Health Care
(*Small Business Times,* September 2005)

Health care costs are rising at 10-15% per year and employers are struggling for ways to pay these costs, which typically represent 15% of their labor costs. Many are shifting the costs to their employees by demanding high deductibles and co-pays, and in some cases contracting with HMOs who make their money more by denying care than providing it.

But what else can companies do? They are competing with manufacturers in countries that have taxpayer-paid universal health care systems, and these competitors need not add health care to the cost of their products. Of course our manufacturers can send their work abroad, but then American jobs are lost.

Rising health care costs are the result of only one thing, a medical community that has switched from being humanitarian medical centers to for-profit corporations. The industry has run amok. They are inefficiently operated and they love it, because inefficiency is where they make much of their profits. Medicare and private insurers are incurring 20% to 30% of their costs from unnecessary and inappropriate medical testing, and another 30% in exorbitant administrative waste. Compare that 30% to Canada's 8% and Medicare's 3.5%. Wisconsinites are supporting 400 for-profit insurance companies compared to the ONE non-profit contractor in each Canadian province.

The 30% waste is not exclusive to government systems; it also exists within the private sector. It is the profit motive that is driving up health care costs, and this motivation exists on all fronts: hospitals, physicians and insurers, including for-profit HMOs. For-profit entities are obligated by law to seek the highest profits possible for their shareholders, and cutting care helps achieve this goal.

The United States and South Africa are the only two industrialized countries that do not have universal health care for their citizens. Over 45 million Americans, 15% of our population, are totally without health care and just show up at the emergency room for treatment, which is the most expensive form of rationing possible. The ER charges sometimes force them into bankruptcy, where the losses are shifted to those who are insured or to the taxpayers. Over 18,000 Americans die prematurely every year because they lack coverage — which is six times more than died on 9/11. Another 50 million Americans are underinsured and are a mishap away from bankruptcy and the societal costs that result.

Why do we allow this? Because our politicians are paid to allow it: it's called "$100 million per year in political contributions given by our health care and pharmaceutical industries." Political money got us into this mess and eliminating political money will be the only way of getting us out of it. Unless, of course, business leaders force the issue and demand change.

The solution is a universal health care system paid for not by employers but by the taxpayers. That's right; the system must be funded by the very same people who are paying the bill today: we the taxpayers. We pay the current medical costs through many circuitous routes, the most obvious being that when employers pay for medical insurance they add those costs to their product price and we pay at the cash register. We also pay with deductibles and co-pays and with the cost-shifting that medical providers do to offset losses resulting from serving the uninsured. We taxpayers are therefore paying 100% of the nation's medical costs already, through our employers, but in the process we are driving jobs out of the country and accepting substandard health care.

We need a universal, single payer system like Canada's, but with better funding and without their wait times. Our most popular single-payer system is Medicare, which has no wait times. But both

Medicare and our private insurance systems are rife with misuse and overuse.

But look at what universal health care offers Canadians:

➤ Canadians have a life expectancy two years longer than Americans (79.3 years compared to our 77 years). They are 5th in the world in longevity compared to America at 26th.

➤ Canada's infant mortality rate is 35% lower than ours, because mothers are not priced out of (i.e., denied) prenatal care

➤ We spend $5,267 per-capita on health care compared to Canada's $2,931, because Canada's administration costs are 8% compared to our 30%.

➤ We spend more dollars on health care than any other country (15% of GDP compared to Canada's 9%), yet our system of care is ranked by the World Health Organization at 37th in the world (France is first, Canada is 5th).

➤ On a per-capita basis the U.S. has twice as many MRI scanners as does Canada.

➤ On a per-capita basis we have fewer hospital days per visit as do the Canadians.

➤ On a per-capita basis we have fewer doctor visits as do the Canadians.

But that's not what the for-profit health care interests will tell you. They are deathly afraid that the U.S. is going to implement a similar, efficient system and their profits will dry up. When they tell us about the long wait times in Canada they fail to tell us they've included all patients with future appointments. They fail to tell us that 90% of Canadians prefer their health care system to ours. They fail to tell us that only a handful of Canadians head south for their elective procedures, and many are already in the States when they decide to order them. And they fail to tell us that "they" includes a group of special interests in Canada that wants to open their system for profit taking too, and are helping to kill the idea in America.

If we do it right, there will be no wait times and we can replace Medicaid, BadgerCare and 40% of worker compensation costs, all for the same dollars we are paying today. And we might even get Medicare to buy into our system, too. Then Wisconsin businesses can compete with the rest of the world. What's not to like about this?

Following is a column by political comedian **Will Durst,** and though his comments are right on target, they are not funny at all:

You Can't Make Stuff Up Like This
By Will Durst

Bush to the Non-Rich: Drop Dead

You know what surprises me most about Bush's new Budget Proposal? I'll tell you what surprises me most about Bush's new Budget Proposal. What surprises me most about Bush's new Budget Proposal is that the front gates of the White House aren't being knocked down by legions of outraged clergy armed with spiked bats and pitchforks and acetylene torches screaming for the head of any of the leering corporate lackeys possessing even the remotest of roles in submitting this moral crime against humanity to Congress. And that the ruling class lets Bush get away with this potentially revolutionary inciting crap. That's what surprises me most about Bush's new Budget Proposal.

And I don't use the term "ruling class" lightly. His tax cuts for the rich: not only do they remain in defiance of the largest deficit EVER, but King Leerer intends to fight to make them permanent. HOWEVER, for any program involving anybody who isn't rich: oh yes, cuts do exist. Severe cuts. Cuts o'plenty. Cuts to the bone, unless those bones happen to be located in the vicinity of the cholesterol laden limb of a fat cat.

Apparently the plan is to balance the budget on the nutritionally deprived uninsured backs of the inadequately medicated poor. That's the deal: budget cuts if you're not rich, tax cuts if you are. Less money for those who don't have any and more to those who do. That's how President Fredo says we're going to get out of the giant deficit hole he's dug. You can't put it any more simply. Rich people richer. Poor people poorer.

Here's just a sample of what he plans for our future with a handy reminder of why. Because you can't hear it too much. For those of you with a strong stomach and a low threshold of infuriation, feel free to read on. For the rest of you, this might be a good time to check out your horoscope or some of the cheerier comic strips like Family Circus.

- ➢ Tighter restrictions on Food Stamp eligibility so rich people can have more money.
- ➢ Federal Drug Administration inspection teams sacked so rich people can have more money.
- ➢ Highway and infrastructure improvement budgets slashed so rich people can have more money.
- ➢ An 11% reduction in Homeland Security funds available to state and local coordination efforts so rich people can have more money.
- ➢ $250 million cut from programs to train child care doctors and other health care professionals so rich people can have more money.
- ➢ Small Business Administration cut from $3.3 billion to $.6 billion so rich people can have more money.
- ➢ Increase on charges for Veterans Health Care so rich people can have more money.
- ➢ Cutting Federal Foster Care Programs so rich people can have more money.
- ➢ Cutting Medicaid and Medicare benefits so rich people can have more money.
- ➢ Ending community services block grants, a $637 million program that helps pay for community action agencies founded more than 35 years ago as part of the fight against poverty so rich people can have more money.
- ➢ Proposed cuts in aid to farmers, seniors, children, students, cops, veterans, the homeless, the hungry, the environment, Amtrak, AND the Center for Disease Control and Prevention so rich people can have more money.
- ➢ Gutting the low income home energy assistance program which is mostly used by the elderly. That's right friends, he's cutting winter heating subsidies to the elderly so rich people can have more money.

What are we now: The Gorgar People? Let's just cut to the chase. You hit 65, we ship you to the Aleutian Islands and place you on an ice floe with matches and a pointy stick. If you're a Republican, we take away the stick, because it's considered an entitlement.

Thanks to Durst for permission to print this article, and don't miss his web site at www.willdurst.com. As he makes the point so well, our political system is not a pretty sight. This is one of the sadder sides of our democracy, and it is up to Americans to drain the swamp.

The failure of politicians to address the concerns of society is the symptom of a runaway disease; eliminating our moneyed political system is its only cure. Public elections should not be financed with private money. If public office holders are to be beholden to anybody, it should be to the taxpayers.

"Politics is the gentle art of getting votes from the poor and campaign funds from the rich, by promising to protect each from the other."
Oscar Ameringer

Appendix A

So what now? Find the groups that you believe have your best interests at heart. Here are a few activist groups I support, but also see the appendix for other groups and resources:

Public Campaign, the national Clean Money advocate, has state contacts listed at: www.publicampaign.org/states

Sierra Club (www.sierraclub.org) is a leading Environmental group with offices in most states

Wisconsin Democracy Campaign (www.wisdc.org) is co-sponsor of www.PeoplesLegislature.org, a strong activist group in my state (you should seek out one in your state)

Wisconsin Citizen Action (www.wi-citizenaction.org) has a large statewide left-leaning activist group, but may also have offices in your state (www.citizenaction.org)

State Public Interest Groups can be found at www.pirg.org, and don't miss its congressional scorecard at www.pirg.org/score2003

Center for Voting and Democracy (www.FairVote.org) specifically tackles voting issues and promotes Instant Runoff elections (IRVs).

Common Cause (www.commoncause.org) is better in some states than others, but overall an excellent group.

League of Women Voters (www.lwv.org) has been very active on the campaign reform issue

Public Citizen (www.citizen.org), founded by Ralph Nader, is a strong web-based action group

ReclaimDemocracy.org (www.reclaimdemocracy.org) has a few local groups, but nonetheless a good resource page.

No, none of these groups are right wing conservatives, and it puzzles me that the right is not concerned with the corruption issue. They have family too, and they tout morals and values. But morals and values are missing from our current political structure.

Appendix B

Suggested national health care changes

Definition of Independent Diagnostic Testing Facility (IDTF): A company that is independently owned and operated and meets the criteria of Medicare's IDTF classification. Such a company could be owned by either independent business people or a hospital, but the IDTF rules should ensure that it cannot have ownership by a hospital employee or physician (or his/her immediate family members), *that refers patients to it.*

IDTFs typically provide mobile testing services, MRI scanning and cardiac monitoring services via the Internet, and must be required to provide appropriately trained and certified testing personnel.

These labs must be required to bill all procedures according to a national fee schedule, less, perhaps, a small facility fee that the hospital or clinic may bill. IDTFs may not bill patients without an independent physician referral, and may not in any way pass money or other assets to their physician or hospital customers. IDTFs must have a staff physician to oversee quality control, and that physician may perform diagnostic interpretations but must bill that component directly. If the number of staff physicians exceeds one, the other physicians may not be referring physicians.

If IDTFs are employed, and expensive equipment or monitors are required for the service, the entity purchasing the service shall not be allowed to purchase the equipment and it must instead be supplied as a part of the IDTF service. This is suggested so that hospitals or clinics do not falsely inflate the number of patient tests they order as a means of offsetting the cost of the equipment. Such equipment costs can be built into the costs of the service, and thus shared among more than one hospital or clinic client, further reducing costs.

The main thrust of the national health care program is the establishment of an independent health care board appointed with staggered 14-year terms to isolate them from political pressure. The board would implement and control all of the following:

Health Care Board

➢ This must be a nonpartisan and nonconflicted board and must not include any current members of the state legislature. Ideally, board members would be retired physicians, nurses, accountants, business leaders or hospital administrators. The board would operate with the same autonomy as does the Federal Reserve Board and with the full authority to establish rules and funding.

Certificate of Need (CON) program

➢ The CON process with a separate board must be re-established (or established if it didn't earlier exist) and its own budget and rules controlled by the above health care board.

➢ All hospital and clinic purchases of high-end technology would be regulated. This is defined as diagnostic equipment which costs over $50,000 ($500,000 for a hospital) or requires, under Medicare's IDTF regulations, credentialed or licensed personnel to operate.

➢ All health care facilities (hospitals, outpatient clinics and services, and independent physicians) must receive CON approvals before adding more than 20 patient overnight beds per year or acquiring (through purchase, lease or otherwise) any piece of equipment meeting the definition of high-end technology of the dollar amounts described above, except with prior permission of the CON board.

National fee schedule

➢ All health care providers (hospitals, physicians, IDTFs) may not charge patients more than that which is listed on the national fee schedule that is maintained by Medicare (though that may be modified from time to time). Physicians and hospitals that cannot operate within this fee schedule may contract the service out to an IDTF.

➢ Reasonable limits on the number of repeat tests must be established either by the same committee that established the national CPT codes (the American Medical Association and Medicare are members), or by a specially appointed board of retired physicians.

> ➢ In the event a new medical service or procedure has been introduced, the health care board may provide a temporary waiver and affix a reimbursement until the costs have been assessed by Medicare, in a time-frame not to exceed 90 days. Once reimbursement levels are determined, the board may apply them retroactively.

Hospitals

> ➢ Must adhere to the new CON regulations with regard to purchasing new high-end technology and adding new hospital beds or functions.

> ➢ Must divest of any currently "owned" clinics and physician employees, and any other facility that has physicians on its staff or as shareholders. The only exception is that hospitals may employ physician administrators that do not refer patients to the hospital.

> ➢ Hospitals shall be compensated using a negotiated yearly operating budget and a second budget for capital expenses. Should extraordinary purchases be required, they may be approved and funded by the CON board.

> ➢ Itemized billing by hospitals shall no longer be needed or allowed. One single-page charge slip to the patient on discharge will include only the number of days stayed, with the approximate cost-per-day absorbed by the Medicare system.

> ➢ In general, and with CON approval, hospitals will purchase the high-end equipment and provide appropriately credentialed personnel, or they may use a contract IDTF to provide all equipment and personnel necessary to service the patient population. Such systems include echocardiography, Holter monitoring, CT scans, MRIs and other High End technologies. However, physicians and their clinics will have the option to employ competitive IDTF services and not be obligated to use the local hospital (this provides an important competitive function, not in price but in quality of care).

> ➢ Must eliminate all forms of television or print advertising, except that which appears on their own web site.

Physicians and clinics

➤ Must adhere to the CON regulations with regard to all purchases of new high-end technology devices or systems.

➤ In general all high-end diagnostic testing must be referred to a hospital or qualified IDTF. Only special CON approval can bypass this requirement.

➤ Physicians and clinics that have previously purchased high-end technology must report and receive CON approval to continue providing such services beyond the typical five year lifespan of the equipment. These entities will be grandfathered for no more than five years from the time of its original purchase. Thereafter they must refer their patients to hospitals or independent IDTFs.

➤ Must divest of all financial interests in hospitals to which they refer patients, and may not refer patients to hospitals in which they or an immediate family member has any ownership.

➤ Shall have the option to refer patients needing high-end tests either to the hospital or to a competitive IDTF, providing that the IDTF is approved and takes full responsibility for billing the payor for the complete test.

➤ Except in rural areas where other qualified physicians may not be available, physicians may not be both the ordering physician and receive payment for interpreting the test.

➤ Physicians must be appropriately certified to interpret diagnostic tests, as established by the health care board.

➤ Physicians shall not receive any form of compensation from pharmaceutical companies, device manufacturers, IDTFs or any other entity which may conflict with their medical judgement in treating patients. This includes industry paid educational trips, seminars, and consulting engagements. If this is useful to the physician's education or practice, they must pay for these expenses themselves.

Insurance or payment system

➤ Should be a single-payer system modeled after the Medicare system or that in Canada. As with Medicare today, only one administrative company per state is needed, and companies can compete for that contract using guidelines established by the health care board.

> If co-payments or deductibles are employed as an incentive for patients not to use the system frivolously, these may be offset by patients who perform community services and receive non-transferable vouchers. These could also be waived for the first 5 visits per year.

Attorneys and tort reform

> The 12-man jury trial must be reserved for criminal trials, which in medical cases would have to be brought by the district attorney or through the federal legal system.

> Otherwise, a three-judge binding arbitration panel would replace the 12-man jury for medical cases, and this panel shall consist of retired judges, physicians and nurses (or when appropriate, retired hospital administrators).

> Members of the arbitration panel must be drawn from a geographical area extending beyond 75 miles of the defendant and must disclose and recuse themselves in the event of a potential conflict of interest they may have in the case (friends with the defendant or family, etc.).

> If awards are not determined by the 3-person panel, a system of final offer arbitration may be implemented.

> The panel shall assess responsibility and awards, if any. In cases of total incapacitation of a patient, awards shall be limited to lifetime costs of care, including nursing, plus a yearly payment equal to three times the U.S. median income (as determined by the U.S. Department of Labor).

> Punitive damages, if any, shall be used to help fund the universal health care system, with any excesses applied to the clean money campaign funding system. Fair attorney fees may be assessed to the losing party.

> A three-strike system should punish bad lawyers, bad doctors and habitually litigious patients when such suits are determined by the panel to be frivolous or unwarranted.

Pharmaceuticals

> All drug research and development shall be approved and funded by the NIH, which will issue contracts to qualified medical colleges, research scientists and physicians.

> All resulting patents shall become the property of the NIH, and royalties to the manufacturing companies will not be charged because they'd get passed to taxpayers anyway.

> Once drugs are approved by the FDA, royalty-free licenses to manufacture and market the drugs shall be issued to at least three qualified U.S. drug manufacturers.

> All radio, TV and print advertising of prescription drugs shall be prohibited, except for the materials directly given to physicians or patients.

> Medicare and any national health plan selected shall be obligated to negotiate with the licensed manufacturers for best price, just as the Veterans Hospitals do.

> Drug companies may not sell the drugs outside of the US at prices lower than they sell in the US.

> If drug companies want to do initial research on animals, they may. But the final product must go through the NIH system established above and become available to other qualified manufacturers in the competitive marketplace. No pharmaceutical company may contract for drug trials on patients; only the NIH can.

> Pharmaceutical companies shall be prohibited from providing physicians with consulting fees, speaking fees, expenses for training seminars, travel or lodging expenses or any other remuneration that creates a conflict of interest with proper patient care.

> Pharmaceutical companies may have, from time to time, legitimate need to obtain physician feedback, and a just compensation system may be created by the health care board. In any event, such compensation shall not exceed the physicians normal practice income.

Food and Drug Administration (FDA)

> Shall only employ physicians who are free of conflicts of interest (i.e., no past or present employment or consulting for a drug company and no stock ownership in a drug company, etc.)

Appendix C
Web Resources

Also located at www.WiCleanElections.org/links

Agribusiness Accountability Initiative:
www.AgriBusinessAccountability.org

Alliance for Better Campaigns: www.bettercampaigns.org

American Medical Student Association: www.amsa.org

Americans Against Political Corruption:
www.pirg.org/democracy/cfr

Americans for Campaign Reform: www.just6dollars.org

Americans for Democratic Action: www.inequality.org

Bermuda Project: www.TheBermudaProject.com

Brennan Center for Justice: www.BrennanCenter.org

Call for Reform: www.CallForReform.org

Campaign Finance Information Center:
www.CampaignFinance.org

Campaign Finance Institute: www.cfinst.org

Campaign for America's Future: www.OurFuture.org

Campaign Legal Center: www.camlc.org

CampaignReform.org: www.CampaignReform.org

Center for Corporate Policy: www.CorporatePolicy.org

Center for Governmental Studies: www.cgs.org

Center for Media and Democracy: www.prwatch.org

Center for Political Accountability:
www.PoliticalAccountability.net

Center for Public Integrity: www.PublicIntegrity.org

Center for Responsive Politics:
 www.OpenSecrets.org and
 www.crp.org/industries/alphalist.asp
 (alphabetical list of contributing industries)

Center for Study of Responsive Law: www.csrl.org

Center for Voting and Democracy: www.FairVote.org

Center on Budget and Policy Priorities: www.cbpp.org

Centre for Corporate Accountability (London):
 www.CorporateAccountability.org/index.htm

Citizen Action:
 www.citizenaction.org and www.citizenactionWI.org
 and www.GrassRoots.org

Citizen Works:
 www.CitizenWorks.org and
 www.CitizenWorks.org/corp/tax/taxbreif.php
 (for a report on offshore corporate tax havens)

Citizens Against Government Waste: www.cagw.org
 (don't miss their Pig Book)

Citizens for Corporate Responsibility: www.c4cr.org

Citizens for Election Reform (CT): www.cfer.us

Citizens for Responsibility and Ethics:
 www.citizensforethics.org

Citizens for Tax Justice: www.ctj.org

Clean Elections Institute: www.azclean.org

Common Cause: www.CommonCause.org

Common Dreams: www.CommonDreams.org

Concord Coalition: www.concordcoalition.org

Congressional Accountability Project:
 www.CongressProject.org

Congressional Observer Publications:
 www.proaxis.com/~cop (House and Senate Votes)

Consumer Project on Technology: www.cptech.org

Corporate Accountability Project: www.corporations.org

Corporate Crime Reporter:
www.CorporateCrimeReporter.com

Corporate Crime Wave:
www.newint.org/issue358/facts.htm (facts)

Corporate Governance: www.corpgov.net

Corporate Research Project: www.corp-research.org

CorpWatch: www.corpwatch.org
(holding corporations accountable)

Democracy 21: www.Democracy21.org

Democracy for America:
www.DemocracyForAmerica.com

Democracy Matters: www.DemocracyMatters.org

Economy.com: www.economy.com

Elections Not Auctions: www.ElectionsNotAuctions.org

Endgame Research Services:
www.EndGame.org and
www.EndGame.org/primer-wealth.html
(on wealth concentration) and
www.EndGame.org/corpcon.html
(on corporate power)

Environmental News Network: www.enn.com

Environmental Working Group: www.ewg.org

Equal Justice Society: www.EqualJusticeSociety.org

Essential Action: www.essentialaction.org

Essential Information: www.essential.org

Everybody In Nobody Out:
www.EverybodyInNobodyOut.org

Fanny Lou Hamer Project: www.flhp.org

FECinfo.com: www.FecInfo.com

FightingBob.com: www.fightingbob.com

Follow the Money: www.FollowTheMoney.org

Follow the Money (Wisconsin): www.FollowTheMoney.us

FundRace: www.fundrace.org (campaign data)

Grandfather Economic Report (a must see web site):
    http://mwhodges.home.att.net

Halliburton Watch: www.HalliburtonWatch.org

How Dare They?: www.HowDareThey.org_

Initiative & Referendum Institute: www.iandrinstitute.org

Investigative Reporters and Editors: www.reporter.org

League of Women Voters: www.lwv.org

Maine Citizens for Clean Elections: www.mainecleanelections.org

Media Matters for America: www.MediaMatters.org

Minnesota Alliance for Progressive Action:
    www.mapa-mn.org

Mother Jones Magazine:
    www.motherjones.com and
    www.motherjones.com/news/special_reports/mojo_400
    /browse.html (400 biggest contributors)

MultiNational Monitor: www.MultiNationalMonitor.org

National Voting Rights Institute: www.nvri.org

People's Legislature: www.PeoplesLegislature.org

Personal Democracy Forum: www.personaldemocracy.com

Physicians for a National Health Program: www.pnhp.org

PoliticalMoneyLine: www.FecInfo.com

Program on Corps, Law and Democracy: www.poclad.org

Progress Report: www.progress.org

Project Vote Smart: www.vote-smart.org

Public Campaign: www.publicampaign.org
    (Clean Elections advocate)

Public Citizen: www.citizen.org

Public Interest Group: www.pirg.org

ReclaimDemocracy.org: www.reclaimdemocracy.org

On Corporate Personhood
www.reclaimdemocracy.org/personhood

On Democratic Elections
www.reclaimdemocracy.org/political_reform/
democractic_elections_primer.html

Reform Institute: www.ReformInstitute.org

Sierra Club: www.sierraclub.org

Stealth PACs: www.stealthpacs.org (Public Citizen)

Tax Foundation: www.TaxFoundation.org

Taxpayers for Common Sense:
www.taxpayer.net and see their *Scorecards* at
http://capwiz.com/taxpayer/dbq/officials/
or search on scorecard

Taxreform.org: www.taxreform.org

Texans for Public Justice: www.tpj.org

The American Prospect: www.prospect.org

TheRestofUs.org: www.TheRestofUs.org

The Umbrella Movement: www.TheRightIsWrong.us

Tompaine.com: www.TomPaine.com

Trips for Judges: www.TripsForJudges.org

United for Fair Economy:
www.FairEconomy.org and don't miss
www.FairEconomy.org/press/2005/EE2005.pdf
(Excellent report on corporate excesses)

White House for Sale: www.WhitehouseForSale.org

Wisconsin Campaign Finance Reform: www.wi-cfr.org

Wisconsin Citizen Action: www.wi-citizenaction.org

Wisconsin Clean Elections: www.WiCleanElections.org

Wisconsin Coalition for Health: www.wisconsinhealth.org

Wisconsin Democracy Campaign: www.wisdc.org

<u>Good links pages for activists</u>

www.cagw.org

www.CooperativeIndividualism.org/links.html

www.corpgov.net/links/links.html

www.corporatepolicy.org/links.htm

www.endgame.org/links.html

www.foe.org/international/shareholder/links.html

www.inequality.org/links.html

www.inequality.org/recommendedreading.html

www.WiCleanElections.org/links

<u>U.S. Govt Roll Call Votes</u>

House Roll Call Votes:

Today that direct link is:

http://clerk.house.gov/evs/2005/index.asp

http://clerk.house.gov/legisAct/votes.html

But if it changes, go to **http://clerk.house.gov**, click "Roll Call Votes" in the Quick Links on the right, click the highest year on the list under Roll Call Votes. In the above case you may be able to replace 2005 above with the year you are interested in researching, but don't count on it.

Senate Roll Call Votes:

Today that direct link is:

www.senate.gov/pagelayout/legislative/a_three_ sections_with_teasers/votes.htm

But if that link changes, go to **www.senate.gov**, click on "Legislation and Records", click on "Votes" on the left, click the highest year in the Roll Call Table.

Appendix D

Sources

1. Center for Responsive Government — **www.OpenSecrets.org**

2. *Milwaukee Journal Sentinel*, August 7, 1997 "Free Thompson Trips Have Risen Sharply"

3. James K. Galbraith, *The New Democracy Project's Anthology* "What we stand for: A Progressive Platform for a Changing America"

4. Paul Begala, *It's still the Economy, Stupid*, and Boston Globe 3/21/01

5. *Critical Condition: How Health Care in America Became Big Business—and Bad Medicine* by Donald L. Barlett and James B. Steele

6. *Health Spending In The United States And The Rest Of The World* by Gerard F. Anderson, Peter S. Hussy, Bianca K. Frogner and Hugh R. Waters (*Health Affairs*, Volume 24 Number 4, Pages 903-924)

Note: Most of the sources will appear on the pages in which they were cited. A lot of good people should be recognized for their hard work on these issues, and I hope that I have not overlooked any citations or used data that was not properly attributed.

Politicians are like diapers. They should both be changed frequently and for the same reason.

Anonymous

Appendix E

Book Recommendations
(Some right wing, some left wing, but all worth a read)

Is That a Politician in Your Pocket:
Washington on $2 Million a Day
by Micah Sifry, Nancy Watzman
ISBN: 047167995X
A must read, this book nails both political parties on paybacks and names the special interests who made out the checks and what they got in return.

Rome Wasn't Burnt in a Day: The Real Deal on How Politicians, Bureaucrats, and Other Washington Barbarians are Bankrupting America
by Joe Scarborough
ISBN: 0060749849
A conservative insider who saw it up close and naked.

Dismantling The American Dream: Globalization, Free Trade, immigration, Unemployment, Poverty,
Debt, Foreign Dependency, More
by Kenneth Buchdahl
ISBN: 0975320718
He watches the dominoes fall, and the outcome isn't pretty.

Exporting America: Why Corporate Greed Is
Shipping American Jobs Overseas
by Lou Dobbs
ISBN: 0446577448
A Republican with his eyes open — perhaps we should export our workers to fill the foreign jobs we are creating. But Dobbs seems not to connect the dots to the moneyed interests, either in his book or on his TV show. He glosses over the fact that campaign contributions have bought our government's hands-off policy with regard to the companies that hire the immigrants to perpetuate low-wage jobs, thus fueling the border explosion.

The Good Fight: Declare Your Independence
and Close the Democracy Gap
by Ralph Nader
ISBN: 0060756047
Heavily Liberal but a thorough analysis. Nader likes neither party's
actions or solutions, and has excellent arguments and ideas.

Running On Empty: How The Democratic and
Republican Parties Are Bankrupting Our Future
*and What Americans Can Do About I*t
by Peter G. Peterson
ISBN: 0374252874
A Republican who nails both parties' failures, an excellent, though
disheartening, read.

Where the Right Went Wrong: How Neoconservatives Subverted
the Reagan Revolution and Hijacked the Bush Presidency
by Patrick J. Buchanan
ISBN: 0312341156
Conservative and mostly right on target (though Buchanan
fails to connect the dots to the moneyed interests).

The People's Business - Controlling Corporations and Restoring
Democracy
by Lee Drutman and Charlie Cray
ISBN: 157653093
Examines corporate power and presents ideas on how ordinary people
can restore citizen control. Citizen Works Corporate Reform

Dime's Worth of Difference: Beyond the Lesser
of Two Evils (Counterpunch)
by Alexander Cockburn (Editor), Jeffrey St. Clair (Editor)
ISBN: 1904859038
Mostly Liberal, but they're not always wrong.(Whatever happened to
the "political middle"?)

Greed and Good: Understanding and Overcoming the Inequality
That Limits Our Lives
by Sam Pizzigati
ISBN: 1891843257
Liberal, but very hard to deny the premise of this book.

Corporate Predators: The Hunt for Mega-Profits and the Attack on Democracy
by Russell Mokhiber, Robert Weissman
ISBN: 1567511589
If you ever had corporate CEOs on a pedestal, this will surely bust that bubble.

Take the Rich off Welfare
by Mark Zepezauer & Arthur Naiman
ISBN: 0896087069
The Welfare Mom doesn't even compare.

Shakedown: How the Government Screws You from A to Z
by James Bovard
ISBN: 0140258191
The title says it all.

America the Broke: How the Reckless Spending of the White House and Congress are Bankrupting Our Country and Destroying Our Children's Future
by Gerald J. Swanson
ISBN: 0385513046
Excellent description of the symptoms but fails to connect the dots.

The Corporation: The Pathological Pursuit of Profit and Power
by Joel Bakan
ISBN: 0743247442
Also see their DVD at **www.TheCorporation.com**

Class War in America: How Economic and Political Conservatives Are Exploiting Low- And Middle-Income American Families
by Charles M. Kelly
ISBN: 1564743489
Even as a Republican, I found it hard to disagree with many of the arguments in this obviously Liberal writing.

Our Media, Not Theirs: The Democratic
Struggle Against Corporate Media
by Robert W. McChesney, John Nichols
ISBN: 1583225498
Politicians controlling big business is bad enough, but controlling our free press is unconscionable.

Critical Condition: How Health Care in America
Became Big Business-and Bad Medicine
by Donald L. Barlett, James B. Steele
ISBN: 0385504543
Don't read this if you have a weak stomach. The Prologue is worth the price of the book.

The Truth About the Drug Companies: How they
deceive us and what to do about it
by Marcia Angell, M.D.
ISBN: 0-375-76094-6
It is frightening what these companies get away with, and you can see the direct tie to the politicians that are on their payroll. Angell is right on target in this excellent expose'.

On The Take - How Medicine's complicity with
big business can endanger your health
by Jerome P. Kassirer, M.D.
ISBN: 0-19-530004-1
A look at how money affects the judgement of physicians charged with treating their patients ahead of their pocketbooks.

Of special note: That the subject of corruption in our health care and pharmaceutical industries, as described in the last three writings, can consume whole 200 to 300 page books is rather disheartening. This is an industry we should be able to hold above all others, but we cannot. Health care providers want to maximize their salaries too, and some are willing to do it at any costs.

Consistent in these book recommendations is that they describe problems that were created by our moneyed political system and can only be cured by eliminating that moneyed system. They don't all connect the dots, but the dots are there to be connected.

Index

!

A

B

C

H

I

J

K

L

M

O

P

R

Z

Additional copies of *Politicians — Owned & Operated by Corporate America* by Jack E. Lohman are available through your favorite book dealer or from the publisher:

Colgate Press
P.O. Box 597
Sussex, WI 53089
Phone: 414-477-8686
Fax: 262-432-0271
Email: CorporateAmerica@exepc.com
Website: www.MoniedPoliticians.com

Politicians — Owned & Operated by Corporate America
(ISBN: 0-9768906-3-1) is $23.95 for hardbound edition, plus $4.50 shipping for first copy ($1.50 each additional copy) and sales tax for WI orders.